THE LOGIC OF MARX

Jindřich Zelený

The Logic of Marx

translated and edited by

TERRELL CARVER

Rowman and Littlefield
Totowa, New Jersey

First published in the United States of America in 1980
by Rowman and Littlefield, 81 Adams Drive, Totowa, New Jersey.

Originally published in German
under the title *Die Wissenschaftslogik bei Marx und
das Kapital*, by Akademie
Verlag, East Berlin 1968.

ISBN 0-8476-6767-7

Karl Marx: *Capital. A Critique of Political
Economy*, Vol. 1, trans. by Ben Fowkes (Penguin
Books in association with *New Left Review* 1976)
pp. 144–6 reprinted by permission of Penguin
Books Ltd. Translation © Ben Fowkes, 1976.

Printed in Great Britain

Contents

Part III

Being, Praxis and Reason

Translator's Foreword

Marx, though not a professional, was no mean philosopher. And to put his views into philosophical context is no small achievement. Professor Zelený has taken this project further, with more success, than anyone else.

The problems are enormous. In comparison with the philosophies of his predecessors and contemporaries, Marx's views were revolutionary in a philosophical, as well as an avowedly political sense. This is still true. It is not surprising that the depth and originality of Marx's philosophical work has only recently been acknowledged, but little has been said beyond introduction and paraphrase. Zelený is one of the first commentators to work with a clear distinction between textual paraphrase and critical analysis, and he rightly observes that the former is no substitute for the latter. The strength of his book lies in his expansion of critical analysis to include an overall characterization of Marx's views on logic and science, not merely in themselves, but with reference to preceding, contemporary and modern schools of thought. Definitions of logic and science are required, and then general characterizations of relevant methods and views in the history of philosophical thinking on these subjects from Aristotle to the present. It takes a brave scholar to work at this level of generalization, and the rewards are substantial. Not only do we have a view of Marx's philosophical work as a whole, we see it in contrast to other views. Some of these – perhaps the classical or transcendental traditions – may be unfamiliar, while empiricism and mathematical logic may seem more familiar to the English reader. But *The Logic of Marx* represents more than a taxonomic exercise in the history of philosophy, since Zelený is successful in pressing us to look critically at whichever tradition seems comfortable. What does it presuppose? What questions are put? How are they answered? What other answers does it permit? What *other* ways are there of asking these questions? What *other* questions might we ask

instead? What *other* presuppositions are plausible? And how do
we justify holding any presuppositions at all?

Zelený is ready with views on logic and science that fall within
a 'clarified Marxist approach'. He is wholly original in the way
that his clarifications incorporate the work of twentieth-century
philosophers outside the Marxist tradition. This is particularly
true with reference to logic. No one else has given such penetrating consideration to the precise tenets of Hegelian logic, and
exactly what Marx adopted from them. Zelený pursues this
inquiry and also reaches stimulating conclusions concerning the
non-Hegelian aspects of Marx's logic, and the relation of that
residue to the work of Russell, Carnap and Tarski. Philosophical
consideration of logic and science need no longer be divided
between Hegelians – and everyone else.

For some, the whole project of putting Marx's views into a
philosophical context will arouse misgivings. Marx was not a
professional philosopher, and he was hostile to philosophy as
practised by professionals. Zelený considers very carefully
Marx's views on the negation and end of philosophy, and
the student of this particular issue will find the essential texts
quoted and assessed. Marx's 'positive science', his 'practical'
materialism, was by his own admission 'not devoid of premises',
and it is from these views that Marx's own work developed.
From that arises the task of making sense of the Marxian
enterprise, and this might legitimately – even for Marx – be
considered a clarified philosophical approach. Marx could
hardly have been hostile to understanding, knowledge and truth,
and he is reported – quite in character, I think – to have said
briskly to an acquaintance, 'Ignorance never yet helped any-
body!'

On his own terms Marx was right in pursuing his critique of
political economy rather than a treatise on his premises – and the
premises for holding premises. In his manuscripts we have notes
made for 'self-clarification', and in his published critique we have
a work that follows on from these studies, alludes to them at
times, and occasionally adds a further clarification. Marx was
highly conscious not only of the reasons for undertaking a critique of political economy but also of the correct methods to
employ. Again, the relevant passages are extracted and given
critical consideration by Zelený, who uses the early works, the
Grundrisse, and the late writings with equal sensitivity. By link-
ing the late works with the early writings in ways that are very
well defended, Zelený is in a position to tackle the philosophical

aspects of *Capital*, a work that contains some of the most philosophically exciting passages in Marx.

Students of contemporary Marxism will also see in Zelený's work a unique capacity to consider recent commentators from both East and West. Soviet philosophers, such as Ryazanov, Rubin, Mankovsky, Il'enkov, Grushin and Mamardashvili; Eastern Europeans, such as Lukács, Ajdukewicz, Filkorn, Sós, Kosík and Cibulka; Western commentators, such as Cornu, Hyppolite, Calvez, Popitz, Löwith, Lefebvre, Marcuse and Althusser. And students of methodological questions in particular will note his extended use of Marx's manuscript *Introduction* of 1857 and his *Notes on Adolph Wagner* of 1879–80.

No writer on the ontological, epistemological, philosophical, logical and scientific issues raised by Marx could hope to satisfy all his critics, and Zelený's work is – quite consciously – no exception. But one of its many virtues is that Zelený is asking the right questions.

In translating Zelený's work I have adopted certain principles that, as it happens, reflect his own philosophical enterprise. Anyone attempting to render philosophical works from one tradition into a language that is the medium for a quite different kind of philosophy runs into this problem: How does one deal with 'foreign' concepts? Does the translator simply render them in the original language, confronting the reader with a mass of incomprehensible italic? Is it perhaps better to create a realm of neologisms – a popular practice at present? I have tried rather to stretch the English language just enough to cover concepts from the German philosophical tradition, without, I hope, lapsing into a discourse that is not English. This does require the representation of thoughts in English that are somewhat foreign to the native philosophical tradition, and this is necessarily not easy reading. But I have tried not to damage the language as such, and I beg the reader to keep this in mind. Zelený's own attempt to render Hegelian and mathematical logic intelligible to students of each tradition bears a certain similarity to my intentions.

In the English text square brackets indicate an insertion by the translator, unless the initials 'J.Z.' appear. It may help the reader to be reminded or informed that a 'determination' is a 'determining attribute', a 'moment' is 'one of the elements of a complex conceptual entity', and that 'ideal' appears frequently with reference to something 'existing only in idea'. Gnoseology is 'the philosophy of cognition', and epistemology the 'science of the methods or grounds of knowledge'. 'Apperception' is 'the mind's

perception of itself as a conscious agent; self-consciousness';
'aporia' are matters of doubt; an 'enthymeme' is a 'syllogism
in which one premiss is suppressed'; and 'praxis' refers to 'the
practice or exercise of a technical subject or art'. For a general
discussion of reflex theory in epistemology see David-Hillel
Ruben's *Marxism and Materialism* (Harvester, 2nd edn., 1979).
Titles of books or articles appearing in a foreign language in the
text are rendered in English, unless the title is such as to defy
translation. In the notes I refer the reader to English translations,
where available. In a very few cases I have translated a passage
from a cited work myself, for example Marx's *Capital*, and then
referred the reader to an English translation for comparison
('cf.'). Some of the amplificatory quotation and comment that
appears in footnotes to *Die Wissenschaftslogik bei Marx und 'Das
Kapital'*, has been omitted in order to produce this translation as
economically as possible. I have kept the numbering in the notes
to this edition the same as in the edition of 1968 (Akademie
Verlag, Berlin), except where the author's revisions (1978) have
indicated otherwise.

In conclusion I should like to thank Professor Zelený very
warmly for supplying me with a useful list of corrections to his
German text, and for his encouragement.

Terrell Carver

Author's Foreword to
the German edition

My 'Introduction' provides a preliminary account of the questions out of which the present inquiry developed and of the way I attempt to examine the problems encountered. Here I merely note that the monograph on the logical structure of *Capital* which was published in 1962 in Czech forms the basis of the German translation. The continuation of my studies led in the intervening years to a more thoroughgoing preoccupation with Marx's critique of Hegel. The present work pursues the results of previous inquiries into the logical structure of *Capital*, while familiarizing the German reader with the Marxian conception of rationality and the supersession of traditional ontology as a whole.

The vitality and breadth of the dialogue which arose in the French periodicals *La Nouvelle Critique, Les Temps Modernes, et al.*, in the mid-1960s concerning my point of view may serve as an indication of the reality and theoretical interest of the problems treated here. The present work may be regarded as a contribution to that debate.

Prague   Jindřich Zelený
31 January 1967

Author's Introduction

The present work is in large part an interpretive study of Marx. Its brief is not, however, purely historical, since it breaks new ground in certain essential respects.

The first part characterizes dialectical–materialist analysis in the specific form in which it appears in Marx's *Capital*. To do this I draw on other Marxian works and manuscripts directly connected with his masterpiece, above all the manuscript of the first draft of *Capital* [published in English as *Grundrisse*].

This inquiry, which takes us from descriptive and explanatory analysis of textual detail to deeper philosophical and logical issues, prepares the way for an investigation of a more general question: in what sense does Marxism constitute a revolution in our conception of science? What is the logical content of this revolution? What has Marx contributed to the discussion of questions raised in modern philosophy by the *Novum Organum* of Bacon, the *Discourse on Method* by Descartes, Locke's *Essay Concerning Human Understanding*, the *New Essays* by Leibniz, Kant's two critiques, and Hegel's *Phenomenology of Mind* and *Science of Logic*? When we inquire into the question of whether the structural–genetic analysis employed in *Capital* possesses a general applicability as a new type of scientific thought, we come swiftly to the conclusion that the answer presupposes a clarification of Marx's relationship to traditional European metaphysics.

In this way the problem of the logic of *Capital* leads us to a consideration of the Marxian critique of Hegel. Marx's critique of bourgeois political economy and his critique of Hegel have an indissoluble inner unity and appear as a coherent whole when we consider in what respect Marx's work constitutes a revolutionary departure in our understanding of rationality.

In my concluding chapters I attempt on the basis of the preceding analysis to establish that Marxism implies the supersession of the traditional opposition of gnoseology and ontology. This yields a new philosophical method for the investigation of the first principles of logic which I call 'ontopraxeologic'.

The present work refers – favourably as well as critically – to previous Marxist–Leninist literature concerned with the question of what new conception of logic is contained explicitly and implicitly in Marx's work.[1] In my opinion there are grounds for regarding as unsatisfactory the results of previous Marxist–Leninist attempts to clarify the relationship of the materialist dialectic and analytical scientific theory. Given the present state of the problem it seems fitting to return to the question of the logical structure of *Capital*, since this – in my view – is the means by which our modern understanding of rationality from the Marxist standpoint can be deepened. It is, to be sure, a new point of view, a return within the perspective of the contemporary problem of so-called dialectical and analytical rationality: *reculer pour mieux sauter*. In this respect the present work takes up Lenin's comment on the necessity and fruitfulness of studying the logical structure of Marx's masterwork.[2]

The return to the problem of the logic of *Capital* makes it possible in my opinion to work out criteria for the debate in contemporary Marxist thought concerning the schism between anthropological and scientistic presuppositions.

Let us now consider an introductory definition. Of course I cannot deal here with all the relevant concepts or with the discussion of other viewpoints. The present inquiry merely endeavours to provide a few preconditions for the answers to questions usually subsumed under the problem of the relationship of formal and dialectical logic. I will not deal here with all these controversies. Rather it is the purpose of introductory definitions to make clear to the reader as far as possible the connotations of the concepts we are using. Hence the reader might reserve judgement on the justification – or lack of it – for these definitions until he has read the complete work.

By logic I mean the science of forms of thought leading to knowledge of objective truth. Logic is concerned above all with the forms of thought which we find in theoretical science, how they are used, and how this appears in the development of the sciences during the last millennium or more, particularly in the modern sciences.

The expression 'to examine the "logic of Marx's *Capital*" ' is obviously metaphorical. It means an inquiry into what sort of logic, what concepts and solutions to problems in logic are contained implicitly in the economic work of Marx.

To think is at the same time to perceive: it is a constituent part of the process of perception, which always exists as an aspect of

human praxis. Since logic as the theory of thought is a constituent part of the process of perception, it is *a part of the theory of
perception*; it forms the primary part of the theory of perception.
The basic problems of the theory of perception and logic understood as questions about the nature and types of rationality are to
be taken as ontopraxeological problems. (The theory of perception includes – besides *logical* problems – those concerned with
forms of thought, the so-called rational stage of perception: from
truth-content up to questions of the dependence of our perceptions on physiological processes, questions of the relativity of
perception to physical conditions, etc.[3])

The Marxist theory of perception returns to problems covered
by German transcendental philosophy in the philosophy of the
identity of thought and being; it returns, on a fundamentally new
level, to an understanding of the relations of thought and reality
which emphasizes their non-identity and the reflexive character
of perception. The copy theory is the foundation on which the
whole Marxist theory of perception and hence the theory of logic
is built. Certain logical problems can be investigated and solved
if we abstract from the copy-projection model of perception, but
the copy theory becomes necessary for the later phases of this
inquiry, when the presuppositions, or more specifically the
limits, of the ('formalistic') inquiry and solution are sought.

Today the logical mode of inquiry is not well understood,
since logic is strictly divided into two parts, of which one is said
to be formal and in no way concerned with content, the other
concerned with content and in no way formal.[4] On the contrary,
it seems correct to classify forms of thought and hence also
logical problems according to their different fields. These fields
possess a relative independence; they are detached from other
questions which the development of logic puts forward. Thus in
the last hundred years the part of logic concerned with entailment (the formal 'consequence') has become distinctly separate.[5]
Some logicians limit the definition of logic exclusively to that
field, so they call the logical problems that remain 'philosophical
problems of logic', 'gnoseological problems of logic', or 'problems of the theory of logic' and distinguish them from the 'purely
logical' or 'properly logical'. The dispute over a comprehensive
or narrow usage of the concept of logic appears to be a terminological dispute without significance – to be resolved by
convention. But in my view there are weighty arguments in
favour of the comprehensive conception, particularly if we take
into consideration the development, contemporary and future,

of Marxist logical investigations. The development of the theory of entailment leads to problems (for example the problem of the limits of formalization, semantic problems of interpretation, etc.) which one can scarcely call 'purely logical' in the narrow sense. If they are located outside the bounds of logic as a specific discipline, then this might restrict further development. There are analogies in other sciences, for example physics, in which there are problems in different fields. There are physical problems, which consist in describing the empirical properties of particular processes (to observe, to measure correctly). There are physical inquiries into the functional constituents of empirical bodies, which characterize physical processes. Moreover there are physical theories constructed with different degrees of generalization using the empirical verification of physical perceptions as a basis. It is clear that these physical theories belong to physics as a whole. The understanding outlined here does not entail the dissolution of the logic of entailment into gnoseological questions. Their relative independence is preserved,[6] and only the sharp delimitation of the so-called purely logical from the rest of the logical – in our sense – is rejected.

The different fields of modern logical investigation can be set out (to illustrate my remarks) as follows:

1. The theory of entailment. Today it comprises the logic of propositions, logic of predicates, logic of classes, etc. Formalization is its most important methodological procedure.

2. The theory of logical probabilities.

3. Formalization is itself an object of logical inquiry. It poses questions of the possibility, limits and logical character of formalization as such.

4. Connected with that is the problem of the interpretation of formal systems (the problem of model-building). It is investigated

(a) in general (= the relationship of syntax and semantics in logic)

(b) in its application to specialized disciplines.

The range of tasks named under points 2, 3 and 4 form, in my judgement, the different branches (implied under point 1) into which logic is differentiated as a consequence of the elaboration, development and supersession of the narrowly 'formalistic' conception of logic. The following points 5 and 6, on the other hand, deal with logical problems from a complex point of view, in that they contain and presuppose in a certain sense the previous points.

5. The problem of the construction of a scientific system in general (not only axiomatic but also systems of the type of Marx's *Capital*, etc.). This and the following point can be designated *methodological* tasks. If in conceiving logical relations the copy theory of perception and the theory of *systems* are emphasized, as is the case in the present work, then 'logic' approaches 'methodology' and becomes, if we press the point, identical with it.[7]

6. The problem of the logical types of scientific thought (the typology of logic).
In this list, which does not attempt an exact classification, certain points overlap in part. But even if an exact classification were proposed as an experiment, no unambiguous arrangement would result, since logic has still more dimensions.

The present study is mainly concerned with the logical problems outlined under points 5 and 6. Hence the fields of logic listed under points 1–4 are merely touched on to a greater or lesser degree.

It is generally recognized that history has generated up to now *different* types of scientific thought. There is less agreement on how to characterize a type of scientific thought, how the difference between those types is to be explained, etc.

As far as Marxism is concerned, it is clear, broadly speaking, that its development was conditioned by a relatively high level of maturity of the capitalist economic social formation and the beginnings of the revolutionary workers' movement.

Up to now more attention has generally been devoted to the dependence of Marxism and bourgeois thought on certain forms of social life than to the analysis of the fundamental theoretical (logical) forms in which a revolutionary break was realized – the break with traditional theory occasioned by the development of Marxism.[8]

A type of logic is characterized in theoretical terms by the logical categories explicitly expressed or used implicitly and by the general methodological procedure which accompanies it. The investigation of logical type in scientific thought is a more abstract question than the investigation of scientific thought within a specific discipline. Thus the 'logic of *Capital*' could be an investigation into the specialized methods of political economy. Naturally one cannot completely separate the two investigations from each other; it is rather a question of priorities. In this investigation we examine the 'logic of *Capital*' with respect to the originality and specific character of the Marxist logical type of scientific thought, the new type of rationality.

The present study is intended to promote further work on the fundamental logical problems of contemporary Marxism–Leninism by means of a clarified Marxist approach.

PART I

Analysis in Marx's *Capital*

CHAPTER 1

Marx on 'scientific explanation'

Marx's answers to questions concerning the goal of the theoretical analysis undertaken in *Capital*, if adduced in isolation from each other, differ at first glance, and at times even contradict each other.

The goal of the analysis in *Capital*, according to Marx, is to give the 'analysis of capital in its basic structure', to present 'the inner organisation of the capitalist mode of production, in its ideal average, as it were'.[1] Marx also formulates, at another point, the goal of his theoretical analysis of capitalism in the well-known formula: '. . . it is the ultimate aim of this work, to lay bare the economic law of motion of modern society . . . '[2] This amounts to the 'illumination of the special laws that regulate the origin, existence, development and death of a given social organism and its replacement by another, higher one'.[3] Emphasis is placed first on the 'inner organisation', the 'basic structure', then on the 'laws of motion', the 'laws of development'. For Marx a structural and genetic analysis presents no contradiction, and does not result in parallel or sequential treatment. Marx was concerned with presenting the capitalist mode of production as a self-developing, self-generating and self-destroying structure. Theoretical analysis which strives towards this goal is a unified structural-genetic analysis.

In the same context in which Marx speaks of 'basic structure', he also refers to relations which correspond 'to the concept of capital', the 'general type of capitalist relations'.[4] Hence 'to understand scientifically' signifies in that context for Marx the representation of the characteristics of a particular self-developing type, organism or whole – *the undertaking of a structural-genetic analysis.*

The originality of Marx's procedure can be demonstrated by comparing it with what his predecessors in theoretical political economy, particularly Ricardo, understood by 'scientific explanation', given that they set out their interpretations of scientific explanation only implicitly (Ricardo) or implicitly and explicitly (Adam Smith).[5]

There are limitations on such a comparative analysis. Comparisons can be made in different ways: either supra-historical and contingent – in which case the comparison leads us away from a correct understanding, rather than towards it – or with reference to origins: then the application of the comparative method, the specification of differences or similarities, is the presupposition and means for accumulating material for further treatment, for a dialectical-materialist understanding of phenomena in their necessary development. We take comparative analysis in the second sense. Between the economic systems of Ricardo and Marx there is a direct genetic connection. Two different types of scientific explanation are embodied in scientific systems covering the same subject. Hence there is a promising point of departure for interpreting the originality of Marx's conception of scientific explanation, that is the Marxist logical type of scientific thought in its first phase of development. I am not, however, concerned with aspects of the wider question of how Ricardo's conception of scientific method, which belongs to the Lockean logical type, is classified in its broad historical setting, what position it occupies there, and what relation it bears to other types of scientific method in modern science, etc.[6] My initial comparative analysis is in any case not concerned with the distinction between Marx's conception and an important pre-Marxist type of scientific explanation, as developed in classical German philosophy, particularly by Hegel. The treatment of the *consequences* of my introductory comparative analysis is of course impossible in further chapters without investigating Hegel's role in the development of the Marxist type of logic and clarifying the originality of Marx's conception with respect to Hegel.

In Ricardo's analysis of capitalism there is an implied conception of scientific explanation which can be characterized as follows:

(a) It distinguishes empirical surface from essence.

(b) Essence is understood as something unchangeable, something given once and for all, analogous to Newton's laws. The empirical forms of phenomena are considered as direct phenomenal forms of a fixed essence, which is partly investigated and then established, and partly taken as an independent presupposition. The empirical forms of phenomena are fixed because of their ahistorical character and at the same time variable with respect to quantitative changes.

(c) The questions to which the whole analysis is addressed appear in a more generalized form:

(i) what quantitative changes in empirical forms take place when they depend on changes in the essence;

(ii) what quantitative changes in empirical forms result if certain empirical forms in a reciprocal relationship vary quantitatively?

The amount of labour required for the production of a commodity is obviously the fixed essence which makes it possible, according to Ricardo, to understand in principle all phenomena of the capitalist economy and 'to determine the laws which regulate this distribution . . . among three classes of the community; namely, the proprietor of land, the owner of the stock or capital . . . and the labourers . . . '[7] which, according to Ricardo, is the chief task of political economy. The original distinction between empirical phenomenon and essence appears at first for Ricardo in the form of a question: what is in reality 'the foundation of the exchangeable value of all things'?[8] If we inquire into the structure of Ricardo's presentation of capitalism, after the determination of the principle that labour is the substance of exchange-value, what we discover is in fact a somewhat illogical division of chapters characterized by questions which Ricardo puts in succession. These questions are the following:

What is the main cause of changes in the relative values of commodities?

Is the existence of different qualities of labour the cause of changes in the relative values of commodities?

Does a greater or lesser use of constant capital influence the relative value of a commodity?

Does the rising or falling of wages affect any of the changes in the relative values of commodities?

What consequences result from changes in the value of money or from changes in the value of commodities which are exchanged for money?

Does the appropriation of land and the resultant development of rent affect the relative value of commodities, independent of the amount of labour which is necessary for the production of commodities?

What is the cause of continual changes in profit and rate of interest resulting from this?

Overall we are inquiring into changes in exchange-value (a

quantitative relationship) under the presupposition that labour is the basis of exchange-value and that it is dependent on quantitative changes in different empirical factors and forms of the capitalist economy.

To term Ricardo's investigation a one-sided *quantitativism* is to overlook the fact that it does not operate with a complete reduction of qualitative characteristics to quantitative. It does not amount to classical mechanics and mechanical materialism.[9] In Ricardo's presentation qualitative determinations do occur, but his theoretical analysis does not treat them as qualitative determinations, since – contrary to the nature of qualitative determinations – they are derived from appearances, from the empirical world, uncritically, as fixed, unchangeable, unmediated. Thus for example wages, profit and rent are qualitatively differentiated forms of income in capitalism. Ricardo does not investigate them, however, with respect to their specific qualities, but considers them as three constant 'natural' sources of three constant 'natural' classes of the population and dedicates the whole inquiry to the question of changes in different quantitative relations between these three forms of income, specifically between different factors in the capitalist mode of production and these forms of income.[10] This shows how the one-sided quantitative standpoint accompanies the ahistorical standpoint.

The quantitative standpoint also enters Ricardo's work in his basic distinction between exchange-value and its essence cited above. Ricardo is not always consistent in that distinction. While most of the time he distinguishes between quantitative relations (in this context *relative* value) and what one might call 'absolute value' which comes to light in that quantitative relation, Ricardo at times confuses matters which Marx later clarified with his distinction between 'value' ('value-substance') and 'exchange-value' ('value-form'). In general Ricardo does not develop this distinction, as would be necessary in order to understand 'the real basis of exchange-value' and to concentrate his analysis properly on the investigation of quantitative changes in exchange-values.

CHAPTER 2

The transformation of concepts

When we investigate how Ricardo's one-sided quantitative standpoint contributed to the new concept of scientific explanation presented in Marx's *Capital* we must bear these points in mind:

(a) Marx did not dismiss Ricardo's investigations into the quantitative relations of commodity exchange as worthless for an understanding of the 'real basis of exchange-value' and the 'character of capital'. He recognized their positive role in the acquisition of scientific knowledge of the objects under investigation.

(b) However, according to Marx, they yielded only a rough and 'deficient representation' and therefore became 'defective', because their subordinate, provisional role in the perception of the object, their limitations, their role as merely one of the individual aspects of the process of perception were not grasped, because they were presented as the whole truth, as knowledge of the characteristics, the essence (the 'nature', as Smith and Ricardo prefer to say) of the objects under investigation. In this case, they are necessarily linked with an ahistorical understanding of categories.[1]

(c) The supersession of Ricardo's one-sided quantitative standpoint by Marx does not mean he devotes less attention to the quantitative aspect of the object. The quantitative aspect of the object is rather perceived more exactly and completely where it is of significance for the scientific perception of the object (that is, the perception of its necessary development, the completion of the structural-genetic analysis of the object). For example Marx's analyses of the quantitative attributes of the average rate of profit are more comprehensive and more precise than those of Smith and Ricardo. Similarly Marx investigates *magnitudes* of value – at first 'absolute' magnitudes, then relative magnitudes, and later magnitudes of value in connection with money, etc.[2]

(d) Marx perceives the *justification* of limiting oneself to and concentrating on the investigation of quantitative changes during a particular phase of science. This limitation and concentration leads to a one-sided quantitative standpoint when it takes place under the conditions outlined in (b). It could, however, be a completely legitimate phase of the epistemological process, a phase based on the higher, genetic conception of scientific explanation (the higher, genetic type of logic), if we are conscious of the place and function of knowledge limited to quantitative analysis.

Now we can take up Ricardo's and Marx's theory of value at a point where the two thinkers are concerned in a similar way with a particular quantitative relationship, and we investigate whether similar forms of thought are used – specifically, whether they are modified by Marx in certain ways. For this study we shall take corresponding analyses of the consequences of changes in the productivity of labour for the exchange-value of commodities.[3]

First, the texts:

Ricardo

To convince ourselves that this is the real foundation of exchangeable value, let us suppose any improvement to be made in the means of abridging labour in any one of the various processes through which the raw cotton must pass, before the manufactured stockings come to the market, to be exchanged for other things; and observe the effects which will follow. If fewer men were required to cultivate the raw cotton, or if fewer sailors were employed in navigating, or shipwrights in constructing the ship, in which it was conveyed to us; if fewer hands were employed in raising the buildings and machinery, or if these, when raised, were rendered more efficient, the stockings would inevitably fall

Marx

The equation 20 yards of linen = 1 coat, or 20 yards of linen are worth 1 coat, presupposes the presence in 1 coat of exactly as much of the substance of value as there is in 20 yards of linen, implies therefore that the quantities in which the two commodities are present have cost the same amount of labour or the same quantity of labour-time. But the labour-time necessary for the production of 20 yards of linen or 1 coat varies with every change in the productivity of the weaver or the tailor. The influence of such changes on the relative expression of the magnitude of value must now be investigated more closely.

I. Let the value of the linen change while the value of the coat remains constant. If the in value, and consequently command less of other things. They would fall, because a less quantity of labour was necessary to their production, and would therefore exchange for a smaller quantity of those things in which no such abridgment of labour had been made . . . Suppose that in the early stages of society, the bows and arrows of the hunter were of equal value, and of equal durability, with the canoe and implements of the fisherman, both being the produce of the same quantity of labour. Under such circumstances the value of the deer, the produce of the hunter's day's labour, would be exactly equal to the value of the fish, the produce of the fisherman's day's labour . . . If with the same quantity of labour a less quantity of fish, or a greater quantity of game were obtained, the value of fish would rise in comparison with that of game. If, on the contrary, with the same quantity of labour a less quantity of game, or a greater quantity of fish was obtained, game would rise in comparison with fish . . . Now suppose, that with the same labour and fixed capital, more fish could be produced, but no more gold or game, the relative value of fish would fall in comparison with gold or game. If, instead of twenty salmon, twenty-five were the produce of one day's labour, the price of a salmon would be sixteen shillings instead of a pound, and two salmon and a half, instead of two salmon, would be given in exchange for one deer, but

the labour-time necessary for the production of the linen be doubled, as a result of the increasing infertility of flax-growing soil for instance, its value will also be doubled. Instead of the equation 20 yards of linen = 1 coat, we should have 20 yards of linen = 2 coats, since 1 coat would now contain only half as much labour-time as 20 yards of linen. If, on the other hand, the necessary labour-time be reduced by one half, as a result of improved looms for instance, the value of the linen will fall by one half. In accordance with this the equation will now read 20 yards of linen = $\frac{1}{2}$ coat. The relative value of commodity A, i.e. its value expressed in commodity B, rises and falls in direct relation to the value of A, if the value of B remains constant.

II. Let the value of the linen remain constant, while the value of the coat changes. If, under these circumstances, the labour-time necessary for the production of a coat is doubled, as a result, for instance, of a poor crop of wool, we should have, instead of 20 yards of linen = 1 coat, 20 yards of linen = $\frac{1}{2}$ coat. If, on the other hand, the value of the coat sinks by one half, then 20 yards of linen = 2 coats. Hence, if the value of commodity A remains constant, its relative value, as expressed in commodity B, rises and falls in inverse relation to the change in the value of B.

If we compare the different cases examined under headings I and II, it emerges that the same change in the magnitude of price of deer would continue at £2 as before. In the same manner, if fewer fish could be obtained with the same capital and labour, fish would rise in comparative value. Fish then would rise or fall in exchangeable value, only because more or less labour was required to obtain a given quantity; and it never could rise or fall beyond the proportion of the increased or diminished quantity of labour required.[4]

relative value may arise from entirely opposed causes. Thus the equation 20 yards of linen = 1 coat becomes 20 yards of linen = 2 coats, either because the value of the linen has doubled or because the value of the coat has fallen by one half, and it becomes 20 yards of linen = $\frac{1}{2}$ coat, either because the value of the linen has fallen by one half, or because the value of the coat has doubled.

III. Let the quantities of labour necessary for the production of the linen and the coat vary simultaneously in the same direction and the same proportion. In this case, 20 yards of linen = 1 coat, as before, whatever change may have taken place in their respective values. Their change of value is revealed only when they are compared with a third commodity, whose value has remained constant. If the values of all commodities rose or fell simultaneously, and in the same proportion, their relative values would remain unaltered. The change in their real values would be manifested by an increase or decrease in the quantity of commodities produced within the same labour-time.

IV. The labour-time necessary for the production respectively of the linen and the coat, and hence their values, may vary simultaneously in the same direction, but to an unequal degree, or in opposite directions, and so on. The influence of all possible combinations of this kind on the relative value of a commodity can be worked out simply by applying cases I, II and III.

Thus real changes in the magnitude of value are neither unequivocally nor exhaustively reflected in their relative expression, or, in other words, in the magnitude of the relative value. The relative value of a commodity may vary, although its value remains constant. Its relative value may remain constant, although its value varies; and finally, simultaneous variations in the magnitude of its value and in the relative expression of that magnitude do not by any means have to correspond at all points.[5]

It is apparent that Marx contributes no new conclusions in principle or distinctive insights on this question. But the analysis is more lucid, more systematic, and more distinct.[6] It is more elegant, more exact, and purer in the sense that Marx does not employ categories more complex than capital, and he distinguishes concepts such as 'magnitude of value' and 'relation of value-magnitudes' more exactly; he does not confuse the two meanings of the term 'relative value'. The most basic distinction between Ricardo and Marx consists in the position they give the analysis just cited in the process of perceiving the object – in other words: what questions they put round this analysis, *before* it and *after* it. Here we see that for Ricardo the text cited is one of the main arguments, if not the main argument for the principle that the exchange-value of a commodity is determined by the amount of labour required for its production. On the other hand, for Marx the text cited is definitely not the main argument for the view that the labour necessary for the production of a commodity is the basis of the exchange-value of the commodity. The main point of the Marxian argument is the answer to another question, namely: under what social conditions does labour turn into value, the sort of labour that creates exchange-value? How is the money-form of value to be explained? How is the principle, according to which labour is the substance of exchange-value, modified by the development of capital?

In Ricardo's understanding of scientific explanation the investigation of the consequences of quantitative changes in the productivity of labour for the exchange-value of the same commodity occupies another position, performs a function other than the one in the Marxian understanding of scientific explanation, although the forms of thought employed in the analysis of these questions virtually coincide in Ricardo and Marx.

When the two thinkers investigate *exchange*, and when – as we have seen in the parallel texts cited above – they work on the investigation of quantitative changes using essentially the same forms of thought, the fundamental distinction between the two is that the Ricardian understanding of the category of exchange is essentially limited and is reduced[7] to the quantitative act of exchange, while in Marx's scientific thought the category of exchange is employed in a new, incomparably richer context. With Marx things, phenomena and qualitative characteristics are themselves grasped as things which develop from other things and are transformed into something else: they are, to put it in Hegelian terms, understood as 'themselves-becoming-another'. Every real form is understood as being in the process of alteration;[8] then 'not only are appearances transitory, alterable, fleeting, only divided from one another by conditional limits, but also the *essences* of things themselves'.[9]

Before analysing these problems further, I shall cite a few examples:

(a) On the investigation of the so-called 'natural price of labour' Ricardo writes:

> It is not to be understood that the natural price of labour, estimated even in food and necessaries, is absolutely fixed and constant. It varies at different times in the same country, and very materially differs in different countries. It depends essentially on the habits and customs of the people.[10]

Up to a point, Ricardo's concepts of wages and the 'natural price of labour' are not completely fixed, fossilized categories. They retain throughout a certain elasticity and alterability which Ricardo calls the (historical and geographical) variability of the 'natural price of labour'. Hence Ricardo's concept of the 'natural price of labour' is a fixed category, as opposed to Marx's category of wages. Ricardo grasps it then only *supra-historically*, as an economic form appropriate for all phases of development of human society: if it alters because of geographical and historical conditions, then it alters only quantitatively.[11] The supersession of this category fixation occurred when Marx grasped wages as an economic form which represents in its particular qualitative attributes something temporary, dependent on historical conditions and on the alterability of the whole of which it is an aspect.

(b) In an analogous way we might, with a small modification, characterize the distinction between the Ricardian and Marxian concepts of 'distribution'. In Ricardo we read:

> The produce of the earth – all that is derived from its surface by the united application of labour, machinery, and capital, is divided among three classes of the community; namely, the proprietor of the land, the owner of the stock or capital necessary for its cultivation, and the labourers by whose industry it is cultivated.
>
> But in different stages of society, the proportions of the whole produce of the earth which will be allotted to each of these classes, under the names of rent, profit, and wages, will be essentially different; depending mainly on the actual fertility of the soil, on the accumulation of capital and population, and on the skill, ingenuity, and instruments employed in agriculture.
>
> To determine the laws which regulate this distribution, is the principal problem in Political Economy . . . [12]

Once again it seems that 'distribution' is understood as alterable in a certain respect and dependent on historical conditions. But this alterability comprises only the quantitative characteristics of distribution; the particular qualitative attributes of 'distribution' are understood by Ricardo as fixed, rigid, given once and for all. Ricardo elevates this historically transitory form of distribution peculiar to the capitalist mode of production into something supra-historical and absolutely inalterable.

Here Marx's supersession of category fixation does not consist in the fact that he revealed the historically transitory character of distribution, in the sense of its belonging only to a particular phase, but not to all phases of human society. As opposed to Ricardo, Marx perceives the elasticity and alterability of concepts, in that he considers transitory, qualitatively different forms of distribution as aspects of qualitatively different modes of production; he sees the particular qualitative–quantitative attributes of specific forms of distribution in context, in mutual transition into one another, affecting particular aspects of the social process. [13]

(c) With Marx the supersession of category fixation has another analogous feature in so far as it deals with logical categories used by Ricardo for expressing the fundamental ontological structure of his understanding of the world. The core of the Marxian conception of the elasticity of concepts and the supersession of fixation in ideas (as in the Marxian category of exchange) is in the last instance a new relationship of relative and absolute, and (in general) a new objectivity, the relationship of objects in objective reality to the process of perception. The basis for that is the historical, practical understanding of man and the social conditions of human life. This Marxian conception is an integral part of structural–genetic analysis as it is employed in *Capital*. I shall examine that analysis in the succeeding sections of this investigation.

CHAPTER 3

Forms of reality and
thought

The Marxian theory of the ontological structure of reality and the logical basis of scientific thought is characterized by, among other things, the solution to the problem of the interdependence between relations and properties.

The relations which we encountered in Ricardo's scientific analysis may be divided up logically into three groups:

1. Relations at the level of appearances, particularly quantitative relations. We have investigated in the preceding chapter Ricardo's and Marx's conceptions of quantitative relations and have come to the conclusion that the forms of thought employed in that field by Ricardo and Marx are essentially similar. We are dealing here with the category 'relation' which is derived from the pioneering work of Leibniz and has undergone a vast development in post-Marxian mathematical logic. The rapid development of that discipline in the twentieth century will doubtless be accelerated, because Marxist thought and praxis, driven by the need for automation in production and for the conscious direction of society and social processes, put mathematical logic increasingly at the service of technology, planning, education, etc.

2. Substantial relations. Ricardo concerned himself very little with these, while Marx devoted great attention to them. This follows from the fact that Marx and Ricardo understand essence differently. While for Ricardo essence is something qualitatively fixed and non-differentiable, Marx sees and investigates the *alteration* of that essence; he understands it as something historically transitory which proceeds through different levels of development and qualitative changes. He understands essence as a contradictory process which has phases of development and different degrees of depth. With respect to scientific knowledge Marx is concerned mainly with the discovery of laws pertaining to substantial alterations.

3. The relations between essence and the level of appearances. With Ricardo these relations are immediately abstracted, so-called 'formal abstractions' (Marx); with Marx the analysis of appearance and essence is an aspect of structural-genetic analysis.[1]

Our task is now to investigate what is meant in Marx's work by the category 'relation', so let us refer critically to the analysis developed by L. A. Mankovsky.[2]

Mankovsky begins with a critique of the logic of relations, as interpreted by positivists. He draws attention to the fact that from a similar positivist position the Russian liberal P. Struve had attempted to misrepresent the Marxian theory of value. Struve maintained that empirically determined price relations are the exclusive, conclusive economic reality in the exchange of commodities. Hence he termed the conception (including Marx's) of price as a phenomenal form of value-substance, a 'metaphysical', 'mechanist–naturalist' conception. The logical structure of the Marxian view is obsolete, Struve maintained, since it rests on an Aristotelian understanding of the S–P [subject–predicate] structure of the proposition.

In the course of his critique of the positivist, non-substantialist conception of the category 'relation', Mankovsky appeals to Marx's famous statement that the *'properties of a thing do not arise from its relation to other things, they are, on the contrary, merely activated by such relations'*.[3] To that Mankovsky appends the following general observation:

> That [passage] was directed against the vulgar economists who spontaneously took up the standpoint of positivism, long before the logic of relations had been worked out as a special theory in logic. The Marxian view explains briefly and exactly the fundamental difference between the logic of materialism and the logic of positivism, between substantialist and relativist logic. The positivist trend towards the 'logic of relations' finds expression in their view on the logical structure of all propositions considered fundamental: They propose in place of the classical formulation of the proposition 'S is P' their own formulation 'aRb' [a 'relation' b]. The classical formulation of the proposition 'S is P', which has become a constituent of dialectical logic, means that perception is directed first of all to the *object* which is expressed by the term S (the subject of the proposition); P (the predicate of the proposition) expresses particular properties of the object.[4]

In its logical aspect Marxian thought has an attributive-substantial orientation and is constructed according to the formula '*S* is *P*'.[5]

Mankovsky is doubtless correct when he maintains that Marx's view on the primary character of the property, as opposed to the relation, alludes to the positivist debasement of scientific thought. But it is questionable whether the general observation is correct that Marx's comments express briefly and exactly the basic antithesis between the logic of materialism and the logic of positivism, between substantialist and relativist logic.

This means that in Marx's work an important question is left unsettled, namely, the distinction between materialist, substantialist logic characteristic of Ricardo, for example, and the materialist, substantialist logic of *Marx*. With Ricardo, materialist, substantialist logic is determined at the outset by his conception of fixed essence, whereas Marx's advance from fixed essence to fluid dialectical essence entails a new conception of materialist, substantialist logic: in Marx's scientific work the materialist – *sit venia verbo* – relativist-substantialist logic is employed. But it is so constructed that it has nothing in common with a relativism which disputes the possibility of perceiving objective reality correctly. It is rather a presupposition of true objective knowledge, following on the collapse of anti-dialectical conceptions of the ontological structure of reality.

When Mankovsky maintains[6] that Marx counterposes the formula '*S* is *P*' to the formula '*aRb*', it must be objected that this simple contraposition of relation- and predicate-structure does not express the Marxian conception. Marx rejects the reduction of exchange-value to a quantitative relation; he grasps and explains the quantitative relation by the deeper property 'of being value'. But this property itself ('of being value') which conditions the quantitative relation and – under contemporary conditions in which commodity production is dominant – every existing exchange relation, arises in a particular phase of human society under particular conditions. It is a particular *relation* between men and their labour, and is *created* by a relation; a material thing is its bearer.

If we were to use symbols we could not say that Marx sets the formula '*S* is *P*' against the formula '*aRb*', but that the whole matter must be explained in a more fundamental way.

Marx proceeds from the empirical surface and agrees at the outset that exchange-value appears at first as a quantitative relation (*is found* in the empirical world of appearances), hence *aRb*.

Marx endorses the formula '*aRb*'. He does not, however, stop at that, but explains that the reduction of exchange-value to a purely relative and in that sense quantitative relation would be incorrect. He recommends: 'Let us consider the matter a little more closely.'[7]

The result of that closer consideration is the distinction of a *dual* relativity, an external and a substantial. That which is relative in substance can appear against external relativity as something absolute and non-relative, but only within particular limits and under particular abstract presuppositions. In that sense Marx sometimes speaks of 'absolute value', opposed to qualitatively and quantitatively determined 'value-forms', as the 'expression', the 'form of appearance' of absolute value. That value, which sometimes appears in Marx as 'absolute value' opposed to the value-form, is *relative* (relative in substance) – (a) in the sense of the historically relative character of the value-substance[8] and (b) in the sense that it is created by the relationship of individual human labour to the total amount of labour that is socially necessary.[9] The relativity of value is contradictory. As in the similar cases which we see in Hegel's *Logic*, an understanding of substance as relation gives way to understanding its contradictory character.

The traditional substantial-attributive structure of scientific thought as conceptualized in the philosophy of the Enlightenment, for example in the metaphysics of Descartes, in Locke or in pre-Kantian German philosophy, is revolutionized by Marx when he relativizes it on the basis of his dialectical interpretation of reality. On that point, which concerns us here in connection with the problem posed by Mankovsky concerning the distinction between substantial and relativist logic,[10] I should like to cite Descartes' substantial-attributive structure, for example in §51 and the following paragraphs of the first part of the *Principles of Philosophy* for clarification. Descartes understands substance as something which exists such that it needs nothing else for its existence. Each of two substances, the spiritual and the physical, possesses its specific constant attribute which forms its essence and is the basis of all other properties (§53). Extension is a characteristic of physical substance; thought is a characteristic of spiritual substance. All *modi, qualitates, differentiae* arise from that basis, and of course under general natural laws, the first of which reads:

Every reality, in so far as it is simple and undivided, always remains in the same condition so far as it can, and never changes except through external causes.[11]

Locke[12] was skeptical of the concept of substance: it is a concept of little use, even obscurantist. Of substance we can only have a dim and confused conception. If we take into consideration how Locke proceeds with the actual investigation of real appearances, we see that in accordance with his gnoseological reservation on the intelligibility of substance and his empiricist critique of idealist rationalism in Descartes, he understands real appearances and their properties in agreement with Descartes. While Descartes puts more emphasis on their mathematical understanding, Locke emphasizes their sensory, empirical understanding, but a similar conception of the ontological structure of reality lies at the basis of the two procedures. With Locke's procedure the categorial apparatus operates with sensory approximations, and with Descartes' procedure, rigorous abstraction from rationally evident principles is given geometrically. This distinction – which is very plain and not without significance in the history of bourgeois thought – cannot hide the fact that we are still dealing in essence with related conceptions. Wolff, against whom classical German philosophy reacted in a very significant way, formulates exactly the rigid, dualistic separation of constant from variable, of absolute from relative properties. In his *Logic* we read in §60: 'If we consider what things consist of, then we first discover constants, which are there when species does not alter; also, alterations which occur, though species is not changed.' §61: 'If any constants pertain to an entity, then this may be expressed absolutely, and the contrary proposition as well.' §62: 'If something is alterable, then this could only be the case under determinate conditions, and the contrary proposition as well.' Wolff's conception of 'relation' as merely external, conceived on the basis of fixed essence and isolated entities opposed to one another, is shown, for example, in §857 of his *Ontology*: 'Relation adds no quality to an entity which it does not contain itself; for no entity exists in dependence, whether real or apparent, of one thing on another.'[13]

What with Descartes or Wolff was fixed and rigid and was represented as a rule in the hierarchical structure 'Substance – Attribute – Mode – Accident', etc., loses its fixedness with Marx, its rigidity and its absolute stability. It becomes dependent on a particular historical phase of development and on its role in real, self-developing totalities (systems).

In Marxian thought the objectively real process, which is uniform in its materiality and comes to be known more deeply and with objective truth, plays the role of substance in the Cartesian sense (as something which needs for its existence nothing other than itself). The category of substance thus understood does not play a role in his thought like the one it plays, for example, in the Cartesian metaphysic. Hence we usually find the term substance in Marx's *Capital* in a transferred sense, in the sense of an essential process, which retains its empirically perceptible form – or its form perceived by mediation – in the different forms of its appearance. The substantial quality of that essential process (the quality of substantiality) is historically relative, but also relative with respect to its role, function, relations in totalities (systems). Confronting Marx was the problem of different levels of the substantial process and also the problem of defining a process by the different relative properties of different substantial levels.[14]

Though Marx, in his critique of the reduction of exchange-value to a quantitative relation, emphasized that in that quantitative relation there is a property not created by that relation, he also indicates elsewhere that the existence of particular properties (also substantial properties) is conditioned and created by particular relations. Marx writes for example:

> As they develop, the interrelations of commodities crystallize into distinct aspects of the universal equivalent, and thus the exchange process becomes at the same time the process of formation of money. This process as a whole, which comprises several processes, constitutes *circulation*.[15]

Marx indicates how bourgeois policital economists transformed the properties of things, which are formed by their relation in a particular whole, by their roles and functions in a particular process, into fixed, substantial properties,[16] independent of relations in a historically transitory whole. That is for example the case, if the means of labour are understood suprahistorically as fixed capital, independent of the relation in which they function.

Marx carefully distinguished cases where entering into particular relations alters the substantial properties of a particular appearance, and cases where it does not alter them, where these substantial properties remain essentially unaltered by their entry into new relations. Thus he writes, for example:

And to this extent Smith is right when he says that the portion of the value of the product created by the labourer himself, for which the capitalist pays him an equivalent in the form of wages, becomes the source of revenue for the labourer. But this does not alter the nature or magnitude of this portion of the value of the commodity any more than the value of the means of production is changed by the fact that they function as capital-values, or the nature and magnitude of a straight line are changed by the fact that it serves as the base of some triangle or as the diameter of some ellipse. The value of labour-power remains quite as independently definite as that of those means of production.[17]

On the subject of how the substantial property 'of being capital' depends on relations in a developing whole, Marx writes:

Money always remains the same form in the same substratum; and can thus be more easily conceived as a mere thing. But one and the same commodity, money etc., can represent capital or revenue etc. Thus it is clear even to the economists that money is not something tangible; but that one and the same thing can be subsumed sometimes under the title capital, sometimes under another and contrary one, and correspondingly *is* or *is not* capital. It is then evident that it is a *relation, and can only be a relation of production*.[18]

Marx's statement of the primacy of the property as opposed to the relation may not therefore be taken as the whole truth; it provides only a particular way of dividing the ontological structure in Marx's work, that is, the relation of the substantial property to surface phenomena, which is expressed by a quantitative relation (proportion).[19] Besides these relations, which are quantitative proportions secondary to a particular social property appearing in the quantitative proportion, Marx recognizes other relations of a very different sort; their connection with properties, with essence, with the remaining phenomenal and substantial relations of the developmental process is not expressed by fixed primacy or fixed abstraction. The most significant characteristic of the Marxian theory of the ontological structure of reality and the logical structure of thought is, in this respect, the *relativization* of the traditional substantial-attributive structure on the basis of dialectical-materialist monism.[20]

Mankovsky attempts to carry on the polemic using a positivist absolutization of the relation – the asubstantialistically understood relation – such that he in fact abandons the essence of relativity[21] and expresses unsatisfactorily the Marxian dialectical-materialist theory of the ontological structure of reality and the logical structure of thought as well as regressing in part to a fixed substantialist logic.

The dialectical-materialist alterability and relativization of the substantial-attributive structure by Marx was preceded by the *Hegelian* critique of the traditional subject–predicate (S–P) mode of thought.[22] When he described the 'character of the knowledge of absolute reality', Hegel emphasized above all that it is necessary to move beyond dead, motionless substance to 'living substance'. 'The living substance', according to Hegel, 'is that being which is truly subject, or, what is the same thing, is truly realized and actual (*wirklich*) solely in the process of positing itself, or in mediating with its own self its transitions . . . '[23] If substance is understood as self-development (as 'becoming', 'becoming another', 'itself-becoming-another', 'self-movement'), then the old S–P structure of the proposition is inadequate for expressing the truth.

> The subject is taken to be a fixed point, and to it as their support the predicates are attached, by a process falling within the individual knowing about it, but not looked upon as belonging to the point of attachment itself; only by such a process, however, could the content be presented as subject.[24]

The truth is the whole and the whole is 'merely the essential nature [of something] reaching its completeness through the process of its own development'.[25] Under the presupposition of appearances as complete and of externally understood alterability, subject and predicate exist in the fixed relationship of superiority or subordination, relative to equal ordering; under the presupposition of substance as self-developing, the predicate must necessarily be understood so that the subject manifests itself in its own movement (= own existence) in the predicate, just as the developing essence is necessarily presented in different phenomenal forms.[26]

All the concepts which are applied in Hegel's critique to traditional subject–predicate thinking (concepts like 'what is truly real', 'self-movement', etc.) are understood in the spirit of absolute idealism, with its principle of the identity of thought and being. In that form they were simply not usable for Marx the materialist, who understood knowledge as reflection. The account of how Marx has superseded the ideas of Hegel contains all the characteristic features of the dialectical-materialist structural-genetic analysis. The chapters in the first part of the present work are concerned with that analysis.

The mathematical and natural scientific thought of the seventeenth and eighteenth centuries is sometimes termed *relational* thought. Filkorn writes, for example: 'The basic property which distinguished the science of the [Galilean – J.Z.] period from the science of slave-holding peoples, is its relationality . . . '[27] It is important to make clear the distinction between the relationality characteristic of Galilean science and the new relationality (the relativization of forms of thought), of which Hegel's *Science of Logic* was the *idealist* manifestation in logic. This new relationality comprises in its *materialistic*, critical supersession of Hegel's ideas a basic element of the Marxian concept of science.

Filkorn draws attention to that distinction[28] and seeks it mainly in the classification of relations into external and internal. 'The science of the Galilean period could not reach the concept of the inner relation . . . It remained on the surface.'[29] It appears that one can characterize that distinction rather by the fact that in Galilean science relationality (the investigation of external and inner relations) was founded on the acceptance of a fixed essence and fixed essential properties,[30] while the relationality of Marxian thought is grounded on the understanding of the relational development of the inner level (essence). This esoteric conception leads to the understanding of contradiction as the essential characteristic of that new relationality in development. If it is said that contradiction is the *source* of change, then old non-dialectical conceptions are obviously confusing us here: for something to change there must exist a source of change, which is something different from the change itself. If we attempt to formulate the Marxian understanding of that ontological question on the basis of our investigation of structural-genetic analysis as employed in *Capital*, then we come to realize that contradictoriness is the innermost property – if one can say that[31] – of the relational and developmental ontological structure in Marxian theory. It is a property which belongs to that structure existentially and is not an external source of change. Rather it is in a certain respect identical with it.

The Marxian relativization of forms of thought on the basis of dialectical-materialist monism could be characterized in this way – if at first we set a negative limitation – that it does not mean a subjectivist relativism (be it only an individualistic type or the 'objective' subjectivism of Kant). Also, it does not mean the limitation of human knowledge to 'merely relative' truth. In a positive sense we can say that it deals with a relativization of forms of thought:

1. in the sense of historical transitoriness;

2. in the sense of perceiving the mutual conditioning, inter-penetration, mutual transcendence of forms of thought, since logical categories are not isolated and not fixed; this is particularly relevant for logical categories in polar opposition;

3. in the sense of the relativization of the antithesis of relative and absolute. The Marxian conception also means the acquisition of the 'absolute' quantity of knowledge, or more clearly, of the object of scientific knowledge (following the Lockean expansion of science under Deism, and the subjectivization of human knowledge in Kant's *Critique of Pure Reason*). We are dealing here with the sole means of acquisition which is possible today. This dialectic of 'relativism' and 'absolutism' is important for the capacity or incapacity of a type of scientific thought to be a concise, logical, *scientific* outlook on the world and life;

4. in the sense of destroying the absolute applicability (and asserting bounds where they could be correctly used) of particular pre-Marxist forms of thought and scientific modes of procedure. Here it is not a matter of historical relativity but of relativity in the sense of limited, non-absolute applicability to and suitability for different fields;

5. in the sense of our understanding the dependence of logical categories on historically developing forms of human society.

CHAPTER 4

The starting point

The problem of the starting point must be investigated from two aspects: 1. The investigation of a given subject; 2. The exposition of a scientific system.[1]

1. Marx proceeds as a materialist, for whom the ideal is the material transposed and translated in the human head,[2] so he proceeds *with the investigation* of an object from objective reality, from empirical observation. This involves the conversion of empirical observations and data into concepts.[3]

Marx's conception of the empirical starting point is different from Locke's (which forms the basis of Smith's and Ricardo's analysis), and is characterized by the following:

(a) To the individual-empiricist, contemplative interpretation of experience Marx counterposes the historical-collectivist, practical conception.[4]

(b) The claim to be free of presuppositions, which arises from unhistorical conceptions of a 'tabula rasa', is replaced by the claim that all presuppositions must be investigated so as to understand them critically, since they are historically and socially inseparable from any scientific approach to objective reality.[5]

(c) Marx's theoretical standpoint applies in all phases of the empirical appropriation of material, and this general philosophical line (the conception of the ontological structure of reality and the character of logical categories) is worked out gradually; political and economic conceptions are grasped theoretically in the form of hypotheses. The role of such 'anticipated' theoretical orientations is limited by their dialectical-materialist character;[6] they are used with an awareness of their open-endedness, their characteristic dialectical operation; in no way is this a simple subsumption of individual cases under a general scheme.

2. Marx was intensively concerned with *the problem of the starting point in the systematic structural-genetic presentation* of the capitalist mode of production. He dealt with this in a detailed way in his methodological discussion in the unfinished *Introduction* of 1857[7]

as well as in his critique of the systems of Smith and Ricardo
in *Theories of Surplus Value*.[8]

(a) Marx connects the problem of the starting point first of all
with the level of development of the science under consideration. The
attempt at the beginning of the seventeenth century to make
political economy scientific began with the living whole (population, nation, state, etc.) as it appeared to the pioneers of the new
science. These living totalities could enter into the works of the
economists of the seventeenth century only as 'chaotic conceptions of the whole'. Their analysis proceeds to work out a few
simple, general concepts, such as division of labour, money,
value, etc.

> As soon as those individual moments were more or less fixed and
> abstracted, the economic systems which ascend from the simple
> [moment], such as labour, division of labour, need, [and]
> exchange-value, up to the state, exchange among nations and the
> world market, began [to be formulated]. The latter is obviously the
> scientifically correct method.[9]

(b) Within the limits of that 'scientifically correct method'
different theories are still possible. Important distinctions concerning the systems of political economy which ascend from
simple determinations to living totalities are formulated in
Marx's critique of the construction of the systems of Ricardo and
Smith. This is a matter of two theoretical orientations:

(i) Ricardo proceeds from the simple determination, which he
understands as *fixed essence*;

(ii) Marx proceeds from the simple concept which he understands as a *cell* and which is a 'simple' (elementary, seed-like)
unity of opposites. On that depends the distinction between the
explanation of a complex whole by so-called formal abstraction
without genetic and structural mediation,[10] and the explanation
of a complex whole through its reproduction in ideas by the
method of structural-genetic analysis.

The cell, the elementary form in the capitalist economy is for
Marx the commodity, the value-form of the product. Through
all the alterations of his plans[11] he stuck to the solution which he
had worked out in the first years of his economic studies, that the
secret of the capitalist production of commodities is hidden in the
commodity as a specific economic form.

Hence the question arises – what qualifies a particular
economic form to play the role of 'cell': its analysis becomes the

starting point of the whole structural-genetic analysis of capitalism. In his popular exposition of the method employed in Marx's economic works, Engels says: 'With this method we begin with the first and simplest relation which is historically, actually available . . . '[12] But there are many such simple, historical, factually given relations. Which of them plays the role of 'cell' and starting point in structural-genetic analysis is not decided by simplicity and priority of historical appearance, nor does the fact that we are dealing with the most usual and most material phenomenon of capitalist society itself decide anything. Only these facts enable Marx to take the commodity as 'cell': the fact that the commodity-form is an economic phenomenon from which there is a historical-genetic connection through to capital and capitalism, as well as the fact that in the mechanism of developed capitalism the commodity-form is the elementary form. The understanding of that elementary form is a presupposition for understanding the complex economic forms of capitalism (or that Marx, as Lenin says,[13] found in the commodity all contradictions, specifically the seeds of all contradictions of capitalist society).[14]

(c) Marx links the problem ('the choice') of starting point for a scientific system not only with the level of development of the science under consideration, but also *with the level of development of the reality under investigation*. Hence for exchange-value and value to be understood as the starting point of the whole system of capitalist relations, a high level of development of the capitalist economy was necessary.[15]

The Marxian conception of the problem of the starting point of a scientific system refers us back to *Hegel* and stands at the same time in sharp contrast. Hegel's critique of previous conceptions of the problem of the starting point of a scientific system has elements of truth in this respect: a self-developing whole is not to be grasped by the transposition of the earlier axiomatic method from mathematics to other objects.[16] This procedure presupposed a fixed essence, while Hegel's new conception consists in this: that, as we have already mentioned, essence is understood to be self-developing. Hegel prepared the way for the Marxian thesis on the starting point of science by his reflections on the circular structure of a scientific system and on the combination of the immediate (the unmediated) and the mediated in reality and thought.[17] At the same time Hegel's solution to the problem of the starting point of a scientific system – his objective-idealist principle of the identity of thought and being –

is predetermined and distorted. Since he considers ultimate reality to be hypostatized logical categories whose embodiment is
the material reality of nature and society, Hegel establishes at the
beginning of his system in the *Logic* the concept of 'being', 'pure
being', 'being without any further specification'.[18] By treating all
definitions very freely Hegel produces [the concept] 'nothing'
from 'pure being'. Science therefore really begins with the unity
of 'being' and 'nothing'; at the same time the principle of immanent necessary change is posited, which leads to more concrete
categories and to the construction of the whole scientific system.[19]

On the basis of the materialist copy-theory Marx analyses
Hegelian dialectical ideas of ascending from the simple, with few
determinations, to the complex, rich in determinations; science
as a circle; and the relationship of the immediate and the mediated. At the same time he revises, in essence, pre-Marxist copy-
theory. He proceeds with the reproduction in ideas of a complex
reality rich in determinations, not from the analysis of abstract
concepts, but from the analysis of some other simple reality, the
elementary concrete as cell, whose determination is abstract
compared to the determination of the complex whole.[20] If then
the concrete appears as a result of ascending from the abstract to
the concrete, Marx is still fundamentally remote from the idealist
conception that concrete reality is the consequence of the self-
movement of any sort of objective thought, self-movement
which ascends from abstract to the concrete, since ' . . . the
method of ascending from the abstract to the concrete is merely
the way for thinking to appropriate the concrete, to reproduce it
as a mental concrete'.[21]

The investigation of the distinction between the materialist,
dialectical conception of Marx and the idealist, dialectical conception of Hegel concerning the problem of the starting point of
a scientific system leads to the problem of their contradictory
conceptions of dialectical development and the relationship between theoretical presentation and actual history.

CHAPTER 5

Theory and history

In Engels's[1] discussion of this question he emphasized that on the whole there is a parallel between theoretical presentation and actual history. The limiting conditions on this fundamental truth amount to a simplified explanation of Marx's interpretation of the components, the agreement and the contradictions of that relationship.[2]

If we investigate the relationship between theoretical presentation and the sequence of real historical events in Marx's theory of capitalism, we discover an interpenetration, a convergence and divergence. Marx acknowledges actual historical events as primary, but he notes particularly that it is *impossible* to see the real course of historical events and to appropriate it mentally through the merely passive, parallel representation of real events in thought. The use of the constructive power of thought in the realm of ideas does not remove us from objective reality; rather without it we cannot give an adequate reproduction of reality in ideas.

To mirroring in the sense of a passive, parallel copy Marx opposed a sense of mirroring as the 'ideal expression' of reality, the 'intellectual reproduction' of reality.

The Marxian conception of successful intellectual presentation as the dialectical-material reproduction of reality in ideas is characterized – in so far as it deals with the relation of scientific presentation to actual history – by several different aspects.

1. Marx's analysis operates simultaneously on two levels,[3] on the level of theoretical development[4] (Marx sometimes speaks of 'logical development') and on the level of real historical events. The level of theoretical development is derived from, and is in a certain respect the same as, real historical events, indeed the fundamental constituents of real history. Activity on the level of theoretical development, in so far as it can diverge from and can also run counter to the events of real history, is no construction *a priori*, but 'mirrors the life of the material'.[5]

It is one of the characteristics of Marxian analysis that theoretical work constantly touches on the facts of historical reality. That is an important point. The continuous oscillation between abstract dialectical development and concrete historical reality pervades the whole of Marx's *Capital*. At the same time it must be emphasized that the Marxian analysis *detaches* itself continually from the sequence and superficialities of historical reality and expresses *in ideas* the necessary relations of that reality. Only thus could Marx *grasp* historical actuality, only by forming his scientific account as the inner arrangement, somewhat idealized and typified, of the historical actuality of capitalist relations. This 'detaching' is not accomplished in the interests of distance from historical reality, and it is no idealist flight from reality. Rather it arises in the interests of the rational appropriation of reality, in the interests of approaching reality. We are dealing here with an integral aspect of the dialectical-materialist reproduction of reality in ideas. It is, according to Marx, 'a product of the thinking head which appropriates the world in the only mode possible for it'.[6] Without that 'ideal' procedure, in merely sticking to real history, it would be impossible to explain the character and essence of capitalism. This 'ideal' procedure of reproducing reality in ideas is *necessary* in order to grasp historical reality, but it would be an error to take it as the direct copy of real historical fact.

References to historical reality occur in Marx's scientific system in two forms. First there are examples which illustrate completed or proposed theoretical development. They illustrate the exposition and refer to the dialectical-materialist understanding of theoretically developed general relations. These historical presentations are mainly undertaken at the same time as theoretical exposition or especially just *after* theoretical exposition in certain sub-sections.[7] The legitimacy and coherence of *those* historical presentations in Marx's structural-genetic analysis are justified by the dialectical-materialist treatment of general forms, according to which general relations only exist as particular, individual forms.

The second group includes such historical events and historical facts which are themselves of no significance for theoretical development, but are introduced consciously into Marxian analysis in the form of established, theoretically underived, historically given presuppositions which are then the starting point of further theoretical development (illustrated by historical events of the first sort).

Marx puts forward certain views on the role and legitimacy of historical events of the second sort in dialectical-materialist structural-genetic analysis, for example in the consideration of original accumulation [of capital].[8] He distinguished (a) the conditions and presuppositions of the existence of capital, which itself creates capital by its own circulation, and (b) the conditions and presuppositions of the existence of capital which belong only to the history of the creation of capital, which are merely phases of development of capitalism, but which disappear as soon as capital takes off on its own accord. The original accumulation of capital, which has a non-capitalist origin, is just such an external presupposition of capital. This historical presupposition of the development of capitalism does not belong to the actual system of production ruled by capital. As soon as capital has developed, money, functioning as money-capital in the hands of capitalists, is built up, and the real conditions for the capitalist process of value creation are no longer apprehended as a historical presupposition but as the consequence of the specific activity of capital; in that way it creates the presuppositions and conditions of its own further existence and growth. To that Marx added:

> . . . our method indicates the points where historical investigation must enter in, or where bourgeois economy as a merely historical form of the production process points beyond itself to earlier historical modes of production. In order to develop the laws of bourgeois economy, therefore, it is not necessary to write the *real history of the relations of production*. But the correct observation and deduction of these laws, as having themselves become in history, always leads to primary equations – like the empirical numbers e.g. in natural science – which point towards a past lying behind this system. These indications, together with a correct grasp of the present, then also offer the key to the understanding of the past – a work in its own right which, it is to be hoped, we shall be able to undertake as well. This correct view likewise leads at the same time to the points at which the suspension of the present form of production relations gives signs of its becoming – foreshadowings of the future. Just as, on one side the pre-bourgeois phases appear as engaged in *suspending themselves* and hence in positing the *historic presuppositions* for a new state of society.[9]

Consequently in a scientific system which attempts the structural-genetic analysis of capitalism (that is, whose goal is to reveal, to 'develop' 'conceptual knowledge', the 'concept' of the capitalist mode of production), there are of necessity particular historical facts taken as established, theoretically non-derivative events. Understanding them theoretically presupposes a scientific task other than the one of developing the concept of capitalism, namely that of working out the concept of feudalism.

It is clear that in all these questions an important role is assigned to the specifically Marxian conception of the logical form which Marx terms 'conceptual knowledge' or the 'concept'.

2. The Marxian conception of the 'concept' expresses a logical form which we do not find in classical English political economy and which is essential for the Marxian dialectical-materialist conception of the reproduction of reality in ideas and for Marxian structural-genetic analysis as a specific type of analysis. The 'concept', according to Marx, is the intellectual reproduction of the inner arrangement, the inner structure of an object, and indeed of that inner structure in its development, its origin, existence and decline. In the 'concept' Marx works out the logical form which unites the structural and the genetic point of view internally in correspondence with the new logical-ontological dialectical-materialist conception. 'Concept' means the rational understanding, the intellectual reproduction, the intellectual appropriation, the intellectual mirroring of the object in its structural-genetic essence, that is in its structural-genetic coherence.[10]

Marx characterizes conceptual knowledge (the 'concept') of the capitalist mode of production as follows:

> We are not dealing with the relation [to each other] which the economic relations take up in the sequence of different forms of society. Still less [are we dealing with] their order of succession 'in the idea' (*Proudhon*), (a hallucinatory conception of historical movement). Rather [we are dealing] with their arrangement within modern bourgeois society.[11]

But this arrangement is (a) not static; it exists only 'in motion'; it is a development on the basis of a developed form and leads to the decline of that developed form, to the development, to the coming into being of a new form; (b) this structural process in the developed form is connected with history in the phases in which the form under investigation has become the 'developed form'. There are throughout no simple connections; they are not to be expressed by a simple parallelism. This means that one may not present scientifically the structural process in the developed form without taking into consideration the historical origins, and the theoretical procedure which allows for the interpretation of structural connections[12] in that developed form and *at the same time* allows for the historical–genetic component *before* the form under consideration becomes the developed form.

If for the Marxian logical form 'conceptual knowledge' (the 'concept') we use the term 'structure', then there is a general[13] and a specific sense which refers us back to Hegel. The Hegelian *Science of Logic* is the work which led in idealist form to a new structural conception of reality, a new concept of structure: it is not to be expressed by one or two categories; only the whole system can express the new conception of 'structure' and give a general theory of structure.[14]

Working out the 'conceptual knowledge' of an object means, according to Marx, taking possession of reality, appropriating reality theoretically, in the sole possible form.[15]

In order to complete the characterization of the Marxian logical form 'conceptual knowledge', we will take the logical structure of the concept of *money*, as presented in *Capital*. At first Marx investigates the *origin* of money; he explains by logical–historical analysis the *development* of money. In his opinion the main difficulty with the analysis of money is overcome as soon as its origin in the commodity and the exchange of commodities is understood.[16] Once that is done, the riddle of money is solved.[17] But when money ceases to be something mysterious, it is still not fully known, our perception of it is still incomplete. Marx pursues the analysis of different functions of money (and the particular forms arising from them),[18] then the analysis of the qualitative and quantitative characteristics of the monetary expression of the exchange relations of the commodity, and the analysis of the transformation of money into capital; in the second volume, the analysis of the monetary phase of industrial capital; in the third volume, the analysis of monetary capital, credit, etc.[19] *All* of Marx's logical categories are there, the whole logical apparatus of Marx's new conception of determinism, for which Hegel's *Phenomenology* and *Logic* prepared the way.[20]

In general Marx uses the expression 'conceptual and historical'. Thus he writes for example:

A greater number of labourers working together, at the same time, in one place (or, if you will, in the same field of labour), in order to produce the same sort of commodity under the mastership of one capitalist, constitutes, both historically and logically,[21] the starting point of capitalist production.[22]

This 'historical and logical' is to be interpreted such that the phenomenon in question was not only the starting point for historical development and the development of capitalist production but also *remains* the starting point in the circuit taken by capital as a developed form; in that role as starting point it operates in the inner structure of capitalist production. We have already mentioned conditions which are to be sure the *historical* starting point but are throughout not '*conceptual*', for example original (non-capitalist) accumulation. Or, for example, merchant capital has towards capitalist production a different 'historical' and a different 'logical' ('conceptual') relation.

When he works out the conceptual knowledge of a particular reality (the 'development of the concept') we encounter in Marx – in so far as he deals with the relation of theoretical progression to the course of actual history – the relation of *parallel correspondence*, where categories have to be developed factually and historically from the abstract to the concrete, for example from the simple value-form to the money-form. But we encounter *incongruence* where development is of a different sort. The path of theoretical analysis is then distinct from the course of history, for example, with the explanation of the average rate of profit.[23]

GRUSHIN'S INTERPRETATION

A noteworthy and in many respects stimulating interpretation of the problem under investigation here has been undertaken by B. A. Grushin.[24]

Even if we could agree in the main with Grushin's exposition, his observations are still problematic on certain points and necessitate discussion. We will concentrate on these points.

In Grushin's interpretation the distinction between the 'history of the object' (*istoriya predmeta*) and the 'developed object' (*stavshy predmet*) plays a fundamental role. With the investigation of the historical process of development of an object, theory is occupied 'with two kinds of materials under investigation – with facts and relations of the empirical history of the object, which develop in a particular temporal sequence, and with facts and relations of the object which are presented contemporaneously to the researcher, often without mediation'.[25] From the two the researcher must proceed with the reproduction in ideas of the development of the object. Hence he distinguishes 'a relation whose components are linked by their temporal sequence with one another, i.e. by the relation of precedence to consequence', from the relation 'which is reproduced continuously in repeated conditions, and components of both relations are given to the researcher simultaneously'. The author points out that this distinction is very relative. 'The concept of the "developed object" contains conceptions of the development of the object, of every point of that development, but only at a given point, i.e. simultaneous connections (independent of the level of their development), but not temporal connections. Perhaps the term "structure of the object" would more usefully apply, but it also has its defects', Grushin adds.[26]

The distinction between the 'developed object' and the 'history of the object' is regarded in Grushin's exposition as the key to the characterization of certain fundamental aspects of Marx's theoretical analysis of capitalism.

Grushin maintains that, depending on the objective character of the process under investigation, Marx's analysis distinguishes such processes as are reproducible in thought by 'historical' investigation from processes reproducible by investigating the 'developed object'. The investigation of alterations in the length of the working day in Marx's history of capital is taken by Grushin as an example of an investigation necessarily founded on the 'history of the object', while the investigation of the process 'money-capital', according to Grushin, bears another character: it must be reproduced in thought by the investigation of 'developed' connections and relations without turning to the historical development of capitalism.[27]

Moreover Grushin recognizes the existence of certain other processes which can be reproduced in thought only by the *simultaneous* investigation of the relations of the 'developed object' and the 'history of the object'. There are also processes which could be reproduced by the investigation of the relations of the 'developed object' *as well as* the 'history of the object'.[28]

If the 'developed object' is given at the same time as the 'history of the object', then the researcher, depending on his purpose, makes the 'developed object' *as well as* the 'history of the object' into a direct object of his research.

Thus we find in Marx's *Capital* not a few cases where one and the same object is analysed doubly, first in its 'developed' connections and relations, at another time in its historical connections and relations. As an example one can cite Chapters 1 and 2 of the first volume. The object under investigation is the same: the developmental process of the commodity. But in the first chapter this process is reproduced through the analysis of the commodity as a

given fact under the conditions of its existence . . . In the second
chapter, on the other hand, the immediate object of investigation is
the concrete historical process of the origin and development of the
commodity.[29]

Grushin bases his classification of 'logical' and 'historical' procedures on his distinction between 'developed object' and the
'history of the object'.

The investigation of the 'developed object' and the 'history of the
object' is in all cases not only essential but also necessary if we do
not want to throw all the procedures and all the processes of
scientific investigation into confusion and if we want to lay down
real laws of the dialectical mode of thought . . . Each investigation is
a *regular process* which presupposes the solution of specific logical
and historical questions, and indeed in a specific sequence. The
division of the materials for investigation into the 'developed
object' and the 'history of the object' opens up, in spite of its
grossness and conditionality, the way to the real analysis of the
logical. The logical is divided now under two rough rubrics:
'logical procedure' and 'historical procedure'. The two serve for
the reproduction in ideas of the process of development. But
logical procedure realizes this task by the analysis of the 'developed
object', while historical procedure analyses the 'history of the
object'.[30]

Grushin's interpretation introduces important distinctions,
whereas preceding expositions of that problem as a rule did not.
But if we subject Grushin's interpretation to a critical analysis of
its limitations, we find that it suffers from standing at a halfway
point and from not pushing its own distinction far enough.

Unaware of all the limitations concerning its conditionality,
Grushin operates with the antithesis 'developed object' and 'history of the object' as alternatives which simplify and confuse the
relationship between the history of the object and the structure of
the object. Actually the concept of the 'historical' appears in
Grushin's exposition in a dual sense: (a) in the narrow sense of
surface processes which exist in temporal sequence,[31] and (b) in
the more comprehensive sense of objectively existing developmental processes and their relations.[32]

It is conceivable that the mixture of those two senses of the
concept 'historical', the transition from one sense to the other in
Grushin's reflections, introduces indeterminacy. Grushin formulates some things ambiguously, for example 'the unity of the
logical and historical', likewise the antithesis 'developed object'

and 'history of the object', on which he constructs his work. To avoid this indeterminacy and vagueness, it is necessary for us to distinguish certain things more exactly than is the case with the antithesis 'developed object' and 'history of the object'. In order to formulate the specific character of the Marxian conception of theoretical analysis in general, and in particular the aspects of theoretical analysis under investigation, we must differentiate the antithesis 'developed object' and 'history of the object' as follows:

(a) the pre-history of the developed object;[33]

(b) the history of the developed object.

(a) and (b) possess the levels:

(i) the factual and empirical, appearing on the surface;

(ii) inner regularities, such as structural and genetic forms, which manifest themselves on the factual empirical surface.

In the Marxian analysis of capitalism all the objective processes of development which lead to the genesis of capitalism and precede the operation of capital on its own basis belong to the pre-history of the developed object. As soon as capital operates of its own accord,[34] the history of the developed object begins. This has different phases: from the opening phases up to classical maturity, to the phases of dissolution, the transition to 'another object'.

If in the light of this richer, more exact distinction we consider the examples of Marxian analysis cited by Grushin, we reach different conclusions concerning their logical characteristics. Grushin's thesis that Marx's 'investigation of the working day is not applicable to the "developed object", which requires instead attention to "historical" material',[35] is untenable.

If we investigate the logical structure of Marx's exposition of the working day[36] with respect to our interests here, we conclude that Marx undertakes first a logical, theoretical analysis of the problem of the length of the working day and of alterations in its length. From research into the essence of the relations of capital and the inner mechanism of *developed capitalism* Marx derives basic knowledge related to the length of the working day and alterations in that length: in fact no limits for the working day are given by the character of commodity exchange and consequently no limits to surplus labour. The capitalist strives for maximal lengthening of the working day, while realizing his rights in accordance with the exchange of commodities. The worker, on the other hand, strives for the limitation of the working day to a 'normal' length.

> Hence, in the history of capitalist production, the establishment of
> a norm for the working day presents itself as a struggle over the
> limits of that day, a struggle between collective capital, i.e. the class
> of capitalists, and collective labour, i.e. the working-class.[37]

This theoretical analysis, this logical derivation is a representation of predictable relationships which exist objectively in real historical processes. In that sense Marx's logical analysis is always – one way or another – embedded in real history; it is the *mirroring* of real history.

The development through logic of the knowledge that the length of the working day and its transformation in capitalism are a result of class struggle, is illustrated in the Marxian exposition by concrete historical events at the empirical level. Hence at the same time Marx expands his theoretical analysis by means of illustration (in that section he does not *merely* stay on the surface). Thus he is concerned at first with the Factory Act of 1850, which he compares with the *Règlement organique* of 1831, the law which directed labour relations in the Danubean principalities. There he expresses perceptions which expand the preceding analysis of the essence of the capitalist appropriation of surplus labour, hence perceptions which belong to *logical* analysis. Further sub-sections reveal that the problem of the working day in mature capitalism is distinguished in many respects from the same problem at the beginning of capitalism, the period in which capital was in the embryonic stage.[38] While in the preceding exposition Marx's logical analysis was expanded by the explanation of the distinction between capitalist (that is, existing in mature capitalism) appropriation of surplus labour by lengthening working time and *pre-capitalist* forms, here it is expanded by the explanation of specific attributes of the different phases of the history of capitalism. The final sub-sections deal with the influence of the Factory Act on other countries, hence on certain phenomena at the empirical level, but here the preceding logical analysis is also expanded by a few new generalizations.

As we have seen, the part of Marx's analysis of capitalism under investigation here has its basis in the analysis of relations in the 'developed object' as well as in the analysis of events of history, indeed the history of capitalism and the history of pre-capitalist forms.

In principle, the same might be said of Marx's investigation of the process 'money–capital'. Grushin sets out his interpretation as follows:

The historical fact that money is the first form of appearance of capital, is at the same time a relation of the developed object, i.e. a relation which is reproduced by conditions which are continuously repeated. [Marx writes that] 'All new capital, to commence with, comes on the stage, that is, on the market, whether of commodities, labour, or money, even in our days, in the shape of money that by a definite process has to be transformed into capital'. It is just this property of the process which permits its reproduction in thought by means of the investigation of 'developed' relations and connections, *without considering the historical development of capital.*[39] (My emphasis – J.Z.)

To support his interpretation Grushin calls on Marx.

As a matter of history, capital, as opposed to landed property, invariably takes the form at first of money; it appears as moneyed wealth, as the capital of the merchant and of the usurer. But we have no need to refer to the origin of capital in order to discover that the first form of appearance of capital is money. We can see it daily under our very eyes.[40]

Marx demonstrates here that money is the first form, the starting point and seed of capital in developed capitalism as well as in the genesis of capitalism: no more and no less. Grushin mistakenly assigns to Marx's words another meaning, namely: it is not necessary to be concerned with the history and development of capital if one presents the process 'money–capital' (that is, the development in logic of capital from money). Actually Marx has emphasized the exact opposite, that the process 'money–capital' cannot be represented theoretically by the investigation of particular, empirically given historical conditions and events, unless those historical circumstances are ordered into a theoretical presentation.[41]

It is also obvious here that Marx's theoretical presentation of the process 'money–capital' presupposes his analysis of relations in the 'developed object' as well as of events of empirical history, and the historical *development* of capitalism above all. In the later phases of his theoretical analysis of the functions of money and the relation 'money–capital in mature capitalism (credit, money-capital as commodity, etc.) theoretical analysis is accompanied by historical and factual data which illustrate Marx's logical work.

By considering Grushin's interpretation as a special case, when reproduction in theoretical terms is accomplished by the simultaneous investigation of the relations 'developed object' and 'history of the object',[42] we have reached the conclusion that it is a generally applicable principle of Marxian dialectical-materialist analysis as a whole and in its individual sections, to investigate the relations of the 'developed object' which are expressed in logical analysis. These relations are *always* in a determinate *unity* (differentiated by the character of the relation) with the history of the object, in which case the 'history of the object' must be broken down according to its different levels and phases.

We have been concerned with analysing insufficiencies in Grushin's antithesis 'developed object' – 'history of the object', particularly the second pole, the 'history of the object', in order to formulate the specific attributes of Marx's dialectical-materialist analysis. So that we can make progress with the characterization of the linkage of the logical and historical in Marxian analysis we must concern ourselves more precisely with the question of what *new conception of the logical*, what connection with the new logical form 'conceptual knowledge', we find in Marx's analysis of capitalism. Then we will return to some of the problems raised above, particularly to Grushin's interpretation of Engels's exposition of the two possible methods of investigation, the logical and the historical.

CHAPTER 6

Dialectical derivation

As well as the traditional method of logical derivation Marx uses a specific method, usually called dialectical (materialist-dialectical). This dialectical derivation, or in more specific terms, the development of ideas, plays a dominant role in Marx's system, while traditional derivation plays a subordinate, supportive role.[1]

The specific features of dialectical derivation in Marx have already been characterized in part in the chapters on the starting point and the relation of theoretical exposition to the course of actual history (particularly in the sections on the Marxian logical form, the 'concept'). Now we will expand this characterization.

With dialectical derivation in Marx we are not dealing with proof in the Euclidean sense. For Marx, derivation *more geometrico* is far from the only or the main form of scientific derivation. Marx refers in this matter to the critique of the axiomatic method as undertaken by classical German philosophy, particularly by Hegel. Yet Christian Wolff posits an equation between scientific method in general and the Euclidean mathematical method. He asserts that science could exist in no other way than through proof by inalterable principles.[2] Kant has attempted to prove that a science so understood is helpless in applications to ontological and certain other questions.[3] Hegel limits the mathematical method, which had been taken at one time for the sole scientific method, to the less important realm of objects of understanding. For objects of reason, to which he assigned many further theoretical questions besides philosophical ones, he considered the new dialectical method, which he developed, to be appropriate.

Marx constructs his scientific system of political economy not by means of the axiomatic method but by using the new, dialectical derivation. He considers his dialectical *materialist* derivation – as is well known – to be not only distinct from the Hegelian one but also its antithesis, its direct opposite.

Before we consider the overall distinction between, and the antithetical character of, the Hegelian and Marxian conceptions of dialectical derivation and dialectical transitions, let us consider more exactly the logical forms and the logical character of certain dialectical patterns of thought in Marx and, first of all, some of their external properties. We shall investigate the logical structure of the Marxian exposition of the theory of value up to the development of money by means of the dialectical derivation of the money-form of value, and we shall be particularly aware whether and how new logical forms are used in it.

The departure from traditional derivation appears most significantly in the part of Marx's theory of value in which he sets down the transitions of the value-form.[4] The object of that part is

> a task . . . the performance of which has never yet even been attempted by *bourgeois* economy, the task of tracing the genesis of this money form, of developing the expression of value implied in the value relation of commodities, from its simplest, almost imperceptible outline, to the dazzling money form. By doing this we shall, at the same time, solve the riddle presented by money.[5]

Hence this dialectical derivation, this dialectical analysis is the investigation of the origin and development of particular forms and thereby the discovery of the secret of a particular object.[6]

Marx begins the analysis with the 'simple, isolated or accidental form of value'. What is this beginning based on? The value relation of the commodity to any other kind of commodity, according to Marx, is '*obviously* the simplest value-relation'.[7] What is the logical character of '*obviously*', of 'evidence'? It has no purely logical character, as if it were derived from non-derivative, presupposed logical and ontological axioms. It possesses – as we have yet to show – a logical-historical character.

Marx continues the analysis of the simple value-form with the observation[8] that the two commodities play different roles. The value of the first commodity is expressed as the relative form of value, or it is found in the relative form of value. The other commodity functions as an equivalent or is found in the equivalent form. They are antithetical and inseparable poles of the same expression of value. Marx gives a detailed qualitative and quantitative characterization of the relative form of value and the equivalent form; then he turns to the *totality* of the simple value-form.

Marx concludes the analysis of the first, simple form of value thus:

> Nevertheless, the elementary form of value passes by an easy

transition into a more complete form. It is true that by means of the elementary form, the value of a commodity A, becomes expressed in terms of one, and only one, other commodity. But that one may be a commodity of any kind, coat, iron, corn, or anything else. Therefore, according as A is placed in relation with one or the other, we get for one and the same commodity, different elementary expressions of value. The number of such possible expressions is limited only by the number of the different kinds of commodities distinct from it. The isolated expression of A's value, is therefore convertible into a series, prolonged to any length, of the different elementary expressions of that value.[9]

Hence we obtain the total or expanded form of value.

Marx expresses the transition from the second form of value to the third, general form of value (after the exposition of the 'deficiency' of the second form) in the following way:

> when a person exchanges his linen for many other commodities, and thus expresses its value in a series of other commodities, it necessarily follows, that the various owners of the latter exchange them for the linen, and consequently express the value of their various commodities in one and the same third commodity, the linen. If then, we reverse the series, 20 yards of linen = 1 coat or = 10 lbs of tea, etc., that is to say, if we give expression to the converse relation already implied in the series, we get, *C. The General form of value.*[10]

Finally Marx says of the transition of the third form into the value-form:

> The particular commodity, with whose bodily form the equivalent form is thus socially identified, now becomes the money commodity, or serves as money. It becomes the special social function of that commodity, and consequently its social monopoly, to play within the world of commodities the part of the universal equivalent. Amongst the commodities which, in form B, figure as particular equivalents of the linen, and, in form C, express in common their relative values in linen, this foremost place has been attained by one in particular – namely, gold.[11]

Thus we obtain the money form.

Now we put the question: what is the logical character of this derivation?

Marx interprets the development of the forms of value as an expression of a particular *necessity*. What is the character of this necessity? It is certain that we are not dealing here with Kantian analytical necessity. Nor are we dealing here with Hegelian dialectical necessity of the immanent development of concepts and forms of thought: that can be seen (though not fully) from what we have cited, but will become evident from further investigation of the logical character of the Marxian derivation.

To the dialectical derivation of the money-form of value (Chapter 1) Marx links the exposition (in Chapter 2) of the essence and the development of the exchange process. Here he is also concerned with the analysis of money. He writes:

> Money is a crystal formed of necessity in the course of the exchanges, whereby different products of labour are practically equated to one another and thus by practice converted into commodities. The historical progress and extension of exchanges develops the contrast, latent in commodities, between use-value and value. The necessity for giving an external expression to this contrast for the purposes of commercial intercourse, urges on the establishment of an independent form of value, and finds no rest until it is once for all satisfied by the differentiation of commodities into commodities and money. At the same rate, then, as the conversion of products into commodities is being accomplished, so also is the conversion of one special commodity into money.[12]

In what relationship does (a) the development of the value-form as it is discussed in the first chapter, stand to (b) the development of the exchange process as it is dealt with in the second chapter? What relationship do the 'necessary result' in (a) and the 'necessary result' in (b), the 'genesis' in (a) and the 'genesis' in (b), bear to one another?

We have before us *two necessary sequences*, inseparably linked. We shall be speaking of the 'dialectical-logical' and the 'historically' necessary sequence (the 'dialectical-logical' and the 'historical' origin).

The dialectical-logical derivation, as used in the Marxian derivation of the money-form of value in the first chapter, expresses in a concentrated way the immanent character of the value-form (that character is a specific contradiction, and the resolution of that contradiction arises from the development in logic of particular forms). This contradiction has the external form of one concept, category or form of thought resulting from another. In content the dialectical-logical sequence is the mirroring of the necessary constituents of real forms and indeed their inner structural process. Hence it depends on a new conception of the ontological structure of reality.[13] The specific character of the Marxian dialectical–logical derivation cannot be understood so long as we take as our basis the ontology of Galilean–Cartesian science (particularly its conception of causality) and the limited understanding of the logical and of logical derivation associated with it. Marx refers to the pioneering ideas on the ontological structure of reality which Leibniz in the *Monadology* and then classical German philosophy, particularly Hegel, have defended against Galilean–Cartesian science and its interpretation of causality.

The genesis of a particular form as it is interpreted by dialectical–logical derivation is therefore not *identical* with its historical origin, but it is also not its simple epitome, its expression free of contingency;[14] it is the *'ideal expression'* of that genesis. In dialectical–logical derivation there is abstraction from the numerous factors and conditions which have played a role in the historical realization of the forms under investigation. This abstraction is not based on the frailty of human understanding (as, for example, Grossmann interprets this);[15] it is necessary as a first step in understanding historical development and real forms in their complexity, their essence and their particularity. Otherwise the 'conceptual knowledge' of real activities could not be worked out. Its existence is confirmed because there is open to the human mind no other way to the theoretical appropriation of any facts, for example the development and essence of money, than the method of working out the 'conceptual knowledge' of reality.

The sequence, which is the logical form of Marxian 'conceptual knowledge' in dialectical–logical derivation, is therefore the historically necessary sequence *sui generis*. The development of the 'ideal expression' of the reality under investigation with the help of the dialectical–logical sequence and the dialectical–logical transition is a presupposition for understanding real history. In this way the 'ideal expression' can only be developed if one proceeds from the investigation of real history.

Engels characterized the dialectical–logical sequence as it is used by Marx in the theory of value, when he admonished Schmidt and Sombart for forgetting 'that we are dealing here not only with a purely logical process, but with a historical process and its explanatory reflection in thought, the logical pursuance of its inner connections'.[16]

To interpret this characterization we must know *how* it is possible for Marx to 'trace the inner connection of the historical process logically' and in this way 'to give an explanatory mirroring of the historical process'. The originality and the specific character of the Marxian logical forms 'ideal expression' and 'conceptual knowledge' are to be found by deciphering Engels's characterization.

We are not dealing here with a purely logical process and at the same time – we might say – with only a pure historical process, but with the 'ideal expression of the historical process'.

To formulate the 'ideal expression' means for Marx 'to discover the inner necessary connection'.[17] 'To trace logically the inner connection of the historical process' is only another expression for 'uncovering the inner necessary connection'. To avoid tautologies we must bear in mind that Marx understood 'the inner necessary connection' in a new way. Marx's ideas on the ontological structure of reality produce a new conception of the specifically logical as well as a new conception of the 'logical investigation of the inner connections of the historical process'.

Let us turn back to our example of the dialectical-logical derivation of the money-form of value. Does it tell us why the simple accidental form of value was necessarily overtaken by the developed value-form? We could answer that this is not the case – or only partly so. Marx's real interest is concentrated here on 'genesis' in another sense, on the inner connection; one could say: on the *essence* of the historical process. It would be still more exact to say that the question is posed imprecisely. Marx distinguishes immanent regularity of development from external causality and investigates the necessary historical genesis of money in the section on dialectical-materialist derivation in the first chapter *and* in the sections on the development of exchange in the second chapter. The two parts form *together* the dialectical-materialist analysis of money (which is later supplemented by the analysis of the particularities and functions of money in capitalism). In this sense we could say that the dialectical-logical derivation in the first chapter is an *aspect* of the dialectical-materialist analysis, which would not be complete if it were not accompanied in the second chapter by the derivation of money in the form of the 'historically' necessary sequence.

Only if we understand this dual derivation, this dual sequence in the spirit of the copy-theory of dialectical materialism (and of the dialectical-materialist understanding of the ontological structure of reality), will we understand the dialectical-materialist analysis of the money-form of value.

If one is severed from the other or if they are opposed to one another, then Marx's scientific explanation is distorted. On the other hand, the knowledge that only the two derivations (and necessary sequences) in their unity give the completed dialectical-materialist analysis of reality puts us on guard against unjustified conclusions being drawn from certain one-sided formulations (taken in isolation) of Marx and Engels on the logical structure of the Marxian analysis, and helps us towards understanding a certain emphasis which frequently turns up in Marx's *mode of expression*.

For example, the sequential account of the money-form of value is formulated by Marx and Engels in the following way:

(a) From the contradiction between the general character of value and its material existence in a particular commodity, etc. – these general characteristics are the same as later appear in money – arises the category of money.[18]

Or:

(b) The immanent contradiction of the commodity as immediate unity of use-value and exchange-value, as the product of useful private labour . . . and as the direct social embodiment of abstract human labour, this contradiction does not rest until it has taken the form of the splitting of the commodity into commodity and money.[19]

This genetic account is formulated by them in another way:

Money is a crystal formed of necessity in the course of exchanges, whereby different products of labour are practically equated to one another and thus by practice converted into commodities. The historical progress and extension of exchanges develops the contrast, latent in commodities, between use-value and value. *The necessity for giving an external expression to this contrast for the purposes of commercial intercourse*, urges on the establishment of an independent form of value, and finds no rest until it is once for all satisfied by the differentiation of commodities into commodities and money. At the same rate, then, as the conversion of products into commodities is being accomplished, so also is the conversion of one special commodity into money.[20] (Note what I have emphasized above – J.Z.)

Or:

In the direct barter of products, each commodity is directly a

means of exchange to its owner, and to all other persons an
equivalent, but that only in so far as it has use-value for them. At
this stage, therefore, the articles exchanged do not acquire a value-
form independent of their own use-value, or of the individual
needs of the exchangers. The necessity for a value-form grows
with the increasing number and variety of the commodities
exchanged. The problem and the means of solution arise simultaneously. Commodity-owners never equate their own commodities to those of others, and exchange them on a large scale,
without different kinds of commodities belonging to different
owners being exchangeable for, and equated as values to, one and
the same special article. Such last-mentioned article, by becoming
the equivalent of various other commodities, acquires at once,
though within narrow limits, the character of a general social
equivalent. This character comes and goes with the momentary
social acts that called it into life. In turn and transiently it attached
itself first to this and then to that commodity. But with the
development of exchange it fixes itself firmly and exclusively to
particular sorts of commodities, and becomes crystallised by
assuming the money-form.[21]

The result is that Marx and Engels formulate the origin of
money at different times in different ways, depending on
whether they want to express the dialectical-logical derivation
(genesis) in the form of the 'ideal expression' of the reality under
investigation or whether they have in mind the 'historical'
genesis. But it must be remembered that these two formulations,
if they are taken in isolation, are one-sided; the dialectical-
materialist analysis is only given by their unification, as is the
case, for example, in *Capital*.

Marx takes account in his preparatory manuscripts of the fact
that it is possible for formulations of the first sort (see (a) above)
to be misunderstood in an idealist way. In the 'Chapter on Money'
(October 1857) in the *Grundrisse*, for example, he writes:

(It will be necessary later, before this question is dropped, to
correct the idealist manner of the presentation, which makes it
seem as if it were merely a matter of conceptual determinations and
of the dialectic of these concepts. Above all in the case of the phrase:
product (or activity) becomes commodity; commodity, exchange
value; exchange value, money.)[22]

As a rule Marx and Engels succeed in avoiding one-sidedness
in their brief formulations of the development of money; they
thus advance to a conception of the genesis of money that is

complex but necessary for the rational understanding of reality, when they arrive at the *specific* unity of the dialectical–logical and historical sequence. For example:

> The gradual extension of barter, the growing number of exchange transactions, and the increasing variety of commodities bartered lead, therefore, to the further development of the commodity as exchange-value, stimulates the formation of money and consequently has a disintegrating effect on direct barter. Economists usually reason that the emergence of money is due to external difficulties which the expansion of barter encounters, but they forget that these difficulties arise from the evolution of exchange-value and hence from that of social labour as universal labour.[23]

Or:

> The fact that the *exchange-value* of the commodity *assumes an independent existence* in money is itself the result of the process of exchange, the development of the contradiction of use-value and exchange-value embodied in the commodity, and of another no less important contradiction embodied in it, namely, that the definite, particular labour of the private individual must manifest itself as its opposite, as equal, necessary, general labour and, in this form, social labour.[24]

Engels expresses himself in a similar way in the Preface to the second volume of *Capital*:

> Marx then investigated the relation of commodities to money and demonstrated how and why, thanks to the property of value immanent in commodities, commodities and commodity-exchange must engender the opposition of commodity and money.[25]

The correspondence between Marx and Engels on the analysis of value throws a light on certain important aspects of the Marxian conception of the unity of the 'dialectical–logical' and 'historical' derivation.[26]

From this exchange of observations and corrections it emerges that Marx assigned greater emphasis to the analysis of the simple expression of value than to the expansion and 'historicizing' of the exposition by historical excursus. He considers it to be the key problem not only for understanding the development of value but all bourgeois economic relations. The focal point of the dialectical-materialist analysis of the money-form of value in

Marx must therefore be the analysis of the commodity and the two-fold character of labour as well as the analysis of the simple value-form.

Since we have concentrated at the beginning of this chapter on the logical structure of the Marxian exposition of the transitions within the value-form as the place at which the departure from traditional derivation and the use of a new method of derivation have come to light in the *clearest* way, we must now supplement and summarize our characterization. The transitions of the value-form (from the simple to the money-form) are only a *part* of Marx's dialectical-logical derivation of money. The *kernel* of this derivation is the analysis of the commodity and the simple value-form. The dialectical-logical derivation of the money-form of value – as contained in Marx's *A Contribution to the Critique of Political Economy* – could be undertaken without *developing* the transitions of the forms of value as Form I into II, II into III and IV (though this could not be done without the analysis of the simple value-form).

Only if we recognize in agreement with Marx that the analysis of the commodity and the simple value-form is the *kernel* of the dialectical-logical derivation of the money-form of value can we understand the logical structure of the exposition of value in Marx. The derivation, the necessary sequence in these transitions, presupposes often implicitly a specific conception of the ontological structure of the phenomenon under investigation, and indeed, a conception (expressed by the analysis of the commodity-form with respect to its substance) of its magnitude and its necessary expression in the simple value-form.[27]

What we have revealed by analysis in the preceding sections, and then in the sections on the transitions of the forms of value (I–II–III–IV) is equally the categorial basis expressing the general and specific ontological structure of the realm under investigation; this categorial basis determines in fact the sequence of the presentation. From this standpoint certain elements of Marx's dialectical-logical derivation in the section on the transitions of the forms of value, which are incomprehensible from the standpoint of traditional derivation (in that they appear arbitrary and foreign, in a way which merely reduces the derivation to traditional derivation) can now be understood.

Thus Marx speaks, for example, in the analysis of Form II, of the 'deficiencies' of that form.[28] Of what significance, from what point of view, of what sort are these 'deficiencies'? From the point of view of the inner connections between the value-substance, magnitude and the value-form already derived, hence from the point of view of the character, the essence of the value-form. Only in that way can the exposition of the 'deficiencies' of Form II serve Marx for mediating the transition to Form III.

The relationship of that 'deficiency' of Form II to the difficulties on which commodity exchange founders in a particular historical phase of its development is expressed by Marx as follows:

> Economists usually reason that the emergence of money is due to external difficulties which the expansion of barter encounters, but they forget that these difficulties arise from the evolution of exchange-value and hence from that of social labour as universal labour.[29]

But what is meant here by 'arise'? If we say that the 'deficiencies' of Form II are a mirroring of difficulties on which the means of exchange in a particular phase of development founders, we express a real relation, but only one-sidedly. It is not the whole truth. At the same time it happens that these difficulties are the expression of the reality that commodity exchange requires the transition to the money-form of value which is entailed by the commodity form of production.[30] Thus the whole dialectical-logical derivation of the value-form in Form I over Form II, and Form II into Form IV, presupposes the results of the previous analysis of the commodity; in that way we reach results which are the exact form of expression of the structure of the inner necessary connections which were already revealed in embryo in the preceding analysis.

In that sense Engels was correct in saying that the exposition of the value-form and the derivation of the money-form of value in *Capital* – as distinct from the presentation which is given in *A Contribution to the Critique of Political Economy* – are distinguished by the 'sharpness of the dialectical development'.[31]

Hence the dialectical-logical presentation of the *genesis* of the money-form of value does not begin in the sections on the transitions of the value-forms but is undertaken in the *whole* of the first chapter. We can set out schematically the course of that analysis in the first chapter of *Capital* in the following way:

Substance of value
Magnitude of value
Form of value

(a) simple value-form
(b) complete or developed value-form
(c) total value-form
(d) money-form
Commodity fetishism

If we were to distinguish the 'dialectical-logical' and 'histori-cal' sequences from one another (remaining conscious of their unity, their complementarity, and the representational character of the dialectical-logical sequence with respect to real history), then the derivation of the money-form of value with the help of the dialectical-logical sequence forms the *whole* first chapter (not just the sections on the transitions of the value-forms); combined with the second chapter on the essence and development of the exchange process, which gives the 'historical' derivation[32] of money, we have the fundamental dialectical-materialist analysis of money.

Marx considered the materialist, dialectical form of the deriva-tion to be correct only under certain *conditions*. The first consists in the requirement for empirical knowledge (of the material to be analysed by means of the materialist, dialectical form of deriva-tion). When, for example, Lassalle used dialectical forms of thought as general schemata, under which he simply subsumed the material of political economy, Marx criticized him not only for misunderstanding the *rational* dialectic, but also for mis-understanding and abusing the *Hegelian dialectic*.[33]

The Marxian requirement for a basic knowledge of the material as a presupposition for the employment of the materialist, dialectical derivation is obvious, if we remember that the materialist, dialectical derivation is only the expression of the inner necessary connections of the object in the specific form appropriate to theory.

The second condition consists in the fact that 'the dialectical form of presentation... knows its bounds'[34] in the sense in which we discussed this in Chapter 4.[35] The theoretical exposition of a self-developing whole by the materialist, dialectical derivation must necessarily touch on factual historical reality as a set of established, dialectically non-derivative *presuppositions* from which materialist, dialectical derivation proceeds.

The third condition consists in the requirement that the totality under investigation, the self-developing totality, has reached *in reality* a determinate point of maturity[36] and that preceding investigations of the self-developing whole have built up an intellectual repository of material. In that respect Marx discusses

the relationship of the dialectical–materialist analysis of capitalism to the theoretical analysis of capitalism as it had been undertaken by the classical political economists, particularly Smith and
Ricardo.[37] We shall concern ourselves in succeeding chapters
with the relationship of the Marxian analysis to preceding types
of analysis.

MARX'S NEW CONCEPTION OF LOGIC

In his new conception of logic, as revealed in the dialectical-
logical derivation just outlined, Marx refers critically to Hegel's
understanding of logic.

The essence of Hegel's discoveries in that field – if we take first
the positive aspect which expresses an advance over the past –
consists in the fact that it brought together a new conception of
the ontological structure of reality with new theoretical conceptions of the logical structure of scientific thought.

The Hegelian understanding of the character of the necessary
connections in reality is expressed by the idea of substance as
self-developing, which was discussed in Chapter 3. The *Science of
Logic*, which replaces the old metaphysics and ontology and
which identifies in the spirit of objective idealism the logical with
the ontological, is developed into a bizarre and totally untenable,
but unusually rich and original system of inverted *observations* on
the ontological structure of reality and on the logical structure of
correct thought already expressed in the Hegelian *Phenomenology
of Mind*, particularly in the Preface 'On Scientific Knowledge in
General'.

Kant offered an influential, though not original conception,
which reduces logical sequence to a procedure with a so-
called analytical character. In the *Critique of Pure Reason* Kant's
question is this: how are general judgements possible which do
not possess an analytical (tautological) character; as well as a
further question: how is a logical sequence possible, which does
not bear an analytical character, which hence – in the Kantian
sense – could possess a synthetic character? It is known that Kant
solves this problem in a subjectivist-agnostic way.[38] Here we are
not dealing with the Kantian solution as a whole. If we are to
understand the specific, historically significant advance of Hegel
over the Kantian position in logic, we must turn our attention to
the fact that the innermost theoretical basis of the total structure
of the Kantian conception of logic is its conception of the
ontological structure of reality, which is characterized by the

principle of the fixed substance and by other conditions[39] corresponding to the world-view of mechanical-mathematical science
of the seventeenth and eighteenth centuries. Hence Kant's
unanswered question: 'How is one to understand that given what
a thing is, it is also something else?' It is conceivable, on the basis
of Kant's ontological conceptions that the question, in so far as
it was understood in terms of the *synthetic* necessary result,
could not be answered. (Here there is no justification for the view
that Kant himself has subjectivized these ontological conceptions
and only considers them as knowledge of phenomenal reality,
specifically as subjective forms of thought, not as forms of
objective reality 'in itself'.)

In the polemic against his predecessors and his contemporaries, mainly with Kant[40] and Schelling, Hegel expressed new
ideas on the character of logic, much valued by Marx in his
theoretical preparation of the dialectical-materialist type of
analysis.

In the Preface to the *Phenomenology of Mind* entitled 'On Scientific Knowledge in General',[41] we encounter for the first time the
new logical form of so-called 'conceptualizing' and the conception of the 'logical sequence' corresponding to it. On a rational
understanding (the 'concept' as God transformed into logic),[42] an
understanding freed of the mystery of absolute idealism, Hegel's
logical form 'conceptualizing' is a stage preparatory to the Marxian logical form 'conceptual knowledge', that is the dialectical-
materialist analysis, as we have characterized it above.

> The systematic development of truth in scientific form can alone
> be the true shape in which truth exists . . . When we state the true
> form of truth to be its scientific character – or, what is the same
> thing, when it is maintained that truth finds the medium of its
> existence in notions or conceptions alone . . . [43]

The 'concept', which is the logical form of ('philosophical')
truth, exists, according to Hegel, only as a scientific system, not
simply as a single concept or single judgement. Hegel has in
mind a scientific system of a new type which is distinguished
from the Euclidean, Newtonian, etc., scientific systems. To the
new type of scientific system belongs a new explanation of the
necessary logical sequence which Kant had not recognized,
which is not to be grasped from the Kantian standpoint. It does
not originate from the specific properties of the knowing subject
and it is also not an axiomatic and mathematically necessary

logical sequence; it is rather the intellectual translation of the structure of the object itself; the intellectual expression of objectively existing necessity, whereby this 'necessity' is newly understood in the sense of substance as self-developing by contradiction. The logical form of truth cannot be the simple aggregation of perceptions, in which they are merely written down and juxtaposed without developmental connection, without the necessary sequence specific to 'conceptualizing'. Such an aggregation of knowledge as, for example, descriptive anatomy, does not, according to Hegel, deserve the name of science.

The ontological structure of reality (in his objective idealist exposition of the forms of thought Hegel would always say: 'the logical structure of reality')[44] has in some respects, but not in the essential respects, the characteristics more or less adequately expressed in mathematical mechanistic science, which lay at the basis of the Kantian conception of logic.

It is with reference to the mutual relation of organic forms of growth and to the analogous relation of philosophical systems in the history of philosophy that Hegel explains the fundamental ontological structure of these basic aspects of reality, true knowledge of which is not possible in any other way than in the logical form 'conceptualizing', hence in a scientific system of the new type:

The more the ordinary mind takes the opposition between true and false to be fixed, the more is it accustomed to expect either agreement or contradiction with a given philosophical system, and only to see reason for the one or the other in any explanatory statement concerning such a system. It does not conceive the diversity of philosophical systems as the progressive evolution of truth; rather, it sees only contradiction in that variety. The bud disappears when the blossom breaks through, and we might say that the former is refuted by the latter; in the same way when the fruit comes, the blossom may be explained to be a false form of the plant's existence, for the fruit appears as its true nature in place of the blossom. These stages are not merely differentiated; they supplant one another as being incompatible with one another. But the ceaseless activity of their own inherent nature makes them at the same time moments of an organic unity, where they not merely do not contradict one another, but where one is as necessary as the other; and this equal necessity of all moments constitutes alone and thereby the life of the whole. But contradiction as between philosophical systems is not wont to be conceived in this way; on the other hand, the mind perceiving the contradiction does not commonly know how to relieve it or keep it free from its onesidedness, and to recognize in what seems conflicting and inherently antagonistic the presence of mutually necessary moments.[45]

Following Hegel we will call such a characteristically onto-logical structure a 'dialectical' ontological structure and the logical form capable of portraying it a 'dialectical' scientific system.

The characteristics of the logic which corresponds to a 'dialectical scientific system' are expressed by Hegel for the first time in his critique of irrationalist attempts to understand the reality of a dialectical ontological structure:

> not the notion, but ecstasy, not the march of cold necessity in the subject-matter, but ferment and enthusiasm – these are to be the ways by which the wealth of the concrete substance is to be stored and increasingly extended.[46]

The logical sequence characteristic of the dialectical scientific system is considered by Hegel to be the 'coldly advancing necessity of the thing'.

'Proof' by means of the dialectically necessary sequence is characterized indirectly by Hegel when he speaks of mathematical proof:

> The process of mathematical proof does not belong to the object; it is a function that takes place outside the matter in hand. Thus, the nature of a right-angled triangle does not break itself up into factors in the manner set forth in the mathematical construction which is required to prove the proposition expressing the relation of its parts. The entire process of producing the result is an affair of knowledge . . . The evidence peculiar to this defective way of knowing – an evidence on the strength of which mathematics plumes itself and proudly struts before philosophy – rests solely on the poverty of its purpose and the defectiveness of its material, and is on that account of a kind that philosophy must scorn to have anything to do with . . . The process of knowledge goes on, therefore, on the surface, does not affect the concrete fact itself, does not touch its inner nature or notion, and is hence not a conceptual way of comprehending . . . In an unreal element of that sort we find, then, only unreal truth, fixed lifeless propositions. We can call a halt at any of them; the next begins of itself *de novo*, without the first having led up to the one that follows, and without *any necessary connexion having in this way arisen from the nature of the subject-matter itself.*[47] (My emphasis – J.Z.)

The 'dialectically' necessary sequence is described by Hegel as 'philosophical' knowledge, and he presents the 'dialectical' ('philosophical') method as the highest level of science, as opposed to the empirical and mathematical methods.[48] The realm where according to Hegel 'philosophical' knowledge is not at home (that is, knowledge in the form of the dialectical scientific system) is the realm of the dead, for

> what is lifeless, not being self-moved, does not bring about distinction within its essential nature; does not attain to essential opposition or unlikeness; and hence involves no transition of one opposite element into its other, no qualitative, immanent movement, no *self*-movement.[49]

The element and scope of 'philosophical' knowledge, that is of knowledge in the form of the scientific dialectical system, is on the other hand, as follows:

> The abstract or unreal is not its element and content, but the real, what is self-establishing, has life within itself, existence in its very notion. It is the process that creates its own moments in its course, and goes through them all . . . [50]

True knowledge in the form of the dialectical scientific system demands that:

> The movement of what is partly consists in becoming another to itself, and thus developing explicitly into its own immanent content . . . [51]

So that:

> True scientific knowledge . . . claims to have before it the inner necessity controlling the object . . . [52]

If one wants to know any kind of reality which possesses a dialectical ontological structure, then using a logical form other than the dialectical scientific system means, according to Hegel, wanting to express reality in an unreal way.[53]

Previous Marxist literature has given a rough critique of Hegelian 'conceptualizing', the *limits* and defects of which are set by the idealist distortion of the relation of thought and being; the antithesis between the Hegelian and the Marxian conceptions of a dialectical scientific system has been explained in that respect.

Hence we shall concentrate on supplementing previous analyses of the difference between Marx's materialist and Hegel's idealist explanations of the dialectical-logical sequence by looking at Marx's *Introduction* of 1857.

Marx does not limit his criticism to the claim that Hegel's outlook is idealist and his – Marx's – is materialist,[54] but investigates in a more detailed way the consequences this has for understanding the essential aspects of the new logical form dialectical 'conceptualizing' which was discovered and mystified by Hegel.

Marx points out that Hegel simplifies and distorts the structure of a dialectical scientific system because of his idealist identification of thought and objective reality. The ascent from the abstract to the concrete in Hegel's dialectical scientific system *coincides* with the development of objective reality (supposedly total and corresponding at every point).[55] The problem of the relation of dialectical-logical derivation, which constructs the scientific system of the object, to real history is wholly omitted. Obviously dialectical-logical derivation, which is understood as the immediate expression of objective reality itself, is taken in a false light, and although it may contain a few elements which mirror objective reality, it gives an image of reality that is idealistically confused.

It is interesting that because of his idealism Hegel exaggerates and enlarges the role of thought (of an objectivizing and hypostatizing sort), but he does not see clearly its role, activity, independence, the specific features of *human* scientific thought which precede the task of knowing reality in its dialectical ontological structure, and he disparages it. Marx, on the contrary, emphasizes that in order to understand reality correctly, as for example the capitalist mode of production, human thought must develop actively and employ certain specific forms which are not just mere parallels to real forms. This emphasis on activity, on the relative independence of human thought and of the specific character of its forms in relation to real forms results not *from abandoning* but on the contrary from *remaining true to the materialist copy-theory* in its dialectical version.

The materialist, dialectical scientific system forms an *artistic whole* with a complex architecture; forays into the historical scene are juxtaposed to one another in an organic unity, a very abstract procedure, yet completely factual and precise; only this complex architecture creates in its totality the theoretical picture of the capitalist mode of production 'in its inner structure'.

The idealist principle of the identity of thought and being also distorts Hegel's 'conceptualizing' in this respect, that in spite of the explanation, clear in principle, of the logical in terms of dialectical concreteness and in spite of the critique of schematism and formalism which – Hegel criticizes them together – attempts to gain knowledge by subsuming things under general logical determinations without considering the concrete basis of the object,[56] Hegel himself very often departs from his declared principles and 'explains' concrete phenomena by their subordination under general logical determinations.[57]

On occasion one sees the difference between Hegel's idealist, dialectical derivation and the materialist, dialectical derivation of Marx in this respect, that with Marx derivation is continually accompanied by historical illustration and is found in continuous *contact* with reality. Indeed that applies in a certain respect to Hegel's *Science of Logic*, but not at all, for example, to the *Philosophy of Right*.

Historical illustrations are not by themselves a distinguishing mark of the Marxian *materialist*, dialectical derivation as opposed to Hegel's idealist dialectical derivation (or Proudhon's confused and sophistic idealist dialectic). Also with Hegel we do find something which we could call historical illustrations of the dialectical derivation. The difference consists in how their relation to the logical development of thought is understood – which is considered primary, and which secondary. As opposed to the idealist interpretation of the dialectical unity of the logical and historical on the basis of the identity of thought and being, Marx posits his materialist conception on the copy-principle. With reference to legal philosophy Marx illustrates the dual 'unity of the logical and historical', for example, as follows: 'Hegel thus provides his logic with a political body; he does not provide us with the logic of the body politic (§287)'.[58]

The distinctive role of mathematical derivation in a dialectical–idealist and in a dialectical–materialist scientific system will be the subject of Chapter 8.

METHODS

Now it is possible to turn back to certain problems introduced in the preceding chapter[59] in connection with Grushin's interpretation of the relationship of the historical and the logical in Marx. Here we are interested in whether Grushin (and many others) are correct in interpreting Engels's views on the possibility of a dual –

historical and logical – form of investigation based on the unified
dialectical–materialist analysis.

According to Grushin the scientific investigation of a self-
developing object like, for example, capitalism, is a complicated
ensemble of procedures of different sorts. Grushin emphasizes
correctly that such an investigation is a strict process which
presupposes the solution of all relevant logical and historical
questions, in no arbitrarily determined sequence. The logical
procedures[60] do not simply exist *alongside* historical procedures; between them there are complex connections: they are
mutually presupposed, sometimes they combine the two into
one, etc.

> Taken as a total organic ensemble these investigative procedures
> form this or that *form and method* of research into an object. Here we
> arrive at the fact that science in the form of theory and in the form
> of the history of an object exists, the fact that in science the logical
> and the historical methods, specifically the mode of investigation
> of an object, exist . . . Logical and historical modes of investigation
> are distinguished from one another as *two different procedures* for the
> investigation of the same object (the analysis of the 'developed
> object' and the 'history of the object'). Hence the logical method is
> the method of investigation of the 'developed object' where
> research into the 'history of the object' is not the *immediate* task, and
> it is the historical method of research into the 'history of the
> object', where the investigation of the 'developed object' is not the
> immediate task of the investigation.[61]

The logical as well as the historical method of research reproduces the historical forms of development. The two contain in
themselves logical and historical procedures which are mutually
connected with one another and form a total process of investigation. The two are forms of the unified dialectical method of
investigation of phenomena.

> But the expression of the mutual effect of the logical and historical
> procedures can be of two sorts: logical (if the immediate task of the
> investigation is the analysis of the 'developed object', while the
> analysis of the 'history of the object' is of subordinate importance)
> and historical (where in the opposite case the immediate task of
> investigation is the analysis of the 'history of the object', while
> analysis of the 'developed object' plays a subordinate and accom-
> panying role).[62]

Grushin's interpretation, striking and inspiring as it is, falls down in that it distinguishes two things insufficiently, and actually confuses them with one another:

(a) the fact that science exists as the theory and the history of an object;

(b) the problem whether the dialectical-materialist analysis of the capitalist mode of production, the scientific goal which Marx has set for himself in *A Contribution to the Critique of Political Economy* and in *Capital*, can be realized in two forms, through two methods (the logical and the historical).

Adding to the confusion is the fact that Grushin, immediately after establishing that science exists as the theory and the history of the *object* (and the existence of the logical and the historical methods of investigation of the object) adds:

It is known that Marx has divided his political-economic work (in its first variants) into theory (first and second volumes) and history (third volume) . . . It is also known that Marx has spoken of *Theories of Surplus Value* as a repetition – in historical form – of the same questions which had been resolved in *Capital* . . . [63]

But the relation of the fourth book of *Capital* to the first three books is something other than the relationship of 'theory of the *object*' to 'history of the *object*'. In the letters which Grushin cites, Marx does not say that he wants to give a theory of the capitalist mode of production in the first books and its history in the fourth book.

In the letters which Grushin cites, Marx writes:

The whole work divides into the following parts:
Book I. Production Process of Capital.
Book II. Circulation Process of Capital.
Book III. Form of the Process as a Whole.
Book IV. Contribution to the History of the Theory. [64]

In the other letter Marx states:

Volume II gives the continuation and conclusion of the theories, *Volume III* the history of political economy from the middle of the seventeenth century. [65]

And finally we read in the third letter (from Marx to Engels on 31 July 1865):

There are still three chapters to be written in order to get finished

with the theoretical part (the first three books). Then there is still
book 4 to be written, which is historico-literary, which is for me
relatively the easiest part, since all questions in the first three books
have been resolved, and the last book is therefore more repetition
[*sic*] in historical form.[66]

The relation of the first three books to the fourth book is not
the same as the relation of the theory and the history of the object.
This means that in the construction of Marx's dialectical-
materialist system the critical analysis of previous literature has a
new role and a new form. The capitalist mode of production is
understood as a self-developing totality, an organic moment of
which is the development of the literature on political economy.
If, as we have seen, the inner connections of mature capitalism are
to be represented scientifically only through dialectical-
materialist structural-genetic analysis, for which it was necessary
to return to forms which either belonged to the prehistory of
capitalism or to the development of capitalism or to developed
capitalism in the phases which precede *mature* (classical) capitalism, then the investigation of the genesis of the literary mirroring of capitalism is equally an organic moment of a scientific
system which presents theoretically *mature* capitalism in theoretically *mature* form. At the same time a scientific system understood in this way is also necessarily a *critique* of previous literature. Hence one must bear in mind that Marx in *Theories of
Surplus Value* is not concerned with the history of political
economy in the usual sense of presenting the history of a particular science. Marx himself says:

> It is in accordance with the plan of my writings to exclude socialist
> and communist writers from the whole of the historical review.
> These latter would only show in part the form in which econo-
> mists themselves criticize themselves, in part the historically deci-
> sive forms in which the laws of political economy were first
> expressed and then developed further.[67]

While as a rule in the work of earlier economists previous
literature has been used only arbitrarily and contingently, mainly
in the form of simple refutation incorporated into real analysis, in
the Marxian dialectical-materialist analysis the critique of previous literature is an organic component of the scientific system.[68] It is – apart from critical remarks on the systematic
theoretical exposition of the object – also undertaken in a
polished literary form, and it considers how previous literature

has gradually approached the correct understanding of the reality under investigation.

The factual structure of Marx's *Capital* does not in itself solve the problem whether Marx's scientific goal, that is, the analysis of the essence of the capitalist mode of production, is to be realized in two forms, the historical and the logical.

Grushin and most Marxist literature answer that question positively. The investigation of the logical structure of Marx's *Capital* leads us, however, to the opposite conclusion.

When Engels, in his review of *A Contribution to a Critique of Political Economy*, speaks of the possibility of undertaking the critique of political economy in a dual mode, historical and logical, he means the critique of economic literature. The historical form of the critique would, according to Engels, refer to the historical development of the literature of political economy. Consequently this would be the *real* development of economic literature. Because the history of economic literature, just like other history, proceeds mainly in leaps and bounds it would be necessary to pursue these leaps and bounds in the development of economic literature through which 'not only . . . a considerable amount of material of slight importance would have to be included, but also . . . the train of thought would frequently have to be interrupted . . . ' Moreover, Engels continues, 'it would . . . be impossible to write the history of political economy without that of bourgeois society, and the task would thus become immense, because of the absence of all preliminary studies. The logical method of approach was therefore the only suitable one.'[69]

This passage from Engels's review does not refer directly to the relation of 'the theory of the capitalist mode of production' to the 'history of the capitalist mode of production', as Grushin interprets it.

Let us formulate this problem more exactly. We ask: how does the dialectical-materialist analysis of capitalism (in the logical form of 'conceptual knowledge', with its unified and complementary 'dialectical-logical' and 'historical' derivations and with its unification of previous literature into the scientific system) relate to the scientific *history* of the capitalist mode of production? Marx was of the opinion that it would 'not [be] necessary to write the *real history of the relations of production*'.[70] The problem, in other words, is *whether it would in general be possible* to discover through the presentation of the history of the capitalist mode of production the laws of capitalism *without* working out the systematic structural-genetic analysis, that is the capitalist mode of production reproduced intellectually in a new, specifically logical form.

The theory of capitalism 'in its inner typical structure' and the real history of capitalist relations of production are conditioned reciprocally and presuppose each other mutually.[71] For the development of the theory of the capitalist mode of production, that is its dialectical-materialist structural-genetic analysis, it is necessary to take into account the history of capitalist relations of production and consequently to conceive this history as continuing. The task of working out the scientific knowledge of capitalism cannot be reduced to the presentation of the history of capitalist relations of production, and one is not to consider the presentation of that history as any kind of *alternative* by which to understand the capitalist mode of production in its inner connections, rather, the scientific system of Marxist political economy must be worked out, and the preceding economic literature criticized. This means that one can only work out the *scientific* history of capitalist relations of production as a whole – in so far as it is not already worked out in parts, which are legitimate aspects of the theoretical knowledge of capitalism – when the theory of mature capitalism has already been developed by means of structural-genetic analysis.[72]

CHAPTER 7

Causal relations

As established in the preceding chapter, the Marxian dialectical derivation presupposes that the relationship of cause and effect takes a new form and role in ontological and logical conceptions which relate to the self-development of the object. Let us consider the problem in more detail.

J. Cibulka,[1] among others, deals with the use of cause and effect in Marxian dialectical-materialist analysis.

We shall attempt to illuminate the problem under investigation through critical reference to Ilenkov's interpretation[2] and to other interpretations in modern Marxist literature which deal perceptively with the Marxian concept of causality (Sós, Filkorn, Lange, Tondl, etc.).[3]

When Cibulka investigates the opening chapter of the third book of *Capital* on the law of the tendency of the average rate of profit to decline, he comes to the conclusion that causal regularities in Marx's *Capital* are understood as effects of deeper dialectical regularities.[4] For example, according to Cibulka's interpretation of Marx, social productivity of labour has two levels.

The basic level of the social productivity of labour is the contradictory process in which relative surplus value arises (or the elements of constant capital become cheaper). This appears as the conversion into value of a given capital, as a diminution of the share of variable capital in relation to constant capital, as a cheapening of the constituents of constant capital, as a decline of the rate of profit and lengthening of that process, a rise in the demand for labour, etc.; each of those phenomena is an integral part of the total process. The surface level of the process is a net of causal relations among independent factors . . . The *inner* contradictory motion contains in itself a mass of individual factors which appear independently opposed and interrelated in causal relations. This fundamental motion, which is essentially contradictory reproduces itself in the net of causal relations as many individual causal motions, each of which possesses a particular direction and intersects the other. The inner contradictoriness of the productivity of labour behaves on this abstract level as an intersection of two causal chains. This abstract level is no mere appearance, rather it is the real surface level of antagonistic contradictions, each member of which is in and of itself independent.[5]

Cibulka thinks that the independence of the individual factors within antagonistic contradictions is a matter of necessity. The causal relations which reproduce the inner contradictory motion represent a significant level of the total process. For purposes of economic analysis it suffices to be content with understanding those causal relations.[6]

Cibulka's analysis represents a step forward, particularly in that it does not stop with establishing the subordination of causal relations to deeper dialectical relations, but attempts to illuminate this subordination in more detail. A positive result of Cibulka's investigation is his critique of certain commonplace conceptions which recall Lenin's thoughts on causality as an aspect of relationships in general, but actually make causality an absolute.[7]

Now let us concentrate on a critique of Cibulka's conclusions. By using a comparative logical analysis of Ricardo's and Marx's explanations of capitalism, we arrive at a somewhat different interpretation. The method of employing causal relations characterized in Cibulka's work is not the only one used by Marx.

1. In the Marxian explanation of capitalism we find the causal relation employed in a way which we might call Galilean or *Galilean–Newtonian*. This is in essence the same understanding of causality which plays a dominant, exclusive role in Ricardo's explanation of capitalism. Marx's use of causal forms of that type is analogous to his transcendence of Ricardo's one-sided quantitative standpoint.[8]

Ricardo, for example, inquires into the causes of variations in the relative value of commodities; Marx puts a similar question, but he does not stop there; he is not limited to it as is Ricardo. In the Marxian analysis the 'Galilean' explanation of causality, in so far as it comes into play, is incorporated as a subordinate aspect into a new context, completely unknown to Galilean science – the monistic conception of reality.

Similarly Marx investigates the relation cause–effect with reference to supply and demand, but advises that the causal effect of supply and demand explains nothing, until we ascertain 'the basis on which the relation rests'.[9]

But before we investigate the 'basis' in Marxian analysis on which causal relations of supply and demand take place, let us illustrate a few further points where Marx's analysis operates with the cause–effect relation in the narrow, essentially Galilean sense.

The causal dependence of quantitative variations of one sort on quantitative variations of another sort is established by Marx, for example, when he speaks of the relation of the quantity of money as a means of circulation to commodity prices:

> that increases or decreases in the amount of currency when the value of precious metals remains constant are always the conse-quence, never the cause, of price variations . . . [10]

In similar cases Marx considers it worthwhile scientifically to establish the *non-existence* of a causal relation. Thus in his polemic against the Proudhonist Darimon he touches on the question whether there is any kind of causal relation between the quantity of paper money and coinage, as the Proudhonists advocated. Marx notes:

> Since the increase in portfolio by 101 million does not cover the decrease in metal assets, 144 million, then the possibility remains open that there is no causal link whatever between the increase on one side and the decrease on the other. [11]

In order to establish whether a causal nexus exists or not between quantities, there is available for Marx the method indi-cated by the Herschel–Mill rule.

2. Besides causality in the narrow 'Galilean' sense Marx uses the relationship cause–effect for characterizing particular aspects of the dialectical process, not only on its phenomenal surface level but also in the levels of the developing essence. The terms 'cause–effect' are used by Marx very freely for different forms of extra-mechanical effect, for labelling different sorts of 'effectual moments', very different sorts of mediation.

One cannot say that Marx has used the relationship cause–effect solely to characterize the phenomenal surface, since we read this, for example, in his analysis of capitalism:

> If, therefore, a certain degree of accumulation of capital appears as a condition of the specifically capitalist mode of production, the latter causes conversely an accelerated accumulation of capital. With the accumulation of capital, therefore, the specifically

capitalistic mode of production develops, and with the capitalist mode of production the accumulation of capital.[12]

When for example Marx investigates small plots held by independent farmers he writes:

> The causes which bring about its downfall show its limitations. These are: Destruction of rural domestic industry, which forms its normal supplement as a result of the development of large-scale industry; a gradual impoverishment and exhaustion of the soil subjected to this cultivation; usurpation by big landowners of the common lands, which constitute the second supplement of the management of land parcels everywhere and which alone enable it to raise cattle; competition, either of the plantation system or large-scale capitalist agriculture.[13]

Modern credit institutions are according to Marx 'as much an effect as a cause of the concentration of capital . . . only form a moment of the latter'[14] (that is, an aspect of the process of concentration). Or another example: capital, according to Marx, has the tendency to destroy pauperism as well as to create it at the same time. This contradictory effect is that first the one tendency and then the other predominates.[15]

Marx generalizes about the non-mechanical conception of causality in a polemic:

> that anything can ultimately destroy its own cause is a logical absurdity only for the usurer enamoured of the high interest rate. The greatness of the Romans was the cause of their conquests, and their conquests destroyed their greatness. Wealth is the cause of luxury and luxury has a destructive effect on wealth.[16]

One cannot say that Marx uses the causal relation only on the surface level; there is just as little justification for the opposite point of view, expressed by Sós, that according to Marx, one 'cannot find the cause on the surface because it is connected with the realm of necessity and essence and belongs to it'.[17]

Now let us review the analysis.

(a) The Galilean–Newtonian conception of the cause–effect relationship is mechanical and quantitative.[18] Causality is understood in the sense of mechanical stasis – one seeks the cause of the disturbance or establishment of equilibrium as a normal condition or – in mechanistic dynamics – one seeks the causes of variations in motion where the load-bearing principle is presupposed. Similarly Ricardo,[19] who presupposes a normal, natural course of the capitalist economy, seeks to find:

1. the cause of the *norm*; he finds it in inalterable laws analogous to Newtonian laws (for example, the 'natural' law of the division of the product among three 'natural' classes; in that respect the labour theory of value is the basic *cause* whereby commodities are exchanged in a given relation);

2. the causes which explain, on the presupposition of the labour principle of value, why the quantitative relation in commodity exchange and the quantitative characteristics of qualitative forms of the capitalist economy are altered;

3. the causes of general deviations from the norm which are, according to Ricardo, usually visible.

Moreover, he recognizes contingent causes[20] which play an important role and are not explicable scientifically.

The fundamental difference between Marx and Ricardo is that Marx opposes his relation of cause and effect based on essence as self-developing to causality based on the conception of a fixed essence.

Marx works *with different forms of effect* from those recognized by Galilean causality. Everything that exists (which is not merely intellectual abstraction), *has an effect* of some sort; to exist = to have an effect. Marx's conception of the different forms of effect is inseparably linked with two principles (is an aspect of those two principles): the principle of the unity of the world and the principle of self-development, that is the view that the absolute[21] 'condition' of things and phenomena is to be found 'in the process of alteration', in 'motion'.[22]

If reality is understood as self-development, then each thing has something in itself which we have earlier characterized as 'substance'; it is – so far as self-development is concerned – *causa sui*. By applying the principle of inertia absolutely he arrives at new concepts of the 'thing', the 'effect', and the 'mutual effect'. When Marx speaks of the forms of effect which are completely alien to Galilean–Newtonian causality, then these characteristics may be understood if we base them on the *whole* of Marx's new conception of the determination of phenomena. The problem of causality for Marx is therefore an inexactly formulated question, which should read: what new conception of determinism (the forms of relationships and the forms of generality and necessity) has Marx developed?

When Marx uses causal forms of thought in order to understand particular aspects of very different relationships and very

different sorts of effects, then the concept 'cause' is used syn-
chronically or as a synonym for the concepts 'condition', 'presupposition', 'basis', etc.[23]

(b) As is obvious from the illustrations cited, we meet in
Marx's analysis 'simultaneous cause and effect' (or: 'simultaneous presupposition and result', 'simultaneous condition and
consequence', etc.). By this usage Marx conceives a relationship
between particular aspects of the developmental process as a
whole.

Hence he distinguishes: (i) the transition of cause into effect
and *vice versa* (the presupposition into the law, the forming into
the formed and *vice versa*, the conditioning into the conditioned
and *vice versa*) in the developmental phase of the genesis of the
object; and (ii) the transition of cause into effect and *vice versa* in
the *development* of the 'developed object'.

In the first case the phenomenon A is only in temporal
sequence the presupposition, cause, condition of phenomenon B;
the realized phenomenon B then necessarily calls forth a new
realization of the phenomenon A whereby the phenomenon A
appears as effect (result, product) of the phenomenon B, which
was the original effect of phenomenon A. Now the phenomenon
A, originally the cause of phenomenon B, turns into the effect,
the product of phenomenon B. The cause turns into effect, the
effect into the cause.

Thus for example in the process of development of capital,
money enters as a presupposition of capital. It is itself the fruit of
a previous complicated process, but with respect to the formation of capital it is clearly a presupposition, condition. As soon as
capital has developed, it produces and reproduces money and its
different economic functions as an aspect of its own motion.[24]

Marx distinguishes presuppositions, causes, and conditions (i)
which disappear after they have served for the development of
the object, and are not reproduced by the motion of the
developed object (for example, original accumulation)[25]; (ii)
which *remain* an aspect of the existence and motion of the
'developed object' (for example, the circulation of money, world
market etc.).[26]

Another case of the transition of cause into effect and *vice versa*
(in the development of the *developed* object) is that the investigated phenomena are *at the same time* cause and effect, in that sense
a moment in the reciprocal effect, the developmental process of
the object which is the unity of many moments. It is obvious that
this 'reciprocal effect' is essentially distinct from the 'reciprocal

effect' investigated in mechanics, for example with the help of the parallelogram of forces (Stevin).[27]

We are dealing with 'reciprocal effect' on the basis of the developing essence. Marx expresses a few general ideas on 'reciprocal effect' and the transition of cause into effect and *vice versa* in connection with the development of capital. Capital creates the conditions and presuppositions of its existence and its growth 'in accordance with its immanent essence'.[28] The presuppositions and conditions of the existence of capital as 'developed object' (that is, in so far as it begins to move on its own basis, in accord with its immanent character) is a consequence 'of its own realization'.[29] It is clear that this understanding of the transition of cause into effect and *vice versa* presupposes the Marxian conception 'knowledge in concepts' and its ontological basis as shown above.[30]

In Engels's view, that one only reaches the causal relationship by taking mutual effect as primary, the concept 'mutual effect' must be necessarily understood as dialectical-materialist in content, that is, in agreement with the new Marxian understanding of determinism.

(c) In Hegel's philosophy and particularly in his logic, which was very significant for Marx in preparing a new understanding of determinism, causality in its Galilean–Newtonian meaning is robbed of its proper place in scientific explanation. It is understood as one of the many forms of 'mediation'.

Hegel has attempted in his *Logic* to give an answer to the problem of determinism expressed by Kant and Jacobi. The two thinkers – each in his own way and with different results – prove that scientific determinism based on the absolutization of mechanical causality is untenable. Kant derives agnostic conclusions concerning the subjective character of the forms of thought (whereby he, as Hegel correctly remarked, left these forms of thought as inalterable essences and accepted them in a determinist form, taking absolute mechanical causality as a basis. Jacobi left the 'final', 'conditioned' objects within the competence of mechanical determinism, and he defined 'conditionality' as 'conditionality in the sense of mechanical causality', 'conditioned in the sense of mechanical determinism'.[31] Objects of any other sort could not, according to Jacobi, be objects of rational cognition; they are merely susceptible to some kind of irrational 'unmediated knowledge'. Hegel adopted (from Fichte, Schelling, etc.) this problematic and attempted to work out a new conception of scientific determinism which could replace determinism based

on the absolutization of mechanical causality. This is Hegelian
logic. Though this attempt in the two volumes of the *Science of Logic*
is, because of idealistic distortions, a 'colossal misfiring', he
nevertheless brings to light worthwhile material to which Marx
could refer critically – as we have already seen in the analysis of
the logical structure of *Capital* – when he created his conception
of the new determinism which superseded determinism based on
mechanical causality.

When Lenin in the *Philosophical Notebooks* remarks that Hegel
subsumed 'history completely under causality and understands
causality a thousand-times more deeply and richly than the mass
of the "learned" of today',[32] he is not supporting the view that
the traditional causal relation has a dominating role in Hegel's
thought. Rather it is a question of emphasizing the Hegelian
determinist conception, which is deterministic in a new way.
Here the term 'causality' is a synonym for 'determinism'. This
interpretation is supported by Lenin's remark:

> If one reads Hegel on causality, it appears strange at first glance,
> why he deals so briefly with this well loved Kantian theme. Why?
> Well, just because causality is for him merely *one* of the determina-
> tions of the universal connection, which he understood more
> deeply and comprehensively at an earlier stage in his *whole* presen-
> tation, *always* in that connection which emphasizes interchange-
> able transitions etc. etc.[33]

Hegel subsumes all forms of connection under the concept
'mediation'; one of these forms, but not the privileged form, is
the causal relation; he gives content to the general concept 'mediation' in his idealist understanding of reality, a content derived
from intellectual mediation and logical connections.[34]

With Marx the concept 'mediation' does not have this general
significance. In general it contains all kinds of effects and connections including 'conditionality', 'connection', 'effect', so that in
the new, rich content of that concept there remains a certain
terminological continuity between Marx and Galilean–Newtonian science. Here we are not dealing with mere contingent
terminological similarities and distinctions: in this concept there
appears the essential difference between Hegel and Marx with
respect to the natural science of the seventeenth and eighteenth
centuries influenced by mathematics.[35]

(d) An important question remains: what role does Galilean
(mechanical) causality play in the Marxian understanding of the

different forms of effect? Marx totally removes the object of his investigation, the capitalist mode of production, from the competence of Galilean–Newtonian science, that is, the type of scientific thought suited to systems of a mechanical character.[36] The capitalist mode of production, according to Marx, is neither 'a solid crystal' nor a self-moving system analogous to a watch; it is an 'organism which has undergone a continuous process of development', each of its aspects exists only 'in motion', 'simultaneously as presupposition and result' of the motion of the object.[37] It is a 'dialectically articulated whole'.[38]

Hence according to Marx analysis leads to knowledge of that dialectically articulated and altering whole, the *constituents* of which may be analysed as mechanical systems, for example systems which are analogous (isomorphic to mechanical systems). That is a subordinate but legitimate element.

In the Marxian analysis of capitalism the analysis of mechanical systems is used (with forms of thought which are essentially similar to mechanical science of the seventeenth century)[39] in particular phases as constituents of the whole dialectical-materialist structural-genetic analysis, which employs the new logical and methodological form 'knowledge in concepts'. They are used where the relation and dependence of particular quantities peculiar to the capitalist economy could be investigated under the presupposition that (i) these quantities are something qualitatively complete (an abstraction from their dialectical character) and that (ii) their dependence is understood as the dependence of independent factors external to one another (which is inseparably connected with (i)). These presuppositions have, to be sure, their basis in objective reality (in the relative stability of the forms of the capitalist economy), but in their pure form they are at first a product of abstraction. The justification for this abstraction is that existing qualitative stability can be sought within determinate limits and can be understood without justifying the view that it is actually a moment of the dialectical process of development. It appears that that is not only a *possibility* but also a *necessity* for analysis. The use of a procedure where mechanical systems are formed from particular aspects of a dialectically articulated whole, systems which are first investigated in that simplified form and are similar to the mechanical science of the seventeenth century, were obviously considered by Marx as an *integrating moment* of the dialectically articulated whole.

It is obvious that as in other cases the analysis of the logical and methodological structure of *Capital* leads us on the one hand to look for a determinate resolution of logical and methodological problems in *ontological* problems mediated by the copy-character of logical and methodological forms: on the other hand, we come again to the relative autonomy of theory which attempts to grasp a dialectically articulated whole as opposed to a known objective reality.

CAUSALITY AND CONTRADICTION

The close connection between these two problems arises from the fact that the basis of the Marxian conception of all relationships and consequently causal relations is the interpretation of reality as self-moving, the deepest principle of which is the unity and struggle of opposites. J. Cibulka[40] has devoted great attention to this aspect of Marx's *Capital*.

To supplement his analysis we incorporate certain considerations related to the comparative logical analysis of Ricardo's and Marx's conceptions of the categories 'antithesis' and 'contradiction', as preparation for the general question: what role does Marx's conception of contradiction play in the supersession of a determinism dependent on mechanical causality, and in the creation of dialectical-materialist determinism?

We are well aware that observations drawn from the analysis of the implicit logical structure of *Capital* represent merely raw material for solving the general question posed above.[41]

(a) One of the essential causes, if not the most essential cause – leaving aside historical and social conditions and concentrating on theory – why Ricardo and pre-Marxist economists in general did not reach a deeper understanding of the essence of capitalism, was their superficial, impoverished conception of the *relation of opposites*. It was also their failure to comprehend that the objectivity, the existence of antithetical determinations in very different relations, including the identity of antitheses, belong to the essence of the object, so that without theoretical presentation of a specific objectivity the object cannot be grasped in its essence, knowledge of the object remains piecemeal, confused (as was the case with the knowledge of capitalism achieved by bourgeois political economy).

When Ricardo encounters an antithesis in the investigation of capitalism – as he must – and formulates it, his formulation is incomplete: Ricardo does not see what he has to hand, he does not understand how to deal with an antithesis; antitheses in such an illogical, unaware formulation do not have their natural flexibility and do not reveal the hidden, changing essence of the object, as is later revealed in the theories of Marx the dialectician.

How does Ricardo understand, for example, the *antithesis* of exchange-value and use-value? Ricardo obviously distinguishes exchange-value from use-value. He criticizes Say,[42] for example, for not distinguishing exchange-value and use-value sufficiently, and operates with a confused concept of an allegedly unified value. In Chapter 20 of his *Principles* Ricardo shows that exchange-value and use-value are so sharply distinguished from one another that their magnitudes can move at the same time in opposite directions. He also emphasizes that exchange-value is linked to use-value,[43] and sees their unity in that use-value is a precondition for the existence of the exchange-value of a commodity.

In that case Ricardo sees antitheses and the unity of opposites, but to a certain point and then only superficially. (In contrast, Ricardo sees only simple labour in connection with the origin of exchange-value. He completely overlooks the fact that the labour which produces commodities and creates value is labour which has antithetical concrete and abstract properties.)[44]

Ricardo's analysis *ceases* with the opposition of exchange-value and use-value and the *unity* of these opposites (which is not false, but only elementary, initial). It is there that Marx *begins* the investigation of the secret of the commodity-form and of money, when he establishes in the first sections of *Capital* that in the commodity, use-value and exchange-value exist *alongside one another* (as two factors of the commodity – saying nothing about their antithetical character) and that use-value is the condition for exchange value, but not *vice versa*.[45] What Marx reveals after further investigation as a polarity, as an inner relation of opposites, as a transition of opposites into one another, as the identification of opposites, etc., is what he introduces at the beginning as distinctions, as distinct properties. When for example he begins to analyse and establish that labour possesses a 'two-fold nature', he explains that 'so far as it finds expression in value, it does not possess the same characteristics that belong to it as a creator of use-values'.[46]

Here – as Marx later explains – the opposition which leads up to the contradiction is presented very freely, openly, boldly. Marx prepares his material for further analysis in order to reveal the deeper relations of those objects, their polarity and their contradictory character.[47]

Marx praised Ricardo, saying that he 'discovers, expresses the economic opposition of classes – as the inner relationship reveals . . .'[48] But at this point Marx has advanced beyond Ricardo in understanding these oppositions, for from the submerged war of classes in capitalist society he concludes that this struggle results inevitably in the dictatorship of the proletariat.[49]

Marx considers it a great service that Ricardo sensed the *distinction* between the price of production and value and that he – unclearly and only as an application of the law of value – formulated the *contradiction* between the determination of the value of a commodity by labour and the existence of the average rate of profit.[50]

Among the theoreticians of classical bourgeois political economy Sismondi, in Marx's opinion, advanced furthest with the anthitheses and contradictions of capitalist economic forms. He nearly came to the conclusion that the capitalist mode of production is contradictory: the possibility of unlimited growth of productivity and wealth and at the same time the need to limit the masses to the necessities of life. He considered crises an expression of the inner contradictions of capitalism.[51]

From our point of view it is important to judge what position is taken by post-Ricardians and by contemporary political economists on Ricardo's and Sismondi's conceptions of the antithetical character of economic forms, how Marx refers critically to it, and what new forms of thought appear in Marx's dialectical-materialist conception of the antithetical and contradictory character of those forms.

James Mill takes the trouble to give Ricardo's theory a systematic form and to work it out, so that it could serve better in lending a basis and support to the capitalist form of production as a 'natural and eternal' form. He understands, even if illogically and unclearly, the antithetical nature of Ricardo's conceptions. He attempts to gloss over the antitheses and contradictions, to present them as merely apparent, so he does not arrive at the essence of the capitalist economy.[52]

When he establishes any kind of economic relation as a unity of *antithetical* determinations, James Mill stresses their *unity*, so that he actually disputes their antithetical character. 'He makes the unity of opposites into the immediate identity of those opposites.'[53] This line was later pursued in the superficial phrases of vulgar apologists (MacCulloch, Bastiat, etc.).[54]

Their disputation of the antithetical character and contradictoriness of capitalist economic forms represents an essential part of their theory. Marx criticized the vulgar economists for merely seeing external differences between economic forms, whereas Smith and Ricardo had already worked out a definite, even if incomplete understanding of their antithetical character.[55]

It is noteworthy that reactionary apologetics do not serve merely to *tone down* and *negate* antitheses, but also to *reveal* and *emphasize* the antithetical character of capitalist economic forms understood undialectically. Malthus, for example, seizes for reactionary purposes on Sismondi's doctrine of the contradictory character of many capitalist forms. He turns that doctrine *against* Ricardo, but not to lead political economy beyond the conception of the contradictory character of capitalism to a higher form, but to fight Ricardo's theory in so far as it was the theoretical expression of forces within the capitalist economy defending pre-capitalist society.[56]

In comparison with Ricardo and Sismondi, who had expressed in pre-Marxist classical bourgeois political economy the antithetical and contradictory character of capitalist economic forms, Marx proceeds further in that he *advances to antitheses and contradictions immanently understood*. Even Sismondi, wholly silenced by Ricardo, lacks the 'immanently understood contradiction', according to Marx. This is a contradiction so understood that, under specific conditions, it implies the identity of opposites,[57] which is linked (falls into place) with the interpretation of reality as self-development. The immanently understood antitheticalness and contradictoriness unknown to Ricardo and to Lockean science were anticipated by classical German philosophy, particularly by Hegel, who criticized the old shallow understanding of antitheticalness and the exclusion of 'contradiction' from science, as formulated, for example, in pre-Kantian German metaphysics.[58]

Marx considered the immanent conception of the contradiction essential for dialectical materialist scientific analysis (and for the jump from the establishment, and the critical judgement of contradictions to an understanding of them). His remark shows that the Hegelian 'contradiction' (that is, the immanently, even if idealistically understood contradiction) is the source of his dialectic.[59]

In Marx we find a movement from external distinction through more or less external opposition to immanently understood contradiction. He proceeds in that way, for example, with the analysis of the commodity and its objective aspects, value and use-value.[60]

Or, for example, in connection with his investigation of the linkage of the individual elements of the value-forming process Marx comments:

> So far in the realization process, we have only the indifference of the individual moments towards one another; that they determine each other internally and search for each other externally; but that they may or may not find each other, balance each other, correspond to each other. The inner necessity of moments which belong together, and their indifferent, independent existence towards one another, are already a foundation of contradictions.
>   Still, we are by no means finished. The contradiction between production and realization – of which capital, by its concept, is the unity – has to be grasped more intrinsically than merely as the indifferent, seemingly reciprocally independent appearance of the individual moments of the process, or rather of the totality of processes.[61]

In Marx's analysis we find the contrary procedure – from immanent contradiction to external antitheses as the phenomenal form of the inner immanent contradictions. For example, Marx writes:

> The opposition or contrast existing internally in each commodity between use-value and value, is, therefore, made evident externally by two commodities being placed in such relation to each other, that the commodity whose value it is sought to express, figures directly as a mere use-value, while the commodity in which that value is to be expressed, figures directly as mere exchange value. Hence the elementary form in which the contrast contained in that commodity, between use-value and value, becomes apparent.[62]

The highest developed phenomenal form of this inner antithesis is the antithesis commodity–money.

(b) What is the relationship of this analysis of contradiction (does it proceed from external differences and antitheses to inner, contrary ones)[63] to causal explanation, for example, in Marxian monetary theory? In the chapter on dialectical derivation where we attempted to explain the relationship of the dialectical-logical and the historical derivation of money, it was said that in the investigation of the origin of money Marx had not put the simple question: what is the cause of the development of money? He investigates general, necessary relations, the different forms of effect and necessary transition characteristic to the development of money, which answer the question how the essence of money is to be understood as a historical (transitory) phenomenon. Hence that is the question which replaces in Marxian determinism the simple question of the 'cause of the origin of money'; essence as self-development must be presupposed.

Though many economists saw the origin of money in the difficulties inherent in barter, Marx formulated the development of money through the immanent contradiction of the commodity form.[64]

We have in Marx's analysis a complex self-developing structure whose basis is the immanent contradiction of the commodity. In the different stages of maturity of commodity production and then in capitalist commodity production it takes different forms. The immanent contradictions find their expression in (relatively) external phenomena of antagonistic social relations; there we are dealing with more than two levels. The relationship between individual levels, individual effects and phases of development is usually expressed by Marx in the concepts 'creation', 'necessary transition', 'necessary form of appearance', etc. – all categories of his new determinism – and occasionally expressed in causal terms. Cause in this case is understood as an 'effective aspect' of a self-developing organic whole. Causal relation is understood here in a comprehensive non-specific sense which explains a particular alteration of a particular reality, a condition or relation which answers the question 'why'. In such cases one may not apply the causal relation to the immanent contradiction; one cannot, for example, rationally ask for the cause when the inner contradiction of the commodity has the character revealed by Marx's theory, and not another. It can be explained rationally *why* the contradictions of the commodity have a given character, while the historical development of the commodity is revealed (and hence also the expansion of the exchange process);[65] this resembles Marx's way of explaining the development of money, that between a product (so long as it is not a commodity) and a product in the commodity-form there is no direct developmental relation as there is between the simple commodity-form and money.

When Marx indicates that 'the development of contradictions of an historical form of production [is] . . . the sole historical way of dissolution and new formation',[66] he means that the main *cause* (though that concept, if applied to a dialectical process, is incapable of comprehending the relations of a self-developing structure) of the transition to a new social formation is the contradictions within the formation, which always exist as a *development of contradictions* and as a contradictory structure *of even more levels*.

The development of immanent contradictions, which is in a certain respect *causa sui*, can appear as the cause of the existence and development of external antitheses.[67] The development of these external antitheses, the development of aspects from the development of inner contradictions, their form of development, has that effect and can appear in individual phases and aspects as the cause of the development of inner contradictions. Hence Marx writes, for example, on the effect of the general extension of the Factory Act:

> By maturing the material conditions, and the combination on a social scale of the processes of production, it matures the contradictions and antagonisms of the capitalist form of production, and thereby provides, along with the elements for the formation of a new society, the forces for exploding the old one.[68]

It is obvious that we are dealing with an effect in an organic process of development; Marx speaks in such cases of 'feed back'.

Sometimes it seems as if Marx considers contradictory character as something which results just as much from another 'basis' of development. He says, for example, in *Capital* that he is dealing not with the higher or lower point of development of social antagonisms 'that result from the natural laws of capitalist production', but with these 'laws themselves', with 'these tendencies working with iron necessity towards inevitable results'.[69] His purpose is 'to lay bare the economic law of motion of modern society'.[70] Or in other words: the mother of antagonism is large scale industry,[71] etc. In reality, contradiction is always taken to be the basis of development. To lay bare the economic law of motion means to reveal the necessary, general forms of development of specific contradictions of capitalism; this development is, as we have just seen, the sole path of transition for capitalism into another formation. Similarly when Marx speaks of 'antagonisms which result from the law', that is only another way of saying that we are dealing with antagonisms which are an expression[72] of the immanent contradictions of capitalism as it develops. The 'law' in this case is the law of value, a conception of the regular development of the immanent contradictions of the commodity and capitalist economic forms.[73]

(c) In the analysis of the *specific* forms of antitheses and contradictions in the commodity and capitalist economic forms Marx formulates certain thoughts on the *general* form of antitheses, which – even if they do not resolve these general questions – are of great significance for further investigations.[74]

Marx, as we have seen, believes that Hegel's conception of 'contradiction', in spite of its idealist distortions, is the source of his dialectic.[75] Hegel discovered the *general* form of the dialectic (that is, the general form of antithesis and contradiction),[76] though it was distorted by idealism.

In general Marx characterizes the dialectical-materialist conception of antithesis and contradiction as including

in its comprehension and affirmative recognition of the existing state of things, at the same time, also, the recognition of the negation of that state, of its inevitable breaking up; because it regards every historically developed social form as in fluid movement, and therefore takes into account its transient nature not less than its momentary existence; because it lets nothing impose upon it, and is in its essence critical and revolutionary.[77]

That is also the sense of Lenin's general view that 'the unity of opposites is relative, the struggle of opposites is absolute'. Thus an essential sign of *all* self-developing processes is understood if we are aware that 'unities of opposites' are distinct and always specific, and that it is just the same with antitheses.[78]

The forms and resolution of such a contradiction could be distinguished in its various phases. In the analysis of the contradictions of commodity-production and capitalist economic forms Marx recognizes on the whole two basic forms:

1. The form which appears to equalize, to renew an equilibrium through which the resolution of contradictions proceeds, retaining the original qualitative basis; through the resolution of contradictions it arrives at qualitative alterations, at the development of qualitatively new forms in which the original contradiction – as a rule in modified form – is reproduced;[79]

2. The form which signifies the abolition of the old contradiction and the creation of a new unity of opposites (hence the development of new forms on a basis other than that of capitalism).[80]

It must be admitted that Marx seldom expressed any general thoughts on antitheses. In the main he emphasized that antithesis and contradiction, as they occur in commodity-production and capitalist economic forms, serve only for *particular* phenomena *in a specific way*, but not for all types of antithesis and contradiction.[81] Scientific knowledge of an object can only be knowledge of the unity of opposites and the forms of contradiction in a specific case.

CHAPTER 8

Mathematics in
Marxian analysis

Marx's scientific system, a structural-genetic analysis, can be distinguished from scientific systems constructed by the axiomatic method, whether classical or modern.[1] On the other hand mathematical derivation plays a significant role in Marx's analysis.[2] Marxian analysis contains as a subordinate aspect certain methods which recall the procedures of model building and mathematical analysis, as developed in the modern axiomatic method. It is not that the Marxian conception of science anticipates mathematical logic of the twentieth century, nor that we want to overlook the qualitative difference between the modern axiomatic method, with its well developed procedures of formalization and model building; we want to elucidate those elements of the Marxian analysis with an affinity to the modern axiomatic method. In *Capital* Marx uses mathematical derivation in a way which was usual in natural science and which in itself is not original. But what is new with Marx is that mathematical derivation is an aspect of dialectical-materialist structural-genetic analysis.

Let us consider in that connection some of Marx's procedures in the third volume of *Capital* on the relation of the rate of profit to the rate of surplus value:

So far as the quantity of profit is assumed to be equal to that of surplus-value, its magnitude, and that of the rate of profit, is determined by ratios of simple figures given or ascertainable in every individual case. The analysis, therefore, first is carried on purely in the mathematical field.[3]

Marx comes to the conclusion that the magnitude of the rate of profit is determined by the formula

$$p' = m' \frac{v}{c} = m' \frac{v}{c+v},$$

where m' is the rate of surplus value, v the variable capital, C the total capital and c the constant capital. Marx continues:

> Let us now go on to apply the above-mentioned equation of the rate of profit, $p' = s' v/C$, to the various possible cases. We shall successively change the value of the individual factors of $s' v/C$ and determine the effect of these changes on the rate of profit. In this way we shall obtain different series of cases, which we may regard either as successive altered conditions of operation for one and the same capital, or as different capitals existing side by side and introduced for the sake of comparison, taken, as it were, from different branches of industry or different countries. In cases, therefore, where the conception of some of our examples as successive conditions for one and the same capital appears to be forced or impracticable, this objection falls away the moment they are regarded as comparisons of independent capitals.[4]

We are dealing with the following cases:
I. m' constant, v/C variable.
　1. m' and C constant, v variable.
　2. m' constant, v variable, C varies with variations of v.
　3. m' and v constant, c and hence also C variable.
II. m' variable.
　1. m' variable, v/C constant.
　2. m' and v variable, C constant.
　(a) The variation of v and m' proceeds in opposite directions, but with the same magnitude.
　(b) The variation of m' and v proceeds in opposite directions, but with different magnitudes.
　(c) The variation of m' and v proceeds in the same direction.
　3. m', v and C variable.
Marx summarizes the conclusions of this analysis as follows:
　1. p' increases or decreases in the same degree as m', if v/C remains constant.
　2. p' rises or falls in a greater degree than m', if v/C moves in the same direction as m', that is, increases or decreases, if m' increases or decreases.
　3. p' rises or falls in a lesser degree than m', if v/C varies in the opposite direction as m', but in a lesser degree.
　4. p' rises although m' falls, or falls although m' rises, if v/C varies in the opposite direction from m' and in a greater degree.
　5. Finally, p' remains constant, although m' rises, if v/C varies in the opposite direction but in exactly the same degree as m'.
　Marx then summarizes a further aspect:

The rates of profit of two different capitals, or of one and the same capital in two successive different conditions,

are equal

1) if the per cent composition of the capitals is the same and their rates of surplus-value are equal;

2) if their per cent composition is not the same, and the rates of surplus-value by the percentages of the variable portions of capitals (s' by v) are the same, i.e., if the *masses* of surplus-value ($s = s'v$) calculated in per cent of the total capital are equal; in other words, if the factors s' and v are inversely proportional to one another in both cases.

They are unequal

1) if the per cent composition is equal and the rates of surplus-value are unequal, in which case they are related as the rates of surplus value;

2) if the rates of surplus-value are the same and the per cent composition is unequal, in which case they are related as the variable portions of the capitals;

3) if the rates of surplus-value are unequal and the per cent composition not the same, in which case they are related as the products $s'v$, i.e., as the quantities of surplus-value calculated in per cent of the total capital.[5]

Engels adds that in Marx's manuscript there are very detailed illustrative calculations of the difference between the rate of surplus-value and the rate of profit which trace their divergence or convergence.

This part of the Marxian analysis of the capitalist mode of production obviously turns on forms of thought treated by mathematical logic in the investigation of the axiomatic construction of elementary mathematics.[6] The logical presuppositions, the presuppositions of axiom and rule implied here are precisely those implied in the elementary arithmetic and geometry of Peano, Russell, Hilbert and others. The logical investigations of Frege, Russell, Hilbert, etc., attempt to explain forms of thought which have a place in Marx's structural-genetic analysis.

Thus we are dealing in the cases under I with a functional dependence of the type

$y = k \times f(x)$, specifically $y = k \times (g(x))$ for $k > 0$, and in case I/1: $y = x/K$ for $k > 0$, where the field is defined $x \, \varepsilon \, (O, K)$

in case I/2: $y = k \times x/c + v$ for $k > 0$, $c > 0$, where the field is defined $x \, \varepsilon \, (O, c + x)$

in case I/3: $y = k \times v/x + v$ for $k > 0$, $v > 0$, where the field is defined $x \, \varepsilon \, (O, \, x + v)$

in case I/4: $y = k \times x/z + x = k \times x \times 1/x + z$, etc.

The next higher mathematical generalizations of which the Marxian formulations are a special case are general models of linear functions. All cases under I/1–4 are special cases of the functional relation $y = k \times f(x)$, specifically $y = k \times f[g(x)]$, where $f(x)$ and $f[g(x)]$ are linear functions. The next–order generalization is the concept of the function. Then we reach the mathematico–logical concept 'relation' and arrive at relational logic.

This part of the Marxian analysis operates – in so far as its logical basis is concerned – within the bounds of mathematical relational logic. This means that the relevant sections of twentieth century symbolic logic are also a part of the logical structure of procedures which are a legitimate, if subordinate, element of Marx's dialectical–materialist structural–genetic analysis. Modern symbolic logic, however, explains the logical structure of that procedure incompletely and non–definitively. Twentieth-century symbolic logic is concerned with the fundamental problems of logic, for example the theory of sets and the general theory of functions built up on it. Novikov remarks, for example: 'it must be recognized that the principles on which set theory is constructed are not satisfactory even if this theory has successfully generated an axiomatic method.'[7] It appears that the investigation of such questions as the logical basis of set theory in connection with the ontological structure of reality and the logical structure of scientific thought, as undertaken by Marx with critical reference to Hegel, and the investigation of the procedures mentioned, remembering that they are a subordinate moment of another procedure, are necessary to solve the fundamental logical problems posed by symbolic logic, as well as to explain the logical basis of contemporary dialectical-materialist analysis.

Although the general investigation of that problem does not fit within the limited space of this study, another question arises: what does our analysis of the logical structure of Marx's *Capital* allow us to say *about the problem of the distinction and the relationship between the 'logical consequence' and the 'logical derivation', employed in the mathematical section we have cited* (which will be designated

'Part B'), *and about the 'logical consequence' and the 'logical derivation',* *investigated with the example drawn from the first chapter of 'Capital'* (Part A)?[8]

1. The concept of the formal-logical consequence, through which essential aspects of the logical structure of the mathematical section of *Capital* and other sections are to be understood, must be outlined and summarized.

S. A. Yanovskaya defines the logical consequence in the commentary on the Russian translation of Hilbert and Ackermann's *Foundations of Theoretical Logic*[9] with the help of the logical linkage '→' (the material implication),[10] which works well enough, she says, for simple cases. It does not function any longer in the logic of propositions, but in its metalogic which investigates the formulae of the propositional calculus. With the help of the formulae of propositional logic, true for all cases, we can define the concept of the logical consequence for propositional calculus. 'We say that the formula B follows logically (is a logical consequence) from the premises $A_1, A_2, \ldots, A_K$, if the expression $(A_1, A_2, \ldots, A_K) \to B$ is always a true formula of the propositional calculus.'[11]

K. Ajdukiewicz defines the concept of the elementary formal-logical consequence with the help of a scheme of derivation, as follows: a conclusion follows logically from the premises if 'it can be derived according to a logical schema (that is, a formal and generally applicable schema)'.[12] Ajdukiewicz defines the concept of the schema (in §17) with the help of propositional and predicate variables and so-called logical constants (negation, implication, disjunction, quantity, etc.). The 'propositional forms' or 'propositional functions' are expressions which, besides words (or signs) with a certain meaning, that is, besides constants, also contain variables and are true or false only if these variables are replaced by corresponding constants. 'A schema whose premises and propositions are propositional in form, which are composed *from logical constants and variables*, we call a formal syllogistic schema.'[13] Such a formal syllogistic schema may or may not be generally applicable. An example of a generally applicable syllogistic schema is, for example, the *modus ponendo ponens*:

If p, then q

$$\frac{p}{q}$$

An example of a formal syllogistic formula *not* generally applicable might be:

If p, then q

$$\frac{q}{p}$$

A formal syllogistic schema, which is generally applicable, i.e. which has the property that we never arrive at a false conclusion from correct premises if we complete the schema correctly, is called the *logical* syllogism.[14]

E. W. Beth's *Semantic Entailment and Formal Derivability* attempts a comprehensive definition.[15] The author considers Tarski's work from the 1930s[16] and analyses logical entailment in its complex form as developed by symbolic logic in the last few decades. Beth believes that the term 'logical consequence' expresses two different concepts, roughly characterized as follows:

(a) *Formal derivability*. There are formal rules of inference producing a particular, direct syllogistic consequence from premises of a particular character. For example, the *modus ponens*:

If p, then q

$$\frac{p}{q}$$

Or the *conversio simplex*:

$$\frac{\text{Some A are B}}{\text{Some B are A}}$$

In these cases V is the *logical consequence* from U_1, U_2, . . . , (follows logically – from U_1, U_2, . . .), if it is *formally derivable* from U_1, U_2, . . ., that is, if it results from the premises U_1, U_2, . . ., and the syllogistic consequence V can be obtained through the rules of derivation. The author adds that the rules of derivation are called 'formal' because they could be presented in purely 'typographical' terms without affecting the meaning of the proposition on which they were employed.[17]

(b) *Semantic entailment*. This is a relation of entailment in which the *meanings* of the terms in the premises and consequences play an essential role. The semantic consequence is therefore inseparably linked with problems of model building and interpretation. It can be defined as follows: we say that V *results semantically* from $U_1, U_2, \ldots$, if one cannot replace the terms in $U_1, U_2, \ldots$ and in V with new terms so that the new premisses $U_1, U_2, \ldots$, are true, while the new conclusion V' is false.[18] If such a term could be found, then V does *not result* semantically from $U_1, U_2, \ldots$, and the discovery of such a model with such a term is proof that V *does not logically result* from $U_1, U_2, \ldots$.

Formulated positively: from the propositions $U_1, U_2, \ldots, U_K$ the proposition V results logically if and only if each model of the proposition $U_1, U_2 \ldots, U_K$ is equally a model of the proposition V. The logically correct proposition and the logically correct formulation are to be defined in semantic terms with the help of the concept 'model': a proposition is correct if and only if all possible replacements of the meaning of its constant (extralogical) expressions are its model. A formula is logically correct if and only if each granting of a constant meaning to its free variable is its model.[19]

In the cases cited above the concept of the formal-logical consequence is inseparably linked with the concept of the logical constant, whether the definition of the logical constants (the logical concepts) is expressed through simple calculation[20] or – as in the latest work by Kemeny – by means of a complex exact analysis.

It is obvious that these and similar observations on the concept of the logical consequence comprehend essential aspects of the logical structure of the mathematical part and other parts of Marx's *Capital*. It is just as obvious that they do not comprehend the type of logical result contained in dialectical derivation as analysed in the light of the Marxian theory of value and money.

Marx speaks of the first chapter as a 'deduction', as a 'derivation of value',[21] but in the sense of 'development' or 'development by analysis'.

2. If we examine Part A and Part B with respect to the logical connection between propositions, we find that there are two types: (a) an intuitive derivation (that is, its rules are not explicitly formulated); and (b) a derivation with an *enthymematic* character. The concept of the enthymeme, as defined by Ajdukiewicz,[22] must be somewhat altered, if it is to cover both cases.[23]

Two sorts of enthymemes must be distinguished:

I. The first (usual) type is a set whose elements are: (a) formal-logical rules (for example the rule of exclusion), in the majority of cases with the property non-A; (b) propositions of the requisite (potential) system with the property A; (c) propositions of the requisite (potential) system with the property non-A, whereby the property A is defined: 'is expressed in the requisite system'.

In the enthymeme of the first type we can arrange a non-enthymematic formal-logical derivation in which the propositions of group (c) also possess the property A.

II. The second sort of enthymeme: a set whose elements are (a), (b), partly (c) above, plus (d) the extra-formal-logical rule with the property non-A.

To the enthymeme of the second type one cannot assign enthymematic derivations formed in ways similar to case I which were at the same time a formal-logical derivation. The corresponding derivation in which the extra-formal-logical rules possess the property A would not be formal-logical.

The task of understanding the logical character of derivation in Part A is identical with the task of characterizing the elements of group (d) in the case of the enthymeme of Part A.

For Part B it is noteworthy that we encounter in it the enthymeme of the first type—the extra-formal-logical rules are simple and were worked out at length mathematically; they are not specific to Marx.

Part A contains on the other hand an enthymeme of the second type in which the elements of group (d) are a rule specific to Marx. Their systematic formulation – in so far as one can speak of a systematic formulation with respect to that rule – has not yet been worked out; Lenin's discourse on the elements of the dialectic[24] can obviously be considered in that sense the most complete formulation up to now, after these 'elements' are transformed into rules.

With dialectical derivation, as revealed by the enthymeme, formal-logical rules are employed; they possess a subordinate significance with respect to the remaining dialectical rules.

The investigation of the distinction between the derivations in Part A and Part B is displaced by the investigation of the rules of derivation. In the case of dialectical rules we are dealing with extra-formal-logical rules which do not (or do not only) concern intellectual operations, but rather 'empirical procedures' in the widest sense of the word. We are dealing with rules derived from the ontological presuppositions of the materialist dialectic and hence depend on the specific character of the object of Marxian investigation.

In principle an additional formalization of Part A might be undertaken. If the rules of derivation are limited to formal-logical rules,[25] the system generated through this formalization will consist of a series of axioms independent of one another, axioms which establish Marxian results independent of one another, and for example possess the form of logical implication and correspond in antecedent and consequence to the Marxian presupposition and result. In such a system formal-logical rules make possible wholly trivial transformations which are not of interest: everything or almost everything new which Marx derived would already be contained in the axioms of the system concerned. In other words: the dialectical logical consequence in Marx is not in this formalization a clear coordinate of the formal-logical result. The logical structure of Part A would not be grasped by such a formalization, while the potential formalization of Part B would give an isomorphic presentation of the corresponding logical consequence and would express the logical structure of the derivation in that part.

The chief characteristic of the dialectical-logical derivation by which Marx, helped by elements of formal-logical derivation, creates a dialectical-materialist scientific system (he considers such a scientific system to be the sole form of theoretical appropriation of the object under investigation, that is, the capitalist mode of production), is that it is based on securing the inner necessary relations of the object. Its character (hence the ontological character of the capitalist mode of production) conditions and determines *for the time being the specific* character of the dialectical-logical derivation. *In general* it may be said of this logical derivation that it is always *concrete*, hence its *concrete character in general* matches the type of logical derivation. Hence, in logical and metalogical considerations on the dialectical-logical derivation, in abstract investigation of the form of that derivation, the specific character of the derivation must be observed (and the eventual use of the symbolic method would have to be accommodated to that specific character). No formalization is possible in that sense, as is possible for many mathematical objects and is so unusually productive for the advance of human knowledge.

3. Sometimes one encounters the attempt to express the distinction between traditional deductive derivation and dialectical-logical derivation through the opposition of 'formal' and 'content' derivation.

The opposition of form and content is a remnant not only of pre-Marxist but also pre-Hegelian, usually Kantian conceptions of the logical. Today it exists mainly in views which put the 'purely logical' and the 'factual' ('empirical') in metaphysical antithesis.

Carnap characterizes formal-logical relations in deductive logic as 'independent of all real factors, thus in the traditional sense formal'.[26] With Carnap the 'logical' is the 'formal' because it is 'independent of all real facts'. Carnap returns to a pre-Hegelian[27] simplification of *verités de raison* – *verités de fait*, 'forms of thought' – 'thought content', 'logical' – 'factual' ('empirical').

Marx refers to Hegel's critique[28] of these simplified oppositions; he develops Hegelian discoveries on the basis of the copy-theory and puts the logic expressed through that critique on a new basis. In the Marxian conception there is no logical typology, hence no formal-logical schemata of derivation and formal-logical relations of derivation 'independent of all real facts, hence in that sense formal'. One cannot say that any type of logic would be a mirroring 'of mere form independent of content'. Logical forms and relations in that case are forms and relations with content.[29] In logic we are dealing with the investigation of forms of thought with content, in metalogic on the other hand it is a matter of forms of thought with content on a higher level of abstraction.[30]

The metaphysical opposition of form and content, logical and factual, is replaced in Marx's work by a new conception: the logical is the copy of factual content; the multifarious types of logic are an expression of the fact that in general the contents of different levels, aspects, fields of reality are distinguishable. The absolute character, the general applicability, for example of 'formal-logical schemata of derivation' is not a property which distinguishes logical relations applying here from logical relations applying in the dialectical-logical derivation.[31] Within limited boundaries and relations one can and must take particular logical relations as absolutes (as 'value-substance' within limits is 'absolute').

There are different levels, fields and aspects of reality with a particular character of form and content. These particular levels, fields and aspects have their specific necessary relations (regularity, structure); they possess specific systemic properties; they are particular systems and structures. The general theory of system and systemic properties is ontology, logic and metalogic, in which logic and metalogic investigate systems with a copy-character.[32]

It is obvious that one cannot investigate the problem of the relationship of formal-logical derivation to dialectical-logical derivation in Marx's analysis without considering Marx's new conception of the *ontological* structure of reality. Without this it is not possible to grasp the new logical forms used in Marx's scientific system, and the shift and transformation of traditional logical forms in pre-Marxist thought cannot be understood, forms which develop by becoming an aspect of a new whole.[33]

In §183 of his *Doctrine of Science*[34] B. Bolzano is concerned with – as he says – noteworthy propositions which express something in the process of becoming. He wants to express the logical character of those propositions by transforming them into a formation which does not presuppose any kind of self-development. He maintains that the proposition '*M* arises out of *A*' or '*A* supersedes *M*' can be transformed into the allegedly logical formula: 'The object *A* has the quality of succumbing to a change whose effect is that it will be turned into *M* at a future time.' If we proceeded with a similar transformation in Marx's dialectical derivation, then what is specific and basic in the Marxian conception of the logical relations in dialectical derivation would be confused and distorted. Similarly recent formal logical literature usually goes astray when it deals with the explanation of phenomena through dialectical derivation. The conception of the logical as contained implicitly in Marx's work proves the opposite, as with the labour hypothesis: namely, formal-logical forms and the formal-logical consequence as given in modern symbolic logic are to be understood as a special case of a comprehensive theory of logical forms (and general methodology) built up from the ontological explanation of self-development.

4. So-called inductive logical relations also belong to formal logic. The definition is significantly less developed than the definition of deductive formal-logical relations.[35] Wright's well-known distinction of five forms of inductive procedure[36] grasps only the elementary procedure as employed in pre-dialectical types of science. The elementary inductive procedures characterized by Wright are employed in the Marxian analysis as follows:

(a) In the *material preparation* which precedes the *presentation* of the object; Marx characterized this as follows:

Of course the method of presentation must differ in form from that of inquiry. The latter has to appropriate the material in detail, to analyse its different forms of development, to trace out their inner connection. Only after this work is done, can the actual movement be adequately described.[37]

(b) In the dialectical–logical derivation as we have it, for example, in the first chapter of *Capital*, these logical procedures do not as a rule appear in their original form, as in the preparation for the dialectical–logical derivation. The development of pre-suppositions for a dialectical–logical derivation and the development of material for it could be a product of the *same* thinker in sequence, but it could also be a product of preceding generations.[38]

In Marx's dialectical–materialist analysis we are not dealing with a new relation of induction and deduction in their original Baconian–Newtonian forms. Rather, for the recognition of the 'inner structure' of capitalism it was necessary to employ new forms of thought *other* than traditional deduction and induction – forms specific to dialectical–logical derivation. *Hence* induction and deduction of the old stamp do play a particular role. In Marxian analysis, elementary induction and deduction (on the basis of the fixed essence and the fixed generalization subsuming the particular and individual) play a legitimate role in so far as one is entitled and required by the relative *stability* of the essence and the universal to treat that stability as fixed within certain limits.[39]

MATHEMATICS

The mathematics used in the science of the seventeenth and eighteenth centuries, whether in the formulations of Galileo, Descartes[40] or Leibniz, is criticized in Hegel's *idealistic* dialectic as well as in the *materialist* dialectic of Marx. These critiques are essentially different.

From his idealist viewpoint Hegel disparages[41] mathematical and natural science of the seventeenth and eighteenth centuries. He links mathematics with lower forms of thought and separates mathematical relations as 'lacking in conceptual content' from other more complex relations known only through 'conceptualizing'.

While he repudiates the pretensions of mathematics, Marx unlike Hegel, does not regard mathematics as 'undialectical' and a 'lower form of rationality' to be comprehended within another sort of 'truly scientific' knowledge. He is for a maximal and potentially growing use of mathematics in establishing dialectical knowledge.[42] It is noteworthy how Marx puts different, very complicated processes into analogous mathematical relations.[43] The scientific work of Leibniz was always highly valued by Marx.[44] In the mathematical manuscripts he is concerned with

the development of mathematics and mathematical procedures.[45] The distinct roles of mathematical knowledge, distinct
in principle, in the *materialist* and the *idealist* dialectics, coincide
with the fact that Marx worked out a concept *of that which (really)
is*[46] different from Hegel's.

Since in Hegel's mystical idealist presentation the essence of
reality, the highest reality, is a type of logic (termed the 'concept'), namely any thoughts which form the transition of one
logical determination into another; since nature, as presented in
empirical form to the observer, is only a secondary, derived
'embodiment' and 'externalization' of the concept; and since
knowledge of the highest reality is knowledge of ideas, and only
knowledge based on ideas may be termed scientific (in Hegelian
terminology: philosophical) knowledge, there is necessarily a
denigration of the value and role of mathematics and of empirical
science of the mathematical type.

But for Marx the reality of material nature is considered to be
primary, beyond which there is nothing more real. Hence those
aspects of nature grasped in mathematics (which concerns inner
processes as well as external ones) are not less important; with
respect to the ontological character of the aspects of reality
grasped in mathematics, such knowledge has a specific character,
but is *not of lower rank*. Hence Marx does not take from Hegel
the hierarchy of the rational, expressed in classical German philosophy as an antithesis of 'understanding' and 'reason', which
Hegel employed crudely on mathematics ('commonsensical',
'lacking inconceptual content') in relation to 'truly scientific',
'philosophical' knowledge ('conceptualizing'). The gradations of
the rational are more complex for Marx and not easily delineated.
Mathematics is not in principle of a lower order (though obviously not of a higher order) than knowledge of other sorts.

The development of Marxist philosophy in the twentieth century did not incorporate mathematics into dialectical-materialist
analysis; this was an expression – which sometimes appears in the
critique of Hegelianizing tendencies in Marxism today – of insuf-
ficient clarity in the distinction between *idealist* and *materialist*
dialectic.

Émile Meyerson has been concerned with the relation of Hegel
to mathematics and natural science.[47] He shows a broad understanding of the historical role of Hegelian philosophy. Hence
Meyerson mentions Hegel's generally negative relation to
mathematics and natural science. Hegel judges Newton, for
example, in natural philosophy, saying that he is satisfied with

mathematical explications which, according to Hegel, are artificial and by and large external to the true essence of the objects under investigation. Hegel wants to abstract the mathematical formulation of the law of free fall 'from the concept of the body'.[48] Similar derogatory judgements on natural science, and similar derogatory valuations of the usefulness of mathematics in science are to be found in many places in Hegel. But what is not grasped in Meyerson's interpretation, or must be explained as illogicality in Hegel and as a contradiction in his view, is that one can also read in Hegel that mathematical laws of mechanical motion are 'undying discoveries', 'which give to the analysis of the object of understanding its highest honour'.[49] Similarly Kepler's laws of planetary motions are 'a discovery of undying fame'.[50] And Hegel writes that the study of mathematics is 'of the greatest importance'.[51]

The following interpretation appears to be tenable: these apparently contradictory expressions do not change Hegel's attitude towards mathematics and natural science. Since Hegel *valued* mathematics and empirical science – and he valued them *highly* in part – what he is saying is that only through them[52] can the human spirit reach 'philosophical truth', 'comprehension'. If this level is reached, then according to Hegel mathematics and empirical scientific knowledge *cease to be important*; they have no significance in the system of 'true reality', but are only of (ontogenetic and phylogenetic) pedagogical significance.

Marx arrives at a completely different result, however, since he develops a wholly new understanding of *reality*.

CHAPTER 9

Appearance and essence

In contrast to a Ricardian analysis of appearance and essence, that is phenomenal forms related to a particular essence and understood as a form of appearance of that essence, as a procedure 'from essence to appearance',[1] Marx's scientific system is not a simple, straight line 'from appearance to essence' and 'from essence to appearance'. Rather it oscillates between appearance and essence, and has a continuous circular pattern from appearance to essence and from essence to appearance, advancing beyond a genetic or structural (or genetic-structural) level to the comprehensive 'conceptual knowledge' of the object. Circular patterns at a given level (for example, the analysis of simple commodity production) are then an aspect of circular patterns of the totality (for example, the analysis of the capitalist mode of production as a whole). From this viewpoint Marx's analysis, for example, in the first chapter of *Capital*, has the following structure:

The first investigation is of forms in history (commodity, value) which in developed, transformed shape constitute the *essence* of the capitalist mode of production, and indeed in the analysis of these elementary forms one has gone *from appearance to essence*.[2] Then value is investigated independently of its phenomenal form (exchange-value), so that a new investigation of exchange-value as value-form is necessary. One advances from the establishment of distinctions and the existence of antitheses to an analysis of their polarities, to the relations of the object, to an understanding of the contradictions in its essence, and finally to an understanding of particular external objects (commodity – money) as a necessary form for expressing an internally contradictory essence.

Thus in the brief first chapter we find circular (or better spiral) patterns analogous to patterns within commodity analysis, for example the analysis of the relative form of value.[3]

It is that sort of constituent spiral that forms the totality of the Marxian analysis, as expressed externally in the division of the whole presentation into further books. If we investigate this whole construction with respect to appearance and essence, then we can say that the spiral-form analysis in the first volume aims by and large at the intellectual reproduction of the essence of capitalist production, while the third volume presents (abstracts) the phenomenal forms of the capitalist economy as phenomenal forms of the essence.[4] The second volume is the mediating element of this structure,[5] while the fourth volume (*Theories of Surplus Value*) is significant for the whole Marxian analysis but adds nothing new.

As we have said, Ricardo attempts to explain phenomenal forms by simply subsuming them in an essential definition. Marx on the other hand usually abstracts phenomenal forms through so-called 'mediation'. What is the logical character of Ricardo's direct 'subsumption' and Marx's 'mediation'?

By investigating these questions we can explain an important aspect of what Marx calls his use of the 'power of abstraction'.[6] At the same time this throws light on Marx's criticism that Ricardo did not understand how to be abstract *enough* and was therefore *too abstract*.[7] Hence this is not a matter of a greater or lesser degree of abstraction but concerns the fact that in dialectical-materialist structural-genetic analysis the role of abstraction is greater and is distinguished from abstraction in the Lockean type of scientific thought. Besides analogies, new forms of abstraction are also applied.

As in Ricardo we find in Marx an elementary form of abstraction which consists in selecting the common properties of a particular class and fixing them in an abstract concept. In that way Marx formulates at the beginning of his analysis the abstract concept 'labour process'.[8] That sort of abstraction, which fixes common properties, takes no account of the phases of development of the phenomenon. It plays a positive role in dialectical-materialist structural-genetic analysis, but only under this condition: one must be conscious of its use, limitations and deficiencies. In other cases it becomes a false and unhistorical hindrance, confusing qualitatively different historical forms and substituting supra-historical forms for historically specific ones, giving them an absolute character. It was for example often employed in that way in bourgeois apologetics.[9]

New, with respect to Ricardo and relevant for the analysis of appearance and essence, is a mode of abstraction which we might characterize roughly as investigating aspects of the inner structure of the object in isolation from one another and from complex (concrete) forms, a presupposition for understanding (that is, the dialectical-materialist derivation) of phenomena.

Abstracting of that sort is integral to dialectical derivation. In that respect Marx emphasizes, for example, the necessity of an abstract investigation of simple commodity production before the derivation of capital and capitalist commodity production;[10] the necessity of an abstract investigation of capital in general before the investigation of capital in its specific forms;[11] the necessity of an abstract investigation of surplus-value in general before the investigation of its specific forms, hence also of profit and the average rate of profit,[12] etc.

An inability to use this type of abstraction goes hand in hand with an inability to employ dialectical derivation. The more concrete forms are then – as with Ricardo – introduced crudely, unmediated by their relations with the other simple forms with which they occur in reality in a mediated form (genetically and structurally mediated). Marx claims, for example:

> Instead of *presupposing* the *general rate of profit*, Ricardo would have had to investigate to what extent its *existence* corresponds in general to the determination of value by labour time, and he would have found that instead of corresponding to it, it prima facie contradicts it, its existence is therefore to be developed through a number of mediating stages, a development very different from simple subsumption under the law of value.[13]

The derivation of the general rate of profit presupposes all the procedures of the dialectical-materialist structural-genetic analysis set down in the first and second volumes of *Capital*. Marx speaks there of 'mediation' and 'middle terms' in a specific sense: a particular economic form is only derived 'through mediated middle terms' when their exposition occupies a corresponding place in the dialectical-materialist structural-genetic analysis of the object. Here 'mediation' is nothing other than the explanation of particular concrete economic forms so that their analysis becomes an aspect of a structural-genetic analysis.

In the correspondence with Engels (letter of 27 June 1867) he illustrates what it means to mediate economic forms like 'price of production' through the middle terms of a derivation:

> In regard to what you say about the inevitable doubts of the

philistine and vulgar economist . . . the whole thing boils down, scientifically expressed, to the following question:

How is the *value* of a commodity *transformed* into its *price of production*, in which

1) *the whole labour seems to be paid* in the form of *wages*;

2) the surplus labour, or surplus value, however, assumes the form of an *increase in price* named interest, profit, etc., *over and above* the *cost price* (= price of the constant part of capital + wages).

Answering this question presupposes:

I. That the *transformation* of, for example, the *value of a day's labour power* into *wages*, or the *price of a day's labour* has been demonstrated. This is done in *Chapter V* of this volume.

II. That the *transformation of surplus value* into *profit*, of *profit* into *average profit*, etc., has been demonstrated. This takes for granted *a priori* demonstration of the *circulation process of capital*, since the turnover of capital, etc., plays a role here. This matter therefore cannot be presented before the third book (*Volume II* contains books two and three). There it will be seen what the philistine's and vulgar economist's *way of looking at things* stems from, namely, from the fact that it is only the direct *form of manifestation* of relations that is reflected in their brains and not their *inner connection*. Incidentally, if the latter were the case what need would there be of *science*?

If I were to *cut short* all such doubts *in advance* I would spoil the whole method of dialectical exposition. On the contrary. This method has the advantage of constantly *setting traps* for those fellows which provoke them to an untimely manifestation of their asininity.[14]

The logical content of the Marxian derivation of economic forms 'through the mediation of middle terms' can be represented only by giving the characteristics of the whole scientific system built up from dialectical-materialist structural-genetic analysis. To that characterization belong the different procedures of genetic and structural mediation, 'dialectical-logical' and 'historical' mediation, appearance–essence mediation, etc.

Different conceptions of the ontological structure of reality underlie the difference between Ricardo's explanation of economic phenomena through subsumption, and their derivation by Marx 'through mediating middle terms'. On the one hand it is a matter of conceiving a fixed essence (and causality, change, relation understood accordingly, together with a simple, qualitatively rigid conception of appearance–essence, etc.), on the other, a conception of essence as a process of contradictory self-development.

(We add that what has been said obviously does not exhaust the characteristics of the Marxian mode of abstraction. On that problem see Gorsky's comprehensive work.[15] We note only that the explanation of Marx's so-called theory of abstraction amounts to nothing more than explaining Marx's new conception of scientific determinism. Broadly one can say that we find in Marx's work as many forms of abstraction as we find categories which express the dialectically articulated whole. Abstraction serves Marx for constructing the 'ideal expression' of the reality under investigation. Marx works with abstractions of different sorts, depending on the aspects and constituents of the 'ideal expression' that concerns him.)

CHAPTER 10

Analysis and synthesis in Marx's presentation

To reveal the specific features and originality of Marxian analysis as employed in *Capital*, we put the following questions: how does the Marxian conception of the structure of a scientific system modify older conceptions of analytic and synthetic procedure in science? What new unity of analysis and synthesis is contained implicitly in Marx's scientific system?

Analytical procedures, if we understand them – broadly speaking – in the original sense of intellectual dissolution, dissection of the whole into parts (terms, aspects), were always linked in Ricardo's work with the opposing synthetic procedures. We encounter different unities of analysis and synthesis, depending on the ontological conceptions of totality ('unity') and the relations of the parts (or terms) and the whole.

In the science of the seventeenth and eighteenth centuries the unity of analysis and synthesis was constructed as a rule on a mechanical understanding of the whole and the part.[1] The unity, the sorts of unity of analysis and synthesis in the Marxian system can be characterized in that they concern a dialectically articulated, self-developing whole in which different sorts of totalities, including elementary mechanical totalities, are subordinate aspects. We might mention certain results achieved by the Soviet philosopher Mamardashvili.[2]

Mamardashvili emphasizes that the task of characterizing the unity of analysis and synthesis in *Capital* is identical with the task of characterizing Marx's dialectical method in its totality. In his case

> analysis and synthesis [are] the result of other thought processes and function in dialectical thought only in connection with those processes . . . The dialectical method forms in its totality the rules for analysing and synthesizing complex systems; it is an instrument for finding the inner connections of an organic whole within the whole ensemble of its relations.[3]

What Marx calls an 'organic, dialectically articulated whole' is, according to Mamardashvili, a historical, self-developing, complex and functionally differentiated system 'of relations and processes which affect each other mutually'.

> Here it is necessary to distinguish not only objects which are linked by simple co-ordinates ('parts'), but the elements, terms ('articulation', in Marx's words) of the structure, that is objects which are linked apart from their co-ordinates so that a whole series of their properties result from their conjunction, mutual effects, origin of one from the other, etc. An object which modifies other objects (whether they originate from it, or are phenomenal forms of it, etc.) and the objects which form the particular dynamic structure in common with it are – to put it strongly – not 'parts' of the structure.[4]

As an example Mamardashvili takes trading profit, which one can scarcely call a 'part' of capitalist economics, since it is not an independent object. From its explanation we see that it is not linear, a matter of understanding its co-ordinates with other parts of the whole, but of illustrating its origin in surplus-value. Hence through the use of analysis and synthesis on an organic whole the concepts whole and part are developed. The structure of the organic whole and its elements come into play, the whole ensemble of its relations, appearances and properties in the roles of 'whole' and 'part'. The relations between elements and aspects of the whole could be of very different sorts (content–form, inner contradiction–external differentiation of antitheses, law–its phenomenal form, genetic relation, etc.). In agreement with that, different procedures of dialectical investigation may be used in which there is no analysis or synthesis in the proper sense of the word. But the result is also the clarification of the relations between the elements within the whole, that is, the place taken by the elements within the whole and the explanation of the whole as a necessary ensemble of elements. 'These procedures clarify and their logical characterizations define, sum up the method (in its logical aspect) of explanation.'[5]

  Mamardashvili's analysis grasps – even if in the construction of a general system based on dialectical materialism certain concepts must be critically examined and abbreviated – the fundamental unity of analysis and synthesis in Marx as opposed, for example, to the unity of analysis and synthesis in Smith and Ricardo. The preceding chapters, which were concerned with different aspects of dialectical-materialist structural-genetic analysis, are also contributions to understanding the analytic-synthetic character of Marx's theoretical presentation.

Since classical German philosophy, particularly Kant, Fichte and Hegel, generated new insights into the problem of the analytic-synthetic character of scientific knowledge, we shall attempt to specify in more detail the Marxian view as opposed to classical German conceptions.

Hegel's view, expressed in abbreviated form in the postulate that the dialectical method 'in every circuit is analytic and synthetic at the same time',[6] seems very near to that of Marx. A more detailed investigation, however, reveals that the distinction and antithesis between the views of Hegel and Marx coincides with the antithesis of idealist and materialist philosophical premisses.

In the cited postulate Hegel expresses a particular aspect of the *idealist* dialectical method as used in its 'absolute form' in the *Science of Logic*. This is not a matter of applying external rules to the material, which would be something other than a method. The content of the *Science of Logic* (that is, the logical theory) is in Hegel's view a presentation of his method because that content is the self-motion of logical categories such that each is the necessary transition to another (*its* other). *Content* understood that way, the content of a logical theory, coincides for Hegel with the method of 'philosophical' perception.

In order to interpret Hegel's postulate that his dialectic is 'in every circuit analytic and synthetic at the same time', it is necessary to apply Kant's distinction between analytic and synthetic methods and judgements, because Hegel's view relates critically to that distinction.

(a) According to the traditional view, formulated in antiquity,[7] analytical procedure was from the given to its principles (*reductio ad principia*) – synthetic procedure, the opposite. The indeterminacy and ambiguity of that abbreviation is caused by the indeterminate and ambiguous significance of 'the given' and 'principle'.

A specific example was the distinction between analytic and synthetic methods in mathematics constructed according to Euclidean and Aristotelian axiomatic principles (with the 'given' and axioms for every case): the procedure from axioms and definitions to complex postulates derived from them was considered synthetic, the opposite of the analytic method.[8]

Kant, in the *Prolegomena*, expounds this traditional conception with a few small modifications when he defines the analytic

method as proceeding from a thing as given to the sole conditions under which it is possible for the thing to be the given.[9]

(b) According to Kant, an analytical judgement is distinguished from a synthetic one in that in the first case the predicate
merely expresses what is in the subject, adds nothing new to it; in
the other case, the predicate expresses more than is contained in
the subject itself. The synthetic judgement transcends the bounds
of what is expressed in the subject of the judgement and furthers
our knowledge.[10]

When Hegel characterizes his dialectical method as 'simultaneously analytic and synthetic', he refers to the Kantian concept of analytic and synthetic in the second sense.

Hegel's idealist dialectical method is *analytic* (has an analytic
aspect) since its use requires 'remaining in the thing itself', 'taking nothing external', 'merely expressing what is immanent in
the thing'.[11] Hegel's idealist dialectical method is at the same time
not merely analytic (it possesses a synthetic aspect), since it is not
a procedure based on formal identity; it is an expression of the
fact that an object (with Hegel a logical category) becomes
through its own contradictory character an other, proceeds
beyond its original bounds.[12] On account of this motion, which
is nothing other than the immanent motion of the thing itself, it is
more than it was at the beginning.

In his idealist dialectical method Hegel hints that the unity of
analysis and synthesis is fundamentally distinguished from the
traditional use of analysis and synthesis in 'ultimate' knowledge.[13] The idealist dialectical method does not embody the
unity of analysis and synthesis in the sense of coexistence
or of a confusion of traditional procedures. It possesses 'analytical' and 'synthetic' characteristics simultaneously; it is
therefore analytic-synthetic in a more specific way, and also
in a *more specific way* the unity (identity) of analysis and synthesis.[14]

One cannot simply say of Marx's dialectical method as used in
Capital that 'it is in each motion simultaneously analytic and
synthetic'. The unity of analysis and synthesis and the analytic-
synthetic character of the Marxian theory of capitalism is of a
specific sort, and it is possible to characterize it – since the
different aspects of the Marxian dialectical-materialist
structural-genetic analysis were at the same time an illumination
of analysis and synthesis – in certain respects:

(a) Although Marx is conscious of the limitations of traditional
pre-dialectical empirical and analytical methods as well as their

inability to give a scientific explanation of capitalism, particularly its historically transitory character, he does not share Hegel's depreciation and devaluation of the analytic method. It is not only that he assigns greater value to its historical significance,[15] but also that he considers the procedures of traditional (empirical) analysis and synthesis, which Hegel omitted from his idealist dialectical method, to be a legitimate, even if subordinate aspect of materialist dialectical method. Here we encounter an analogy to what we have already seen in the distinctive positions of Marx and Hegel on mathematics.

(b) If we understand by analysis the division of a whole and the investigation of its parts, and by synthesis the unification of the parts into a whole and the investigation of the object as a totality, then one can speak justifiably of an analytic or synthetic character of different phases of Marx's theoretical analysis of capitalism. Thus for example in the second volume the investigation of the individual capital is abstracted as a part-motion of the total capital, and it includes the investigation (in the third part of the second volume) of the total social capital which is formed from just those part-motions previously investigated in abstract terms (in the first and second parts of the second volume).[16] Individuation and integration are specific here, as they are also specific to other articulated wholes which we encounter in Marx's investigation of capitalism. This also appears in the specific relation of analysing and synthesizing to the whole and hence also in a particular unity of analysis and synthesis in that or any case.[17]

(c) Overall the Marxian theoretical presentation of capitalism moves from simple to complex (intellectually more concrete), hence in that sense it is a *synthetic* procedure. This synthetic procedure is distinct from the view of synthesis in Descartes and Leibniz,[18] as well as from the trichotomous 'concretization' of Hegel.[19] Marx's scientific system is constructed on a synthetic motion *sui generis*, created by the spiral of analysis to synthesis, from a new (genetic or structural) level of synthesis back to analysis, and vice versa. These spirals have a character similar to appearance–essence analysis.[20]

CHAPTER 11

Structural-genetic
analysis

We have seen how Marx links his method to (i) the material under investigation, (ii) the level of development of the science in question, that is the scientific investigation of given material, and (iii) the level of development of the object under investigation. Hence it is not admissible to regard structural-genetic analysis as employed in *Capital* as a pattern of scientific analysis for just any kind of object.[1]

What then of the problem of the *general* significance of the analysis used in *Capital*? When we put this question we must distinguish:

(a) between the method of *Capital* in its specific form, as given by the material under investigation (the character of the capitalist mode of production);

(b) and the method of *Capital* in relation to the general problem of the logical basis of scientific thought. In that respect one can ask whether Marx, through his critique of political economy, a structural-genetic analysis, laid the basis for a new level of scientific thought, a new type of logic, a new rationality.

It would be useful with respect to pre-Marxist levels of development of human knowledge to employ the concept 'logical type of scientific thought', which can be characterized in the following way:

(a) categorial equipment (basic logical categories, that is the resolution of the relation of thought and reality, the ontopraxeological problem);

(b) the related procedures of research and explanation ((a) and (b)) are mutually conditioned and merge in a certain respect with one another;

(c) the connection with society, especially classes;

(d) the connection with the world view of men at a particular historical level of development of society.

The different logical types of scientific thought are distinguished from one another by their conceptions of explanation, proof, the relation between the rational and irrational, etc. The concept of the 'type of logic' presupposes a *stability* of categorial and general methodological conceptions.

From what has been said about the logical structure of *Capital* it is clear that Marxism does not recognize that stability and abstract, supra-historical generality of categorial and methodological conceptions which marks, for example, the Galilean or Lockean type of scientific thought. A stable element (and a new relative stability of another sort) is rather the super-session of relative stability at the first level, likewise of an aspect of individual and social praxis.

In Marxism one finds in that respect a new logical type, a scientific rationality of a new sort. The basis for methodology in the traditional positivist and Hegelian sense (*Science of Logic* – general methodology) disappears.

When we establish that Marx recognizes nothing *a priori*, no logic external to the object, and no 'concreteness', and that he pursues instead the discovery of the 'specific logic of the specific object', then we go back in a radical way on all attempts to abstract from *Capital* a 'dialectical' methodology applicable to all objects (hence the attempt to understand Marx's dialectic in Lassalle's sense). At the same time we open up a whole realm of problems to do with method – second-order problems, so to speak. How are we to understand the concreteness just mentioned? How is traditional logical procedure to be integrated with the new – too new – body of dialectical analyses? This also opens up a range of practical problems which touch on the historicity of the Marxist logical type of scientific thought.

A study of the *general* characteristics of the rationality implied in the Marxian critique of bourgeois political economy presupposes a study of the new conception of the relationship of being, praxis and reason in Marxism. But for that, however, the analysis of the logical structure of *Capital* does not suffice. Marx himself has explained his relationship to traditional ontology and gnoseology in the critique of *Hegelian* philosophy. It will accordingly be the task of the following section to relate the analysis of the logical structure of *Capital* to the general question of the Marxian explanation of reality and rationality as expressed in his critique of Hegel.

PART II

The Marxian critique of Hegel

CHAPTER 12

The critique of Hegel
in the Paris
manuscripts

The problem of the stages in which Marx came to grips with Hegelian philosophy deserves particular attention. The most important stages of the Marxian critique of Hegel – and the most difficult to interpret – comprise the intellectual development in the Paris manuscripts of 1844 (*Economic and Philosophical Manuscripts*) up to *The German Ideology*.

THE NEGATION OF THE NEGATION

The Marxian critique of Hegel in the Paris manuscripts[1] is an attempt to fulfil a theoretical task which – as Marx says – could not be omitted if clarity with respect to the 'method of criticism' was to prevail in the revolutionary movement.[2] *The German Ideology* also faulted the young Hegelians: they did not examine the philosophical presuppositions of their critique; if they had done that, they would have got to grips with Hegel's philosophy.[3] This clarification of the method of criticism, this investigation of the philosophical presuppositions of the critique, Marx understood as a theoretical task; it forms the positive content of his belief in the end of (speculative) philosophy, and it has a metaphilosophical scope; it is among other things a revision and a new conception of being, reality, truth.

In the critique of Hegel in the Paris manuscripts Marx initially takes a Feuerbachian line. But then he distinguishes himself from Feuerbach in his interpretation of the Hegelian 'negation of the negation'. Feuerbach – in Marx's opinion – overlooks significant aspects of the Hegelian conception of the negation of the negation: he understands the negation of the negation only as an intellectual operation which made it possible for Hegel to affirm theological philosophy (that is, rationalized theology), after he had previously negated it. Hegel's negation of the negation made possible, according to Feuerbach, an apparent negation, but in essence an affirmation and apologetic defence of religion and theology as an expression of the alienation and unfreedom of man.[4]

Marx perceived a deeper meaning in Hegel's negation of the negation: a new conception, revolutionizing philosophy itself, of being as becoming and as history; Hegel had 'merely discovered the *abstract, logical, speculative* expression of the movement of history. This movement of history is not yet the *real* history of man as a given subject, it is simply the *process of his creation*, the *history of his emergence*.'[5]

Hegel understood this movement of history uncritically, abstractly, while – according to Marx's view in 1844 – communistic theory, which proceeded from the Feuerbachian critique of religious alienation, had taken a critical view; it concentrated on economic alienation in wage labour and private property and understood communism as the retrieval and appropriation of alienated human essence. 'Communism is the act of positing as the negation of the negation, and is therefore a *real* phase, necessary for the next period of historical development, in the emancipation and recovery of mankind.'[6] For communist man previous world history is 'nothing more than the creation of man through human labour',[7] a proof that man has created himself. In the Paris manuscripts Marx sees communism as 'the *positive* supersession of *private property* as *human self-estrangement*, and hence the true *appropriation* of the *human* essence through and for man . . . It is the solution of the riddle of history and knows itself to be the solution.'[8]

From that standpoint Marx valued Hegel's *Phenomenology of Mind* in these respects, that it (i) understood the true man as the result of his own labour, and (ii) grasped the self-creation of man as a process of alienation and transcendence of alienation.[9]

1. 'Labour' is understood here in a comprehensive sense as human activity which not only produces things but the whole milieu. Previous Marxian analysis in the *Economic and Philosophical Manuscripts* referred to the fact that bourgeois political economy since Adam Smith did not consider lifeless things but labour itself as the source of wealth. Labour is the subjective essence of wealth. In classical political economy, says Marx, '*labour* has therefore been elevated in its absolute – that is, abstract – form to the *principle*'.[10] Land as capital is also an aspect of labour.[11] Labour as production is the realization and actuality of

man. Religion, family, state, law, morals, science, art, etc., are only particular forms of production.[12]

In an analogous way, things, historical institutions, concepts and such like were understood as products and aspects of production by Hegel at a philosophically more general level.[13] In that respect 'Hegel adopts the standpoint of modern political economy'[14] as well. If we substitute man for Hegel's 'self-consciousness', we can say that Hegel grasps labour, the act of producing, as the essence of man.[15]

To be sure, Marx perceives this: 'The only labour Hegel knows and recognizes is *abstract mental* labour.'[16] But it is obviously not the case that Hegel failed to recognize labouring activities other than intellectual ones. Not only from the Jena manuscripts, which were unknown to Marx, but also, for example, from the fourth chapter of the *Phenomenology*, the opposite is clearly the case. Rather all production, all objective labour is in Hegel's view finally and exclusively a labour of the mind, that is, a production and self-production of mind. By means of human labour something else, more significant, deeper than human labour and human life is manifested.[17]

2. In 1844 Marx recognized the starting point for a critical view of history in Feuerbach's æsthetic theory, according to which the development of mankind rests on his own self-generation and leads from his original unity with nature through a necessary[18] objectification and alienation of 'essential human powers' to the transcendence of alienation by the appropriation of those essential human powers. It is obvious that Feuerbach's view – in spite of its polemical stand against Hegel – is inconceivable without German idealism and that it is particularly under the spell of Hegel's *Phenomenology*. So far as Marx – influenced by the contemporary communist theories of Engels and Hess – employed Feuerbach's atheistic theory of the alienation and retrieval of human species being within a critique of bourgeois political economy, a so-called 'critical' understanding of previous history as the self-generation of man appeared in this way in 1844:

Man cannot become man in the complete sense by a one-off decision, through individual education or the like, but only through a historical development in which he expends with other men all his 'species powers' on collective action and 'treats them as objects'.[19] The idea that men only get beyond objectification to real human self-consciousness is one of the central ideas of German classical philosophy and is used in modified form by

Feuerbach and by Marx in his communist theory of 1844.
According to Marx:

> the objectification of the human essence, in a theoretical as well as a
> practical respect, is necessary both in order to make man's *senses
> human* and to create an apropriate *human sense* for the whole of the
> wealth of humanity and of nature.[20]

According to Marx's communist theory of 1844, objectification
has necessarily taken place under conditions of alienated labour,
hence of private property – that is, the 'human essence' has been
objectified 'in an inhuman way'.[21]

> This fact simply means that the object that labour produces, its
> product, stands opposed to it as *something alien*, as a *power indepen-
> dent* of the producer. The product of labour is labour embodied and
> made material in an object, it is the *objectification* of labour. The
> realization of labour is its objectification. In the sphere of political
> economy [that is, under the conditions which are described in
> classical political economy – J.Z.] this realization of labour appears
> as a *loss of reality* for the worker, objectification as *loss of and bondage
> to the object*, and appropriation as *estrangement*, as *alienation*.[22]

Marx emphasizes that in Hegel's *Phenomenology* the self-
generation of man is understood as a process, objectification as
coming into opposition, as externalization, and as transcendance
of that externalization.[23] He praises the *Phenomenology* on points
where it is in accord with the tenets of communist theory,
specifically on points at which communist theory in 1844
remained within certain fundamental conceptions of the Hegelian
Phenomenology.

In the Marxian critique of Hegel in the *Economic and Philosophical Manuscripts* we are presented with a conjunction of different
intellectual motives. Without the Hegelian clarification of history as alienation and the transcendence of alienation, Feuerbach's critique of religion and his theory of a so-called 'real' man
are inconceivable. Without Feuerbach's anthropology, the
communism of Engels, Hess and Marx from 1844 is not conceivable either. But only Marx's communism of 1844 was capable of
a thorough-going critique of Hegel, whereas Feuerbach's theory
of religious alienation was not. Only to Marx in 1844 did Hegel's
Phenomenology appear as the mystified theory of 'communism'.
At first Marx wanted, by offering a more penetrating critique of
Hegel than Feuerbach, to affirm and substantiate its philosophi-

cal discoveries.[24] The *Economic and Philosophical Manuscripts* prepared and presented in part such a breakthrough.

For Marx in 1844 the Hegelian 'negation of the negation' is an 'abstract, speculative, logical' expression for the movement of history. Feuerbach overlooks this side of the Hegelian negation of the negation, though he grasps the movement of history, from which Hegel had abstracted a speculative, logical content. In certain measure he agrees with Hegel; for Hegel as for Feuerbach, previous history is a movement of an original unity (the immediate unity of man and nature) to separation and alienation, and then through the transcendance of alienation to a higher unity which rests on the return of man to himself (with Hegel: the return of self-consciousness to itself).

This structure of movement, unknown to contemporary natural science and to the ontology and logic related to it, was abstracted by Hegel from real history;[25] he puts it on the supratemporal level of 'eternal' logical determinations and explains it in terms of the structure of the 'absolute' mode of being, the mode of being of the absolute. In that way, according to Marx, Hegel reaches logical determinations such as 'concrete generality', 'contradiction', 'self-differentiation', 'concrete identity', among others. In a mystified way this expresses a revolutionary metaphilosophical conception contrary to traditional European ontology, according to which there is no such thing as the historical process; for Hegel the historical itself is the fundamental level of being. Thus we have arrived, thanks to Marx, at a source of Hegelian mystification: history and the structure of movement proper to history were conceptualized by Hegel, and this conceptualized structure is acknowledged as a primary, supra-temporal, higher reality. Actual history taking place in time is understood then as the embodiment of the supratemporal conceptualized structure of the historical.

Since Feuerbach does not see these relationships, Hegel's philosophy is for him only rationalized theology, and Hegel's speculative philosophy as a mystified theory of history remains wholly outside the scope of his critical judgement (and appreciation), that is, as an attempt to revolutionize traditional ontology. Contrary to that, Marx is concerned with Hegel's negation of the negation, in which Hegel attempts to grasp 'the true and only positive' in a new way,[26] namely history. This affects all being, and is an attempt to express rationally 'the self-activating act of all being'.[27] According to Marx the end result of the *Phenomenology* is the dialectic of negativity as a moving and generating principle,[28] that is the attempt to understand history.

Hegel only attained an 'abstract, speculative, logical' expression for the movement of previous history, that is he did not attain a critical understanding of historical movement, since with respect to the essence of alienation and its supersession he made a serious 'mistake' from the standpoint of Marxian communism of 1844. This happened because Hegel was only concerned with an 'alienation of pure, that is abstract philosophical thought'.[29] The different forms in which alienation occurs are only different forms of consciousness and self-consciousness.

> It is not the fact that the human essence *objectifies* itself in an *inhuman* way, in opposition to itself, but that it *objectifies* itself in *distinction* from and in *opposition* to abstract thought, which constitutes the essence of estrangement as it exists and as it is to be superseded.[30]

The history of alienation and its supersession in *Phenomenology* is but the history of 'absolute knowledge', logical speculative thought. In a critical account the appropriation of the objective world by man presupposes that 'religion, wealth, etc., are only the estranged reality of *human* objectification, of *human* essential powers born into work, and therefore only the *way* to true *human* reality . . . '[31] In Hegel's conception – according to which the true essence of man is 'spirit' and the true form of spirit is the thinking spirit, speculative conceptual movement – the appropriation of the objective world by men appears in that religion, wealth, political power and such, are, like objectivity in its 'truth', confirmed as aspects of spirit, spiritual essence.

The supersession of alienation is understood as the transcendance of objectivity, specifically as the extraction of philosophical thought from the subjective (spiritual) character of objectivity of any sort.

HEGEL'S 'APPARENTLY CRITICAL' POSITION

Though Hegel's conception of the essence of alienation and the supersession of that alienation in the *Phenomenology* is obviously speculative and idealist, it does offer – according to Marx's Paris manuscripts – the theoretical starting point for the critique of the social relations and concepts that obtain.

> in so far as it [the *Phenomenology*] grasps the *estrangement* of man –

even though man appears only in the form of mind – *all* the elements of criticism are concealed within it, and often *prepared* and *worked out* in a way that goes far beyond Hegel's own point of view.[32]

Thus far in the *Phenomenology* the appropriation of human essential powers and the supersession of alien objectivity hostile to man is finally and conclusively reduced to conceptual movement, hence to an activity which leaves existing objective alienation untouched. In that way the critical force of the *Phenomenology* is considerably devalued. According to Marx there is in Hegel's *Phenomenology* a critical position in which something else is hidden:

> the uncritical positivism and equally uncritical idealism of Hegel's later works, the philosophical dissolution and restoration of the empirical world, is already to be found in latent form, in embryo, as a potentiality and a secret.[33]

Here we have a critique 'in alienated form', since the continuous negation of existing conceptions and relations, as we meet them in the *Phenomenology*, is for Hegel not the historical activity of men as the sole subjects of the historical process but a teleological process of the idea which is realized by the mediation of generations of men. In the *Phenomenology* Marx finds the elements of a critique prepared in a way that prefigures later development and projects beyond the Hegelian standpoint;[34] these are the elements of a critique of pre-bourgeois and bourgeois economic and political relations and culture from the position of the communist theory of 1844.

By comparison with Feuerbach Marx recognized more deeply and with greater discrimination the philosophical puzzle of Hegel's apparently critical position. Feuerbach glimpsed its essence in Hegel's relation to religion: traditional religion is banished but then reintroduced in the form of rationalized theology. One must understand this in general, and Marx surmises[35] – and illustrates in his analysis of the last chapter of the *Phenomenology* – the specifically Hegelian modifications to an indirect apology for existing reality. 'Self-consciousness in being another is still within itself' – Hegel maintains. When Marx replaces self-consciousness with man, he obtains as a hidden sense of the Hegelian thesis, the general thesis that mankind is in alienation with itself, or the economic, political and cultural relations characterized by alienation are 'absolute' for human life and accordingly eternal, unalterable relations. That is what is maintained in less philosophical language by the classical bourgeois political economists. In that respect 'Hegel adopts the standpoint of modern political economy.'[36] 'Man, who has realized that in law, politics, etc., he leads an alienated life, leads his true human life in this alienated life as such.'[37] Externalization can remain, if it is recognized and known as such. It is overcome and at the same time maintained. Hegel's dialectic is part of a standpoint according to which alienation is 'abolished and transcended' in a two-fold sense, namely superseded (in thought) and given justification (in reality). The philosophical roots of an apparently critical position that turns into an apologetic positivism, are found, according to Marx, in the illusions of dialectical speculation, the idealist understanding of 'negativity'.

The last chapter of the *Phenomenology*, entitled 'Absolute Knowledge', holds Marx's attention in the Paris manuscripts to such a degree that he makes extensive excerpts and devotes a detailed critical commentary to it. In Marx's view this chapter contains in combination the spirit of the *Phenomenology*, its relation to speculative dialectic, and at the same time Hegel's knowledge of these two things and their mutual relations.[38] It is seen by Marx as the most appropriate basis for demonstrating the one-sidedness of Hegel and his limitations.[39]

It is noteworthy that Marx does not only deploy a critique of the *Phenomenology* in the economic manuscripts, as is sometimes claimed. He presents a critique of the 'treatment of the dialectic in the *Phenomenology* and *Logic*,'[40] and more: he deals with Hegel's whole philosophy.[41] He begins with a critique of the *Phenomenology*, the true birthplace and the secret of Hegelian philosophy,[42] that is the secret of Hegel's philosophical system; from here he moves on to a critique of the *Encyclopedia*, even though he does not develop his critique of Hegelian logic, natural philosophy and speculative philosophy as penetratingly as his critique of the *Phenomenology*.

OBJECTIVITY AND OBJECTIFICATION

In his critical commentary on the last chapter of the *Phenomenology* Marx investigates the Hegelian thesis that the alienation of self-consciousness posits objectivity.[43] In that way he formulates his conception of objectivity and man as objective man.

At first he adopts the essential points of the Feuerbachian

critique of Hegel's speculative conception of objectivity. In 1839 in his work *The Critique of Hegelian Philosophy* Feuerbach objected that Hegel does not know real objectivity outside the mind and presupposes – the first chapter of the *Phenomenology* is proof of this – a Fichtean idealist conception of the 'objects of experience'. For Feuerbach the reality of things outside the mind is 'a truth sealed with our blood'.[44]

According to Feuerbach and Marx, all objects are active as natural objects, objectively acting natural essence, and at the same time passive essence, since they are exposed to the objective effects of other natural objects.

Marx writes, in agreement with Feuerbach:[45]

> The sun is an *object* for the plant, an indispensable object which confirms its life, just as the plant is an object for the sun, an *expression* of its life-awakening power and its *objective* essential power . . . A non-objective being is a *non-being*.[46]

For Marx, man is 'directly a natural being'.[47] That does not itself suffice for the concept of man, but it is however an important aspect of the truth about man. Real corporeal man is an objective essence which only creates and posits objects, 'because it is established by objects, because it is fundamentally *nature*'.[48]

For Feuerbach human, religious, alienated objectification is a problem of the first rank. When he speaks of different types of objective relationship, for example, the mutual relations of non-human natural things, the human, noetical relation to objects, he emphasizes analogies, the threads common to different types of objective relationship.[49] He likens their features to one another, applies to human objectification (in the reduction to religious, alienated objectification) what in his opinion is true of objectivity in non-human nature, and as a reversal applies to different types of objective relationship certain aspects of that which forms for him the essence of religious objectification.

Feuerbach passes over a noetically limited, contemplative understanding of objectivity by assigning great significance to the emotional relations of human individuals to objects and to one another, and further by introducing elements of a practical relationship into the investigation of human relationships with objects.[50] In actual analysis he abstracts, however, from these elements of a practical relationship and investigates human objective relationships in their noetical, contemplative form.

Feuerbach finally glimpses the source of the Hegelian understanding of objectivity in the role[51] – historically very significant, by the way – of speculative philosophy as the negation of theology within the realm of theology, in the attempt to rationalize and hence to humanize theology within the realm of religious alienation. In so far as he derives the most important conceptions of speculative philosophy from history, history is reduced for him to a history of religion, to a history of the alienated objectification of man in religion and the supersession of religion by the generation of 'species man'. He does not recognize any alienated objectification other than the religious and modifications – in part critical, in essence however apologetic – of it: the self-objectification of the I (self-consciousness, mind) in speculative philosophy. Feuerbach's 'real' man is in any case an objective, because sensual, essence; he is however not a being who objectifies himself through social labour, as is the 'real' man for Marx. The question whether economic and political objectification in history leads or does not lead to alienation, that is, under what circumstances the economic and political world[52] created by man does or does not have the character of an alienated objectivity, is not very important for Feuerbach.

For Marx speculative philosophy is a theory based on alienation – not only religious, but also and above all social and economic, an expression and aspect of human objectification and the creation of history under conditions of 'alienated labour'. Only from the Marxian standpoint does the critique of Hegel's conception of objectivity take on these new dimensions: (a) the Hegelian conception of 'thingness' is explained as a mystified expression for the production of real objectivity by human economic and political activity; and (b) a sharp light is thrown on the Hegelian identification of objective action with action, activity, positing, the subject of which is thought, 'pure' activity in itself, positing in itself, specifically that positing whose 'bearer' is substantializing thought – the idea.

In his critique of Hegelian speculative philosophy Feuerbach attained certain fundamental perceptions. But his critique of Hegel's *Phenomenology* as a whole remained completely incomprehensible and puzzling. Everything that Feuerbach had to say is said in his commentary on the first chapter of the *Phenomenology* on sense certainty.

Marx valued and criticized Hegel's *Phenomenology* not only with respect to the supersession of religious alienation, but also the supersession of economic alienation. Only from that point of view does Hegel's dialectic reveal its hidden sense, which remained undiscovered by Feuerbach, and one can recognize the 'positive moments of the Hegelian dialectic'[53] not only as preparation for the Feuerbachian supersession of religion but also for the Marxian communist theory of 1844.

What Feuerbach assigned to man as opposed to animals is an alienated objectification in religion and its supersession – the acquisition of an atheistic species consciousness and with that a species life. It is otherwise with Marx: man has the capacity for a productive economic and political objectification, alienated under certain conditions, thus producing the objective world to which man is subject. Religious alienation is a derivative aspect of that basic, practical objectification and alienation. Man produces in a different way from the animals.[54]

Hence Marx proceeds from Feuerbach's understanding of the *human* natural essence but goes further in the Paris manuscripts in certain essential respects, which brings him eventually – with further clarification in the *Theses on Feuerbach* and in *The German Ideology* – to a critical confrontation with Feuerbach.

LOGIC AND ENCYCLOPEDIA

Marx's critique of the *Phenomenology* in the Paris manuscripts forms the starting point for a critical interpretation of the *Logic* and the *Encyclopedia*. In the *Logic* and the *Encyclopedia*, according to Marx, the 'self-generation of man' is expressed at a higher level of abstraction and formalization than in the *Phenomenology*.

For Marx the critical analysis of the Hegelian 'negation of the negation' forms the key to a critical understanding of the *whole* of Hegelian philosophy. In the course of this critical analysis the Marxian interpretation of Hegel's basic conceptions is broadened to cover different aspects and sources.

(a) *At the beginning* Marx believes that the Hegelian negation of the negation reveals its hidden sense if it is understood to be the 'abstract, logical, speculative expression' for the movement of history as the alienation of labour up to the supersession of alienation (that is, to communism as in the Marxian–Feuerbachian communistic theory of 1844).

(b) Under the presupposition that the *Phenomenology* is interpreted primarily as a theory of the generation of communist man by his own labour – through the supersession of alienated labour as the appropriation of communist species consciousness and human species being – it appears to Marx as Hegel's 'mistake'[55] that alienation and the supersession of alienation in the

Phenomenology are reduced in essentials to the alienated externalization of thought and its supersession, so that with Hegel alienation is transcended when all objectivity outside the mind is
understood as an aspect of the self-generating activity of 'spirit'.

> *Estrangement*, which thus forms the real interest of this alienation
> and its supersession, is the opposition of *in itself* and *for itself*, of
> *consciousness* and *self consciousness*, of *object* and *subject* . . . [56]

Here Marx confronts a second primary source of the Hegelian
negation of the negation, namely Kant's synthetic unity of
apperception which Hegel conceptualizes in the negation of the
negation (the identity of subject and object in the identity of
opposites) as the 'principle of speculation'.

(c) Marx probably returns in that connection to the beginning
of his critical analysis of the Hegelian dialectic in the Paris manuscripts, and justifies and summarizes his comments on Feuerbach. At the margin of the manuscript he adds: 'Feuerbach still
conceives the negation of the negation, the concrete concept as
thought overreaching itself in thought and as thought wanting to
be direct perception, nature, reality.'[57] In the later parts of the
manuscript text[58] Marx works with this conception of the
Hegelian negation of the negation, and unites it with his initial
interpretation of the negation of the negation as the 'abstract,
logical, speculative expression for the movement of history'.

The hypostatic, abstract understanding of the act of self-
generation or self-objectification of man[59] reduced to movement
within thought, as Marx found it in the *Phenomenology*, is – according to Marx – further abstracted and formalized in the *Logic* and
Encyclopedia; its alienated form is developed further. In what
specific sense is the Hegelian conception in the *Logic* and *Encyclopedia* an 'abstract', 'formal', 'alienated' one, according to Marx?

In the Paris manuscripts an abstract conception is any conception which is separated from actual man and his historical
development and is made independent against actual man, with
'real man' and 'the historical development of man' understood in
the sense of Marxian, Feuerbachian communism of 1844.

From that standpoint Marx finds in Hegel's philosophy a
multi-level abstraction:

(a) 'Self-consciousness' in place of 'real man'[60] – the first level
of abstraction. In the sense, says Marx, that the historical
development of actual man by Hegel is presented *abstractly* as the
development of consciousness and self-consciousness. The nega-

tion of the negation as the development of actual man (according to the Marxian theory of communism of 1844) is understood by Hegel 'abstractly' (at the first level of abstraction) as the historical self-generation of true self-consciousness (absolute knowledge).

(b) Higher level of abstraction: the fixation of negativity as an independent activity whose 'content' is exclusively logical categories. This procedural unity and identity of content and form is the Hegelian 'concept', 'absolute form of the life of the spirit'. The idea is then a 'self-realizing concept':

> The inexhaustible, vital, sensuous, concrete activity of self-objectification [that is, the generation of man through his own labour – J.Z.] is therefore reduced to its mere abstraction, *absolute negativity*, an abstraction which is then given permanent form as such and conceived as independent activity, as activity itself. Since this so-called negativity is nothing more than the *abstract, empty* form of that real living act, its content can only be a *formal* content, created by abstraction from all content. Consequently there are general, abstract forms of *abstraction* which fit every content and are therefore indifferent to all content; forms of thought and logical categories torn away from *real* mind and *real* nature.[61]

Schematically this multi-level abstraction of Hegel may be expressed as follows: the practical history of actual man is understood abstractly as the motion of self-consciousness, the motion of self-consciousness as the motion of thought, the motion of thought as the motion of logical categories, whose 'absolute' form of motion and form of existence is 'negativity'.

Or expressed in terms of alienated theory: The *Logic* and the *Encyclopedia* are a further alienated abstraction (that is, a separation from 'real man' and his historical development) from the alienated theory presented in the *Phenomenology* of the historical self-generation of man, which Hegelian philosophy as a whole turns into a version of the theological conception of man and the world.

What has meaning only as an aspect of man's life in nature, which is a product of actual man, is separated from man in alienated conceptions and is made autonomous; man is then understood as dependent on his product. In that sense for Marx Hegelian philosophy is the speculative philosophical expression 'of the general alienation of human essence'[62] and it is also – as an aspect of the alienation of life in practice – the alienation of human thought. As far as the understanding of logical categories is concerned, the fact that Hegelian philosophy is a philosophy of alienated human labour is expressed by assigning logical categories a certain independence against nature and human history; that they are fixed in that sense, but in another sense opposed to the Kantian understanding of categories, for example, they are robbed of their fixed character and presented as moving, hence they interact with one another and are counterposed to human history conceived idealistically. Their relations are presented as a necessary motion (self-movement, self-differentiation) whose fundamental structure, whose 'absolute' form of motion, is the 'negation of the negation', the 'absolute negation'. The form in which Hegel frees logical categories from fixation and raises them to totality is not arbitrary, according to Marx, not the result of a contingent theoretical imagination, but rests on the structure of previous human history, the history of the development of human consciousness, and the development of philosophy in particular. The special role of self-consciousness and philosophy means that for Hegel the previous development of mankind is a means for the self-realization of the absolute subject, the idea of the god-man.

The 'negation of the negation', 'negativity', 'supersession' reaches, according to Marx, a dual level of abstraction in Hegelian philosophy: on the one hand as a sort of phenomenal life of the spirit – as 'negation of the negation' in time; on the other hand – at a higher level of abstraction – as a form of motion for logical categories, that is the general structure (method) of the self-generation of the absolute idea in its own logical element. This is a kind of supra-temporal, extra-temporal historicity, which according to Hegel is fundamental; the idea as absolute subject makes use of time as a means for its self-realization.

In this multi-level alienated abstraction Marx glimpses the source of Hegelian formalism, which is different from mathematical formalism, for example the universal mathematics of Leibniz.

In conclusion I would like to move on to two questions, though I can only sketch answers for them.

(a) Is there in the *Theses on Feuerbach* and *The German Ideology* the same critical use of Hegelian philosophy as expressed in the *Economic and Philosophical Manuscripts*?

(b) And further: can the Marxian critique of Hegel in the Paris manuscripts stand up in the light of contemporary developments, the theoretical work of several generations, even though

we possess Hegelian manuscripts which preceded the
Phenomenology and were completely unknown to Marx?

On (a): as far as the development of the critical relation of
Marx to Hegel is concerned, it seems to me decisive that in *The
German Ideology* Marx eliminates from his theory of communism
eschatological and 'ideological'[60] elements of Feuerbachian
provenance, particularly the conception of 'species being' as the
final goal of history. In *The German Ideology* communism is not
understood as the definitive 'solution to the riddle of history',[64]
the realization of the 'species man,' rather this conception, which
reappears in degraded form in the theories of the 'true socialists',
is sharply criticized. Marx distances himself from the views of
the 'true' socialists, of that – in his words[65] –

> unquestioning faith in the conclusions of German philosophy', as
> formulated by Feuerbach, viz., that *'Man'*, 'pure, essential man', is
> the ultimate purpose of world history, that religion is estranged
> human essence, that human essence is human essence and the
> measure of all things

He distances himself from their view that

> money, wage-labour, etc., are also an estrangement of human
> essence, that German socialism is the realisation of German philo-
> sophy and the theoretical truth of foreign socialism and commun-
> ism . . .

In connection with that, as Marx makes concrete his conception
of alienation and alienated labour, frees it of eschatological and
'ideological' elements and deepens his economic analysis of
bourgeois society, he ceases to value the Hegelian *Phenomenology*
as a mystified theory of communism. He justifies his earlier
view, according to which Feuerbach's anthropology represents
the philosophical basis of communism, and departs at the same
time from his earlier view that Hegel grasps 'the essence of
labour' and 'the self-generation of man by labour'. He disclaims
the conception of the 'self-production of the species'[66] and calls it
a speculative, idealist mystery. As a sign – in his opinion – of the
demystified understanding of reality he writes in the third thesis
on Feuerbach: 'The coincidence of the changing of circumstances
and of human activity or self-changing can be conceived and
rationally understood only as *revolutionary practice.*'[67]

Marx sees the essence and measure of Hegelian philosophy in
that it worked out a mystified theory of the historical, practical

unity of man and natural social objectivity,[68] a theory which created the intellectual presuppositions for the supersession of all speculative, 'ideological' philosophy, including 'abstract' materialism based on 'practical materialism', the 'concept of praxis'.

Marx's interpretation of Hegel in the Paris manuscripts contains statements which contradict one another at a decisive point: (a) Hegel grasps man ('species man') as the result of his own labour; he grasps the self-generation of man through his own labour; (b) Hegel knows only an abstract, intellectual labour.

Perhaps the first thesis could be put more clearly: Hegel grasps philosophical self-consciousness – in this sense: *species-man* – as a product of his own activity. The substitution, usual in Young Hegelianism, of 'man' for 'self-consciousness' provides a warrant for the conception of 'real man' as 'species man' in the Feuerbachian sense, which has an eschatological, teleological element. In Marxian, Feuerbachian communism of 1844 history is the self-production of 'actual species man' on analogy with the self-production of philosophical self-consciousness in Hegel's *Phenomenology*. With the understanding of 'real man' as expressed in *The German Ideology*, that analogy and hence the warrant for a substitution is essentially weakened. The emphasis in interpreting the *Phenomenology* and the whole of Hegelian philosophy is shifted: Hegel is a great figure in that he understood being as producing, as historicity, that in particular he created certain theoretical presuppositions to which Marx's 'new materialism' could relate critically. But in that Hegel ultimately knows only the labour of the mind, he does *not* grasp the essence of labour and praxis as the way to human emancipation. In that sense Marx notes in *The German Ideology* in the passage on the task of communist theory to grasp real men in their practical activity: 'With the theoretical armament inherited from Hegel it is, of course, not possible even to understand the empirical, material attitude of these people.'[69]

On (b): from a standpoint which sees in the revolutionary communist movement a contemporary form of human emancipation and in Marx's theoretical accomplishments the theoretical basis of its opening phase, the Marxian critique of Hegel in the Paris manuscripts, in spite of its depth and weight, appears one-sided and incompletely developed.

1. Marx appraises Hegel's 'absolute negativity' for the most part as a conceptualization of certain forms of world history. The source of Hegel's conception in Kant's synthesis of apperception

remains unexplored. In the Marxian critique of Hegel there is little mention of Hegel's intention to create, on the basis of Kantian transcendentalism, a consistent philosophical theory over the complete range of experience and at the same time a more consistent philosophy of freedom than was possible for Kant, Fichte and Schelling. Like Fichte, Hegel proceeds from Kant in grasping objectivity and experience, particularly from the 'transcendental deduction of pure concepts of understanding'; as a result, objectivity is understood above all as the product of the I.[70] From here the idealists proceed to transform and unfold Kant's view of 'the act of the I'. They attempt to work out a new metaphilosophical theory of being, experience and truth. If this set of problems – the Kantian deduction of the concepts of understanding, radicalized by Fichte, as the source of the Hegelian dialectic – were properly considered, it would no longer appear as a mere 'mistake'[71] that Hegel reduced all objectivity to the content of self-consciousness; one could pursue the immanent logic of the direction taken by Kant and Fichte in which – it seems to me – an important aspect of the 'secret' of the Hegelian dialectic would be revealed.

2. It remains a mere indication in the Marxian critique of Hegel, although important material is implicit in Marx's later works, that Hegel's conception of dialectical negativity has one of its sources in an attempt to clarify the question how life becomes the self-conscious life of human individuals.

The real point to be treated critically in Hegel is his attempt at a synthetic clarification of all historical, natural and inter-personal reality through his conception of dialectical negativity.

CHAPTER 13

The Holy Family

While the *Economic and Philosophical Manuscripts* first valued the positive theoretical contribution of Hegel's *Phenomenology* and only then formulated objections and analysed 'mistakes', *The Holy Family* put negative criticism into the foreground. That obviously follows from the thrust of the work, the critique of Bauer's philosophy of critical self-consciousness. As revealed in the foreword, Marx and Engels mount a polemic against Bruno Bauer, convinced that 'real humanism' in Germany has no more dangerous enemy than speculative idealism, which replaces the real individual with 'self-consciousness' or 'spirit'. In Bauer's philosophy the authors of *The Holy Family* saw a caricature of German, particularly Hegelian speculative philosophy. The point of their polemic was to unmask the illusions of speculative philosophy and the 'meaninglessness of German speculation' before a broader public.[1]

In the passage in which Marx discusses Hegel's *Phenomenology* explicitly,[2] he criticizes the Fichtean reduction of any objectivity to self-consciousness. Because Hegel puts *self-consciousness* in place of *man*, different forms of human social reality appear to him as mere forms and manifestations of self-consciousness.

> In Hegel's *Phenomenology* the *material, sensuously perceptible, objective* foundations of the various estranged forms of human self-consciousness are allowed to *remain*. The whole destructive work results in the *most conservative philosophy* because it thinks it has overcome the *objective* world, the sensuously perceptible real world, by transforming it into a 'Thing of Thought', a mere *determinateness of self-consciousness* . . . Moreover, everything that betrays the *limitations of general self-consciousness* – all sensuousness, reality, individuality of men and of their world – is necessarily held by him [Hegel – J.Z.] to be a limit. The whole of the *Phenomenology* is intended to prove that *self-consciousness* is the *only reality* and *all reality*.[3]

The theory of the liberation of man which rests on that

philosophical premiss can only be a theory of an illusory freedom.

> Hegel makes man the *man of self-consciousness* instead of making self-consciousness the *self-consciousness of man*, of real man, i.e. of man living also in a real, objective world and determined by that world. He stands the world *on its head* and can therefore *in his head* also dissolve all limitations, which nevertheless remain in existence *for bad senuousness*, for *real* man.[4]

The theory of liberation must be made free of speculative illusions and must grasp that

> there is a world in which *consciousness* and *being* are distinct; a world which continues to exist when I merely abolish its existence in thought . . . i.e., when I modify my own subjective consciousness without altering the objective reality in a really objective way, that is to say, without altering my own *objective* reality and that of other men. Hence the speculative *mystical identity* of *being* and *thinking* is repeated in Criticism as the equally mystical identity of *practice* and *theory*.[5]

The positive content of the *Phenomenology* is asserted here only in a shortened form such that the scientific value of Hegel's speculative philosophy is distinguished from the young Hegelian caricature:

> Finally, it goes without saying that whereas Hegel's *Phenomenology*, in spite of its speculative original sin, gives in many instances the elements of a true description of human relations, Herr Bruno and Co., on the other hand, provide only an empty caricature . . . [6]

In a similar passage in *The Holy Family* Marx emphasizes the critical exposure of idealist mystification in Hegelian philosophy. Hegel's *Phenomenology* gives a 'speculative theory of creation'.[7] The Hegelian understanding of history

> is nothing but the *speculative* expression of the *Christian–Germanic* dogma of the antithesis between *Spirit* and *Matter*, between *God* and the *world* . . . *Hegel's* conception of history presupposes an *Abstract* or *Absolute Spirit* which develops in such a way that mankind is a mere *mass* that bears the Spirit with a varying degree of consciousness or unconsciousness. Within *empirical*, exoteric history, therefore, Hegel makes a *speculative*, esoteric history, develop. The history of mankind becomes the history of the *Abstract Spirit* of mankind, hence a *spirit far removed* from the real man.[8]

It appears that in his enthusiastic polemic against Bauer's anti-Feuerbachian philosophy, Marx's critique of Hegel in *The Holy Family* is identified with Feuerbach's critique of Hegelian speculation and its limitations are not distinguished to the degree that they were in the Paris manuscripts.[9] Here Feuerbach is the thinker

> who completed and criticised *Hegel from Hegel's point of view* by resolving the metaphysical *Absolute* Spirit into *'real man on the* basis of nature' . . . [He] was the first to complete the *criticism of religion* by sketching in a grand and masterly manner the *basic features* of the *criticism of Hegel's speculation* and hence *of all metaphysics.*[10]

Also Marx's exposition of the secret of Hegelian speculative philosophy, in the example of the apple, pear, almond and 'fruit',[11] remains within the limits of what Feuerbach had already said in criticism of Hegel. The rhetorical and journalistic aspects of Marx's polemic impoverish the analysis of fine distinctions and lead to simplified formulations, whereas the earlier analysis done by Marx *pro domo suo* had developed a deeper, more differentiated analysis.

On the other hand in the development of Marx's critical encounter with Hegel *The Holy Family* was of great significance, since it emphasized explicitly, perhaps in the plainest way of all Marx's early writings, the necessity to break with the transcendental idealist principle of the identity of subject and object, thinking and being, whether this principle is understood objectively or subjectively, in the Hegelian or Fichtean mode.[12]

From the same period as *The Holy Family* there is surviving a Marxian fragment on Hegel's *Phenomenology*,[13] written on sixteen pages of the same notebook as the *Theses on Feuerbach*.[14] This fragment – in agreement with the critique of Bauer in *The Holy Family* – advances the distinction between the critical, intellectual activity identified by Hegel, and objective action, praxis, real activity.

In *The Holy Family* Marx formulates for the first time an historical and philosophical valuation of Hegelian philosophy which is then developed in *The German Ideology*. This also proved fruitful for later phases of Marx's development, where his evaluation of Feuerbach is altered, and hence his evaluation of Feuerbach's critique of Hegel.

In Hegel there are *three* elements, Spinoza's *Substance*, *Fichte's*

Self-Consciousness and *Hegel's* necessarily antagonistic *unity* of the two, the Absolute Spirit. The first element is metaphysically disguised *nature separated* from man; the second is metaphysically disguised *spirit separated* from nature; the third is the metaphysically disguised *unity* of both, *real man* and the real *human species*. [15]

The German Ideology is also addressed to these historical and philosophical issues. [16] In what respect does this manuscript work represent a new phase in the Marxian critique of Hegel?

CHAPTER 14

The German Ideology

When we investigate whether *The German Ideology* represents a new stage in the Marxian critique of Hegel, we encounter a set of problems already summarized at the conclusion of our interpretation of the Paris manuscripts.[1]

Marx (together with Engels) developed a general concept of 'ideology' and the 'ideological' conception of reality,[2] a metaphilosophical view capable of distinguishing the revolutionary theory of Marx (and Engels) not only from Hegel's idealism and the Young Hegelians but also from the materialism of natural science and from Feuerbach's anti-Hegelian anthropology. At the same time Marx's conception is distinct from the 'end of philosophy' as expressed by Feuerbach in his *Preliminary Theses* and *Foundations of the Philosophy of the Future*.

Marx's conception of *critical method* is altered, and the remaining elements of a teleological, eschatological understanding of communism, history, human essence and reality are dropped.

There is also a shift in emphasis in Marx's evaluation of the Hegelian idea of 'self-creation through labour', and alienation and the supersession of alienation.

Before concerning ourselves with those problems we must take into account that *The German Ideology* addresses itself at length only once to the *Phenomenology*; this occurs in the polemic against Stirner, an attempt to prove that Stirner's conceptions are bound, in spite of his denials, to the 'old' Hegelian philosophy. 'In the *Phenomenology*', we read in the *The German Ideology*,

the Hegelian bible, the 'Book', individuals are first of all transformed into 'consciousness' [and the] world into 'object', whereby the manifold variety of forms of life and history is reduced to a different attitude of 'consciousness' to the 'object'. This different attitude is reduced, in turn, to three cardinal relations: (1) the relation of consciousness to the object as to truth, or to truth as mere object (for example, sensual consciousness, the religion of nature, Ionic philosophy, Catholicism, the authoritarian State, etc.); (2) the relation of consciousness as *the true* to the object (reason, spiritual religion, Socrates, Protestantism, the French Revolution); (3) the true relation of consciousness to truth as object, or to the object as truth (logical thinking, speculative philosophy, the spirit as existing for the spirit).[3]

In the *Phenomenology* Marx no longer seizes on the self-creation of man by labour, and he values the positive contributions of Hegelian philosophy more soberly:

One who, like Hegel, creates for the first time such a design for the whole of history and the present-day world in all its scope, cannot possibly do so without comprehensive, positive knowledge, without dealing at least in some passages with empirical history, without great energy and keen insight. On the other hand, if one is satisfied with exploiting and transforming for one's own purposes . . . then absolutely no knowledge of history is necessary.[4]

Implicit in the whole manuscript of *The German Ideology* is the view that Young Hegelian ideology is derived from and dependent on Hegelian philosophy, an acknowledgement of the originality of Hegel's intellectual labours. *The German Ideology* deals with something already expressed in the Paris manuscripts, namely, that it is necessary for the clarification of the 'critical method' in revolutionary communist theory to come to grips with Hegelian dialectic. Only after clarifying that Feuerbach is also a thinker in the grip of German ideology can one dispense with correcting and expanding his critical efforts: the need for an independent critical encounter with Hegel from the standpoint of dialectical and historical materialism stood before the theorists of the proletarian revolutionary movement. This was not somehow accomplished by writing a historical and philosophical work on Hegelian philosophy but by further theoretical and practical clarification of the *method of revolutionary critique* – and its use – by theorists and organisers of the revolutionary communist movement.

THE CRITICAL METHOD

In a letter to Ruge of September 1843, later published in the first number of the *Deutsch-Französische Jahrbücher* (which appeared in February 1844), Marx formulated his conception of the critical method, from which it is obvious that he had already surpassed the Feuerbachian critique.[5]

We do not want to deal here with the distinction between the Marxian and the Feuerbachian conceptions of critique during the period of Marx's enthusiasm for Feuerbach. Our attention is focused on alterations and modifications in Marx's own conception of critique, and the new results presented in *The German Ideology*.

In the letter Marx formulates his programme for a 'ruthless critique of everything that exists',[6] and outlines his method. It is not a matter of anticipating a new world dogmatically and constructing it from 'absolute science'; rather he wants 'to find the new from the critique of the old'. It is necessary to begin with the critique of religion and politics, to link theoretical critique with real political struggle and to identify the critique with it.[7] New principles must necessarily be derived from principles already in the world. It must be shown to the world what it is really struggling for and that this consciousness is something which it *must* appropriate, even if it does not want it.

> The reform of consciousness consists *entirely* in making the world aware of its own consciousness, in arousing it from its dream of itself, in *explaining* its own actions to it. Like Feuerbach's critique of religion, our whole aim can only be to translate religious and political problems into their self-conscious human form.
>
> Our programme must be: the reform of consciousness not through dogmas but by analysing mystical consciousness obscure to itself, whether it appear in religious or political form, it will then become plain that the world has long since dreamed of something of which it needs only to become conscious for it to possess it in reality. It will then become plain that our task is not to draw a sharp mental line between past and future but to *complete* the thought of the past. Lastly, it will become plain that mankind will not begin any *new* work, but will consciously bring about the completion of its old work.[8]

For the critical method there is significance in Marx's conviction that reason has always existed

> but not always in a rational form. Hence the critic can take his cue from every existing form of theoretical and practical consciousness and from this ideal and final goal implicit in the *actual* forms of existing reality he can deduce a true reality.[9]

In that sense Marx thinks of the *Deutsch-Französische Jahrbücher* as the spokesman for 'critical philosophy', and hence striving to make clear to the present its own struggles and desires.[10]

What philosophical presuppositions are to be found in the Marxian conception of the critique and critical philosophy in 1843? They are the same as those used in the manuscript commentary on Hegel's *Philosophy of Right* from the same year and are for the most part clearly formulated.

The critique of religion – hence the Feuerbachian anthropological critique of religion and speculative philosophy as a rationalized theology – is in the period of the *Deutsch-Französische Jahrbücher* 'the presupposition of all critique'.[11] The concept of critique and 'critical philosophy' in this period presupposes the Feuerbachian theory of alienation based on politics, 'society'. Fundamentally the critique of religion is the recognition that man, human essence and its alienation, is the secret of religion. Once the religious self-alienation of man is stated, then it is the task of philosophy 'to unmask self-estrangement in its *unholy forms*'.[12]

> Thus the criticism of heaven turns into the criticism of earth, the *criticism of religion* into the *criticism of law* and the *criticism of theology* into the *criticism of politics* . . . To be radical is to grasp things by the root. But for man the root is man himself . . . The criticism of religion ends with the doctrine that *for man the supreme being is man*, and thus with the *categorical imperative to overthrow all conditions* in which man is a debased, enslaved, neglected and contemptible being . . . [13]

From Hegelian speculative philosophy we reach 'critical philosophy', once we see through a mystification consisting in the inversion of subject and object, subject and predicate.[14]

The principle of 'the true critique' is already for Marx the comprehension and explanation of the genesis of the object, its necessity and specific attributes.

> Similarly, a truly philosophical criticism of the present constitution does not content itself with showing that it contains contradictions: it *explains* them, comprehends their genesis, their necessity. It grasps their *particular* significance. This act of comprehension does not however consist, as Hegel thinks, in discovering the determinations of the concepts of logic at every point; it consists in the discovery of the particular logic of the particular object.[15]

Hence the requirement that criticism has to bear a concrete, historical character, something known to Marx in all his phases of development. What then is the difference in Marx's understanding of the concrete historical character of the critique in the *Deutsch-Französische Jahrbücher, Economic and Philosophical Manuscripts*, and *The German Ideology*?

In the period of the *Deutsch-Französische Jahrbücher* the central critical concept is the *political* self-alienation of man,[16] and in the Paris manuscripts it is economic self-alienation ('alienation of labour'). But in *The German Ideology* (a) the concept of the 'self-alienation of man' ceases to be the central critical conception. In order to understand the forms of human praxis and the relation of active men to their products, new, more exact concepts are gradually worked out – more exact with respect to their concrete historical character as well as to a general understanding of history and reality. (b) The critical method is freed of teleological and eschatological elements; its concrete historical character is in that way modified and deepened.

(a) When, for example, the authors of *The German Ideology* state[17] – without using the concept of alienation – how the forms of the human life process have altered historically, and together with them the relationship of men to nature, to one another, and to the products of their own activity, they add:

> This fixation of social activity, this consolidation of what we ourselves produce into an objective power above us, growing out of our control, thwarting our expectations, bringing to naught our calculations, is one of the chief factors in historical development up till now.
>
> And out of this very contradiction between the interest of the individual and that of the community the latter takes an independent form as the *State*, divorced from the real interests of individual and community, and at the same time as an illusory communal life . . . The social power, i.e., the multiplied productive force, which arises through the co-operation of different individuals as it is determined by the division of labour, appears to these individuals, since their co-operation is not voluntary but has come about naturally, not as their own united power, but as an alien force existing outside them, of the origin and goal of which they are ignorant, which they thus cannot control, which on the contrary passes through a peculiar series of phases and stages independent of the will and the action of man, nay even being the prime governor of these.
>
> This '*estrangement*' (to use a term which will be comprehensible to the philosophers) can, of course, only be abolished given two *practical* premises.[18]

Similarly, after presenting the different economic and political forms[19] developed spontaneously in history and created by civilization, Marx and Engels comment:

> The individuals, who are no longer subject to the division of labour, have been conceived by the philosophers as an ideal, under the name 'Man'. They have conceived the whole process which we have outlined as the evolutionary process of 'Man', so that at every historical stage 'Man' was substituted for the individuals and shown as the motive force of history. The whole process was thus conceived as a process of the self-estrangement of 'Man' . . .[20]

(b) We are obviously not dealing with a Wolffian teleology, which presupposes an external correspondence with divine intentions, but with the anthropological version of Hegelian teleology. For Hegel absolute truth, absolute reality, is the process of the idea becoming itself, an inner correspondence with a movement from 'in itself' to 'in and for itself'. Feuerbach's atheism is dependent on Hegelian teleology: he understands human history as the process of human self-realization as species-being over alienation in religion.[21] In so far as Marx understood communism in the Paris manuscripts as the retrieval of human species-being,[22] or in so far as he understood history as the self-creation of communist man out of his alienated species powers and hence the suppression of alienation,[23] the critique of the Feuerbachian anthropological teleology, which leads *The German Ideology* on to 'true socialists' and Stirner, must be directed in a self-critical way against certain earlier views held by Marx, namely the teleological and eschatological understanding of critique which resulted from the view that critics can 'deduce a true reality . . . from every existing form of theoretical and practical consciousness and from this ideal and final goal implicit in the *actual* forms of existing reality . . .'[24]

The concept of the 'true' or 'truthful' form of an object (human essence, political order, social order, etc.)[25] – a Hegelian concept containing a teleological and eschatological aspect – is dropped in *The German Ideology*. It is explicitly criticized in Marx's example of the 'true', the 'real' essence of man in *The German Ideology* and in the *Poverty of Philosophy* and *Communist Manifesto*.[26]

After the eschatological and teleological aspects of the 'retrieval of the human species essence' are excised from *The German Ideology* naturalism and humanism no longer coincide in Marx's work as they did in the Paris manuscripts. If human nature, human species-being is considered in the Feuerbachian manner more or less analogous to the natural, organic attributes of the species, then communism which promotes the 'retrieval' of the 'human species-being' so understood would be at the same time the completion of naturalism and the fulfilment of humanism.[27] *The German Ideology* offers instead an historically differentiated understanding of the relationship between naturalism and humanism, what is 'natural' and 'unnatural', 'human' and 'inhuman'. What appears at each of the stages of history to be natural or unnatural is historically conditioned, for example 'natural human affinity'. Thus 'this "natural human affinity" . . . is daily changed at the hands of men; it has always been perfectly natural, however inhuman and contrary to nature it may seem, not only in the judgement of "Man", but also of a later, revolutionary generation.'[28]

From Marx's standpoint in *The German Ideology*, criticism is understood as 'new positive science' which arises from the supersession of speculation and an 'ideological' understanding of reality. This positive science is 'the representation of the practical activity, of the practical process of development of men'.[29] This science, which has developed historically and is historically self-conscious, addresses itself to whatever occurs; it has thus 'ceased to be doctrinaire and has become revolutionary'.[30] What are the logical and ontological presuppositions of Marx's new conception of science? This question is the object of our investigations in the next part of this work.

THE END OF PHILOSOPHY?

The 'negation of philosophy' was expressed at the beginning of the 1840s – in different ways – by a series of thinkers: Feuerbach,[31] through Ruge,[32] Hess,[33] Stirner[34] and Bauer, up to Marx. The authors of *The German Ideology* formulate their views on the end of philosophy, or rather the end of the previous type of philosophizing, very radically. They think that philosophy 'as an independent branch of knowledge loses its medium of existence'.[35] The difference between philosophy and the study of reality is likened to the difference between masturbation and sexual love.[36]

In order to grasp the Marxian conception of the negation and end of (speculative) philosophy as expressed in *The German Ideology*, we must consider the development of Marxian views on this question from 1843 to 1845.[37] Let us distinguish these phases more clearly.

1. While Marx's introduction in the *Deutsch-Französische Jahrbücher* speaks of 'critical philosophy'[38] as a replacement, the
article 'Towards a Critique of the Hegelian Philosophy of Right.
Introduction' speaks at the turn of the years 1843–4 of the 'negation of philosophy', its 'supersession', the negation of 'philosophy up to now, of philosophy as philosophy'.[39]

Marx is dealing with 'German political and legal philosophy',
that is, the Hegelian philosophy of right. The critique of German
political and legal philosophy means – according to Marx[40] – the
negation of the speculative philosophy of right, which mirrors
the bourgeois state. Such a theory which abstracts from real man
is only possible because the bourgeois state itself abstracts from
real man in real life.[41] The negation, that is the critique of German
speculative philosophy is the negation of 'philosophy as philosophy', for it results in '*tasks* which can only be solved in one way
– through *practice*'.[42]

On the other hand, the critique (negation) of speculative philosophy in Marx's work is still *philosophy*, the philosophy of the
revolutionary movement for freedom which strives for *human*
(not merely political) emancipation. The emancipation of Ger-
mans into *men* – according to the view Marx held then – can only
come to fruition through the unification of philosophy and the
proletariat: the head of that emancipation is philosophy, its heart
is the proletariat.[43] It appears that a politicized sociologized
Feuerbach is once again on Marx's mind – Feuerbach's identification of the realization and negation of speculative philosophy.[44]

2. Marx's views on the end of speculative philosophy as formulated in the *Economic and Philosophical Manuscripts* are based on
Feuerbach.

> Feuerbach's great achievement is:
>   (1) To have shown that philosophy is nothing more than religion
> brought into thought and developed in thought, and that it is
> equally to be condemned as another form and mode of existence of
> the estrangement of man's nature.
>   (2) To have founded *true materialism* and *real science* . . . [45]

Here we notice that Marx speaks simply of 'philosophy', instead
of 'speculative philosophy', although it is really a matter of
speculative philosophy as opposed to Feuerbach's new philosophy *toto genere*, anthropology. Or it is rather the Feuerbachian
antithesis between speculative, 'absolute' philosophy and the
new philosophy, the philosophy of man.[46]

3. This abbreviation ('philosophy' instead of 'speculative

philosophy') is used by Marx mainly in *The Holy Family* and *The German Ideology*. Hence he says, for example, in *The Holy Family* that philosophy distorts reality,[47] so 'real humanism', inspired by Feuerbach's 'new philosophy', is obviously not subsumed under 'philosophy'.

4. In *The German Ideology*, after the critical attack on Feuerbach and his 'philosophy of man', Marx's conception of the negation of philosophy takes on new aspects. Even Feuerbach's 'new' philosophy of man, with its 'ideological' basis, is not judged to be an offshoot of the old, speculative philosophy. In that the solution to practical and theoretical problems 'in human practice and in the comprehension of this practice'[48] is seen in an ever-renewing praxis, the Marxian conception of the 'negation of philosophy' in *The German Ideology* opens up a new sphere of theoretical investigation which takes the place of traditional metaphysics and first principles and is concerned with the presuppositions and bases of the science of human praxis, the science of 'the practical process of development of men'.[49]

MARX AND STIRNER

The polemic with Stirner in *The German Ideology* can be considered an expression of the Marxian view discussed at the opening of the correspondence between Marx and Engels in the years 1844–5.[50] At the beginning Engels took a more positive view of the 'ego' and linked it with the Marxian standpoint.

Besides Hess Stirner was probably the first of the Young Hegelians to see the end of speculative philosophy and proclaim a philosophy of *praxis*.[51] Because of this – and a series of further premisses – it is only with difficulty that we can accept the broad view formulated, for example, by Ryazanov, that the philosophical significance of Marx's polemic against Stirner is not proportional to its scope.

For Stirner not only Hegel but also Feuerbach and communist theory based on Feuerbachian anthropology are 'old' philosophy, the philosophy of alienated man. He wants to pursue to its end the critique of alienation begun by Feuerbach, and to create a radical philosophy of man which would really be no *philosophy* at all and no philosophy of *man*, but the completely free action of the individual 'ego'. He wants to create a philosophy of creative human life, a consistent philosophy of freedom as the supersession of every form of alienation, even of what in his view Feuerbach, Bauer and Hess, as well as Marx and Engels (in the critique of Bauer in *The Holy Family*) had left untouched and uncriticized.

What are the philosophical (or anti-philosophical) presuppositions of these two forms of the radical critique of the past and present, that is, Stirner's and Marx's critiques?[52] What break with scientific and philosophical tradition, what conception of the negation of speculative philosophy, and of the critique of Hegelian philosophy, is implied in each?

Stirner turns Feuerbach's critical method back on Feuerbach himself. Feuerbach maintained that speculative philosophy (Hegel) is rationalized theology or the 'negation of theology from the standpoint of theology',[53] and Stirner is in agreement,[54] but he goes further in the same direction when he proclaims that Feuerbach's atheism is liberated from theology only on the basis of theology. The theological element in the Feuerbachian philosophy of man is, according to Stirner, the idea of 'man in general' ('man', 'the essence of man') as the highest being, as something 'holy'.[55]

If the real man is to be made free of servitude, then it must follow, as in Feuerbach, that 'spirit' must be done away with[56] in its original religious form 'holy spirit', as well as in its Hegelian philosophical form. The 'absolute idea' has developed through various forms from the 'holy spirit'.[57] Hegel prizes, as does Goethe, the dependence of the subject on the object and his subordination to the objective world.[58] In his philosophy concepts rule; real man, that is the ego, is enslaved and lost.[59] 'Absolute thought' is a thought that forgets that it is always *my* thought, that I am its master: I can negate and transcend it at every instant.[60] Even the Fichtean I is supra-individual, overlooks and subordinates individuality, and hence remains for Stirner inside the sphere of philosophical and Christian preconceptions.[61]

Stirner criticizes communism, that is, what he knew of the communist theory of his time, in a way similar to his criticism of Feuerbachian humanism. Communists in the end are just like Christians, their 'heaven' is 'society', and they want to sacrifice real individual man to a generality alien to the individual.[62] The critique of bourgeois property by communists is justified,[63] but what the communists propose instead is no solution.[64] Communism would make the individual man depend on the whole in a way that means a new servitude.[65] The duty to labour for all who are capable of it is an illiberal element in communism;[66] Stirner demands instead the 'self-realization' of the real ego, which is not only justified against the state but also against 'society'[67] and its 'institutions'.[68] Marxian ideas of human emancipation in the *Deutsch-Französische Jahrbücher* were expressly criticized by Stirner[69] as based on Feuerbachian humanistic religion.

The polemic which Marx mounts against the progenitor of the 'ego' attempts to prove that Stirner, who sets out as a radical critic of speculative philosophy and for whom neither Feuerbach's nor any other departure from traditional philosophy is radical enough, is in reality *dependent* on Hegel and remains in essential aspects within the boundaries of the 'old' philosophy.

For Marx, Stirner is a critic of 'ideology' when, for example, he sees in Feuerbach's anthropology the realization of a generality ('man'), but at the same time he is an 'ideologue' for these reasons:

1. Because in his interpretation of past and present, in his historico-philosophical construction of the 'ego' as a necessary result of previous history, he, like Feuerbach, pursues the same anthropologizing of the Hegelian conception of history, that is, he inserts 'man' where Hegel spoke of 'self-consciousness'.[70] Stirner takes issue, to be sure, with Feuerbach, that we do not reach the truth by merely transposing subject and predicate in religious writings, but he himself confuses the issue by adopting Feuerbach's predicate without alteration, as a real possibility for controlling the world, hence the

> phrases about relations as actual relations, attaching the predicate 'holy' to them, *transforming this predicate into a subject, the 'Holy'*, i.e., doing exactly the same as that for which he reproaches Feuerbach. And so, after he has thus completely got rid of the definite content that was the matter at issue, he begins his struggle, i.e., he discloses his 'ill will' against this 'Holy' which, of course, always remains the same.[71]

Stirner claims that Feuerbach's philosophical anthropology is only apparently anti-Christian and that it retains in fact the whole content of Christianity,[72] while Marx says of Stirner's 'egoism' that it is only the apparent supersession of speculative philosophy. Stirner's observations on previous history as the history of 'man', who from the stages of childhood (realism, dependence on things, Negro and Jewish principles), and youth (idealism, dependence on thought, Mongol principle), turns into man (egoism as the supersession of realism and idealism, Caucasian principle) – are considered by Marx as an example of a speculative understanding of history deriving from Hegel.[73] Different historical stages are reduced to the relationship of consciousness to the world.

> Three simple categories: realism, idealism and absolute negativity as the unity of both (here named *'egoism'*), which we have already encountered in the shape of the child, youth, and man, are made the basis of all history and are embellished with various historical signboards; together with their modest suite of auxiliary categories they form the content of all the imaginary, pseudo-historical phases.[74]

History is transformed into an incarnation of the history of philosophy.

> But even the latter [philosophy] is not conceived as, according to existing sources, it actually came about – not to mention how it developed under the influence of real historical relations – but as it was conceived and described by recent German philosophers, in particular Hegel and Feuerbach. And from these descriptions again only that was selected which could be adapted to the given end, and which came into the hands of our saint by tradition. Thus, history becomes a mere history of pseudo-ideas, a history about spirits and spectres, while the real, empirical history that forms the basis of this ghostly history is only utilised to provide bodies for these spectres; from it are borrowed the names required to clothe these spectres with the appearance of reality.[75]

Stirner's model of the freely creative individual as the unity of creator and created is really the structure of the thought process as reflexive self-consciousness ('reason'), formulated by German transcendental philosophy, and in particular by Hegel's presentation of 'being' in the *Science of Logic*.[76] Stirner's understanding of freedom is really a modification of the speculative conception of freedom as absolute, self-creating thought without presupposition.

2. Stirner is an 'ideologue' for Marx because he succumbs to the illusion that it is possible to alter forces outside the mind through the alteration of thought;[77] 'the physical and social changes taking place in the individuals . . . are, of course, of no concern to Stirner',[78] so that he also understands the 'relation of consciousness'[79] in a speculative, mutilated form, that is, confuses the process of theoretical perception.

With all the brilliance of his pseudo-radical stand against previous *thoughts*, Stirner's attitude to reality is unrevolutionary, conciliatory and conservative.[80] He leaves the world as it is and only interprets it in another way.

Marx's basic theoretical advance beyond Feuerbach and Stirner concerning the negation of speculative philosophy is formulated in thoughts which criticize Feuerbach and Stirner at the same time: both fail to understand man properly as producer of his world,[81] both muddle man's thoughts (including illusions, mystical objectifications *à la* religion) and the world of man with one another, reducing the heavenly (Stirner: the holy) to the earthly (Stirner: the human 'egoistical'). Hence Marx believes that their 'man', whether he is understood as 'species man' (Feuerbach) or as 'ego' (Stirner), is not the real man but an abstract man, since he is understood by them non-practically, since they abstract from praxis as an active–passive relationship to social and natural relations. Feuerbach's 'man' is something abstract and general, because he is conceived on analogy with the organic generality, the species; Stirner's 'man' is something abstract and singular, severed in an illusory manner from society and united by the intellect only in a negative way with social relations. One can only reach the real man and real humanity by explaining the *relationship of active individuals* to social and natural *relations*. Stirner knows only 'things' on the one hand, and the 'ego' on the other; about the 'ego' he knows nothing except the contemplative 'relation of consciousness', hence he does not reach real individuals.[82]

THE ACTIVE INDIVIDUAL

Even during the time when Marx was influenced by Feuerbachian philosophy and valued its role in the supersession of speculative philosophy, he distanced himself from conceptions of society and history in which the active individual did not figure as the primary subject.

Hence in the manuscript commentary on Hegel's *Philosophy of Right* (1843) we find the *leitmotiv* that in absolute idealism the idea plays the role of primary subject, is distinct from human activity, while the real subjects are powerless and demoted.[83] Hegel understands the function and activity of the state abstractly; he forgets that they are human functions, that the creators and bearers of political functions and state power are individuals.[84]

Similarly, the Paris manuscripts require that an abstraction 'society' should not be opposed to the individual.[85] In *The Holy Family* Marx emphasizes that real humanism does not separate humanity from the individual personality;[86] it must be shown how the 'state, private property, etc., turn human beings into abstractions, or are products of *abstract* man, instead of being the reality of individual, concrete human beings'.[87]

The German Ideology summarizes the relations between active individuals in connection with an explicit critique of Feuerbach's abstract-general and Stirner's abstract-individual conceptions of 'man'; it deepens our understanding of these relations.

Relations are always created by the activity of individuals, because they 'relate'[88] themselves to one another in some way. When Marx speaks of 'relations' or the 'relations of production', etc., we must note that the reactionary character of so-called objective (that is, objectivistic) history consists in a severance of historical relations from human activity.[89] Human activity in reality is always the activity of human individuals – even if they are not always individualities – who are conscious of themselves as singled out from the whole.[90] A theoretical conception of the historical development of social relations must respect this character of the individual human life.[91]

> Individuals have always and in all circumstances 'started out *from themselves*', but since they were not *unique* in the sense of not needing any connections with one another, and since their *needs*, consequently their nature and the method of satisfying their needs, connected them with one another (relations between the sexes, exchange, division of labour), they *had to* enter into relations with one another. Further, since they entered into association with one another not as pure Egos, but as individuals at a definite stage of development of their productive forces and requirements, and since this association, in its turn, determined production and needs, it was, therefore, precisely the personal, individual behaviour of individuals, their behaviour to one another as individuals, that created the existing conditions and daily reproduces them anew.[92]

Under particular historical conditions – especially under the division of labour – the activity of the individuals is necessarily transformed from personal relations into class relations, to which personal relations are subordinate; further, this makes 'relations' (that is, the results of men's behaviour) independent of active individuals. The personal relations and *mores* of men are transformed into a thing-like relation, an extra-human objectivity. Independent relations, ruling over individuals and appearing in thing-like form, appear as something which is not the product of the activities of the individual, which is given by 'nature' (classical political economy) or 'reason', the 'absolute character of spirit' (Hegel). That is an ideological mystification which necessarily accompanies pre-communist phases of the historical process.[93]

> In the present epoch, the domination of material conditions over individuals, and the suppression of individuality by chance, has assumed its sharpest and most universal form, thereby setting existing individuals a very definite task. It has set them the task of replacing the domination of circumstances and of chance over individuals by the domination of individuals over chance and circumstances. It has not, as Sancho [Stirner – J.Z.] imagines, put forward the demand that 'I should develop myself', which up to now every individual has done without Sancho's good advice; it has instead called for liberation from one quite definite mode of development. This task, dictated by present-day conditions, coincides with the task of the communist organisation of society.[94]

In previous history it is possible to recognize three types[95] of relations between active individuals and the 'world', that is, nature and social relations, social natural objectivity. In the first type the life and activity of individuals are dependent on nature, so that they are scarcely differentiated from organic processes; men adapt to conditions and circumstances, and they are altogether subsumed under nature. In the second type active individuals are subsumed by the products of their own labour and activity, subjected to them. The power of man over nature increases, yet the individual man is subjected to the growing power of his own products. The third type is characterized by communism, the transformation of labour ('labour', namely wage-labour and other forms linked to the epoch of wage-labour) into free activity. The conscious appropriation of the active relation of man to nature and social individuality, without subsuming personal relations under class relations and without making relations independent of persons leads to a new unity of active individuals and relations. According to Marx, pre-communist forms of life could only be abolished

> on condition of an all-round development of individuals, because the existing character of intercourse and productive forces is an all-round one, and only individuals that are developing in an all-round fashion can appropriate them, i.e., can turn them into free manifestations of their lives.[96]

The basis of communist relations would be a new man, a new

mode of life. In communist revolutionary activity self-alteration and the alteration of circumstances coincide.[97]

While all previous revolutions were merely concerned with the division of activity rather than its type, the communist revolution is directed against the previous mode of activity.[98]

For Marx one aspect of the unity of the active individual and his relations is *the 'relation of consciousness' or the 'theoretically cognizant attitude'*. In *The German Ideology* Marx characterizes his conception by a departure from the standpoint of Feuerbach as well as Stirner, and also from Bruno Bauer, since Bauer's 'philosophy of self-consciousness', which made subjectivity absolute, had been subjected to a detailed critique in *The Holy Family*.

Marx admonishes Stirner and Feuerbach for conceiving the relationship of human consciousness to the world in a confused way. For both, the historical stages of human life – in spite of their mutual disagreements – are in essence an objectification of different *philosophical* positions: for Stirner, Realism, Idealism, and 'Egoism', for Feuerbach theology, including theological philosophy, and anthropology. Consciousness is taken as primary, hence the way to human emancipation is in the alteration of consciousness, the replacement of one theoretical view by another.

If our understanding of the relation of consciousness to the world is to be freed from 'speculation',[99] then we must give up a conception of man as theoretician but not producer of his world.[100] Consciousness is an aspect of the historical unity of the active individual and his relationships; the content and forms of consciousness must always be understood in connection with praxis. In that way the authors of *The German Ideology* sum up, for example, the philosophy of Holbach:

Hence Holbach's theory is the historically justified philosophical illusion about the bourgeoisie just then developing in France, whose thirst for exploitation could still be described as a thirst for the full development of individuals in conditions of intercourse freed from the old feudal fetters. Liberation from the standpoint of the bourgeoisie, i.e., competition, was, of course, for the eighteenth century the only possible way of offering the individuals a new career for freer development. The theoretical proclamation of the consciousness corresponding to this bourgeois practice, the consciousness of mutual exploitation as the universal mutual relation of all individuals, was also a bold and an open step forward, a mundane *enlightenment* as to the meaning of the political, patriarchal, religious and sentimental embroidery of exploitation under feudalism . . .[101]

Similarly, the bases of thought are 'the individuals and their empirical relations . . . '[102] Thought is always the thought of a particular individual; it is determined 'by his individuality and the conditions in which he lives . . . '[103]

Stirner separates the 'image in ideas' of real conflicts from those conflicts and makes it independent. He thus transforms practical conflicts, that is, the struggles of individuals against their practical conditions of life into struggles with conceptions created by individuals. That makes it possible for him to transform actual conflicts, which are the origin of their ideal image,[104] into the consequence of ideological appearances. Thus he arrives at the conclusion that it is not a matter of transcending conflicts in practice but only of giving up the conception of those conflicts.[105]

Here, as in other places, the Marxian terms 'mirroring' and 'image' – though seldom together – are used to characterize epistemology as subordinate to a new conception of theory as an aspect of praxis. This has an anti-ideological function which emphasizes the non-identity of thought and reality within a unity of active, hence perceiving thinking individuals and their relations.

When Marx opposes consciousness and being to one another he often defines 'being' as the 'practical life of real men under determinate historical conditions'.[106]

Marx and Feuerbach both accept the thesis that the concepts of religion and speculative philosophy have empirical reality as a basis.[107] They would however state this differently, in ways corresponding to the difference between Marx's practical understanding of reality and Feuerbach's naturalistic, contemplative conception. Feuerbach reduces the heavenly to the earthly.[108] For Marx this method of reduction is not materialist. Feuerbach – in Marx's opinion – proves the earthly world to be the foundation of religious illusions, but since this earthly world in his work lacks form and concrete qualities, he does not inquire in general into how it is conditioned, since men are said to posit religion and speculative illusion 'in the head'. Stirner also omits this question:

How is it that personal interests always develop, against the will of individuals, into class interests, into common interests which acquire independent existence in relation to the individual persons, and in their independence assume the form of *general* interests? How is it that as such they come into contradiction with actual individuals and in this contradiction, by which they are defined as *general* interests, they can be conceived by consciousness as *ideal* and even as religious, holy interests? How is it that in this process of private interests acquiring independent existence as class interests the personal behaviour of the individual is bound to undergo substantiation, alienation, and at the same time exists as a power independent of him and without him, created by intercourse, and becomes transformed into social relations, into a series of powers which determine and subordinate the individual, and which, therefore, appear in the imagination as 'holy' powers? If Sancho had only understood the fact that within the frameworks of definite *modes of production*, which, of course, are not dependent on the will, alien practical forces, which are independent not only of isolated individuals but even of all of them together, always come to stand above people – then he could be fairly indifferent as to whether this fact is presented in a religious form or distorted in the imagination of the egoist, for whom everything occurs in the imagination, in such a way that he puts nothing above himself. Sancho would then have descended from the realm of speculation into the realm of reality, from what people imagine they are to what they actually are, from what they imagine about themselves to how they act and are bound to act in definite circumstances. What seems to him a product of *thought*, he would have understood to be a produ⁀t of *life*. [109]

Marx does not formulate the task of the critic of religious ideas and speculative, philosophical ideas in the same way as Feuerbach, Stirner, etc., because he does not separate the theoretical activity of man towards the world from the totality of human praxis: 'from real, active men, and on the basis of their real life-process we demonstrate the development of the ideological reflexes and echoes of this life-process'. [110] Or as it is also formulated in a note on methodology in *Capital*:

It is, in reality, much easier to discover by analysis the earthly core of the misty creations of religion, than, conversely it is, to develop from the actual relations of life the corresponding celestialised forms of those relations. The latter method is the only materialistic, and therefore the only scientific one. [111]

We have sought to establish that in *The German Ideology* Marx had already adopted this conception of scientific method.

HEGELIAN PHILOSOPHY AS A UNIFICATION OF SPINOZA AND FICHTE?

Now we shall attempt to interpret Marx's assertion that Hegelian philosophy is a unification of Spinoza and Fichte. This, as we have seen, is stated for the first time in *The Holy Family*: Spinoza's substance is nature, metaphysically disguised and separated from man; Fichtean 'self-consciousness' is spirit, metaphysically disguised and separated from nature; Hegelian philosophy is an attempt to unify these two elements into a metaphysical conception 'absolute spirit'. Hence what is metaphysically disguised in Hegelian 'absolute spirit' is 'real man' and 'real human species'.[112]

The German Ideology also addresses itself to these considerations.[113] Let us observe a few of Marx's own corrections which reflect the advance in the practical-materialistic standpoint set out in the *Theses on Feuerbach*.

If we want to judge Marx's philosophical, historical diagnosis of Hegelian philosophy formulated in *The Holy Family*, we must take into consideration that his views on the secret of Hegelian philosophy and the essence of its method in his polemical writings (*The Holy Family*, *The German Ideology*, *Poverty of Philosophy*) are adapted, limited, and simplified with the immediate controversy in mind. Marx is simply concerned to prove that the authors he criticizes are dependent on Hegel, that between their ideas and Hegel's there is an overlap or similarity; but proof is often subordinated to the polemic. Thus for example the statement of the 'secret of speculative constructs' in *The Holy Family* (the example of the types of fruit and 'fruit') is directed towards the polemic with Szeliga. The passage begins: 'The mystery of the critical presentation of the *Mystères de Paris* is the mystery of *speculative*, of *Hegelian construction*.'[114] Marx ends with the words: 'These preliminary remarks were necessary to make Herr Szeliga intelligible.'[115] His statement of the Hegelian 'substance-subject' is adapted to his immediate polemical goal.

In that respect the last chapter of the *Economic and Philosophical Manuscripts* (and likewise the 1843 manuscript commentary on Hegel's *Philosophy of Right*) are particularly significant. In those works the critique of Hegel is the main theoretical task.

Hegelian philosophy as a contradictory synthesis of Spinoza and Fichte is asserted by Marx in connection with his polemic against Bruno Bauer. The concepts 'substance' and 'self-consciousness' which Marx uses here do not reflect their full historical richness but are obviously intended in the sense employed in Young Hegelian literature and in contemporary philosophy derived from Hegel. Thus, for example, for Bruno Bauer in his *Posaune*[116] each substantial relation is a relation of man's dependence on something external, hence – as formulated by Young Hegelians – a relation of human alienation. The substance is a generality opposing the human ego as an independent and absolute power.[117] Only an anti-substantialist philosophy can – as Bruno Bauer thought – lead to human emancipation and be the philosophy of men as they truly are. In this Schillerian stage of his intellectual development, expressed in the *Posaune*, he presumes to find such an anti-substantialist philosophy in a Fichtean interpretation of Hegel's philosophy. Hegel – Bauer maintains – created a philosophy which sacrifices the individual, not God or external nature (substance, absolute idea as substance), which does not understand the creation of history, hence individuals become the puppets of the 'world spirit'.[118] 'Only the I is substance for him (Hegel), it is everything to him', but it is also an I which posits itself as 'generalized, unending self-consciousness'.[120] Self-consciousness is the sole power in the world and in history, and history has no other sense than the comprehension and development of self-consciousness.[121] Later Bruno Bauer formulates the same philosophy in essence, the philosophy of self-consciousness as a *critique* of Hegel[122] and 'philosophy', obviously under the influence of Feuerbach, Stirner, and Marx. In Stirner's 'ego' he recognizes the attempt to settle accounts with 'substance'.

In the *Posaune* Bauer speaks explicitly of the connection of Hegelian philosophy with Spinoza and Fichte: 'If Spinozism serves him [Hegel – J.Z.] as the necessary beginning of philosophy, then the Fichtean conception of the I serves as the completion.'[123]

The dispute over the interpretation of Hegelian philosophy as substance or subject began originally with Strauss and Bauer as a dispute over the applicability of Hegelian method to Biblical interpretation. It quickly encompassed more comprehensive questions: particularly the problem of the dependence and independence (heteronomy and autonomy) of man, that is, whether men are creators or merely puppets in history, a connection between the visible activity of men and historical necessity, human freedom, etc.

Hegel himself did not consider his philosophical work to be the unification of Spinoza and Fichte. He thought that the philosophical and historical connection between his philosophy and the philosophy of Spinoza and Fichte was mediated by a series of thinkers. Towards Spinoza, Hegel always expressed great approval: Spinozism is the turning point of modern philosophy, the essential beginning of all philosophizing,[123] the *causa sui* is the basic concept of any speculation.[124] The defect of the Spinozistic conception of substance is that it lacks 'the principle of subjectivity, individuality, personality';[125] any particularity and singularity, according to Spinoza, is lacking in essence, lost in one static substance.[126]

Hegel sees Spinoza's opposite number in the philosophy of Leibniz, rather than Fichte.[127] For Hegel Fichte is above all 'the completion of the Kantian philosophy'. Fichte's specific opposition of Spinozism (as the philosophy of natural necessity in which human freedom is lost) to a transcendental philosophy of self-consciousness (as the philosophy of human freedom) is not adopted by Hegel.[128] Spinozism, opposed to Kant, Fichte and Jacobi as the 'fulfilment of the forms of reflexive philosophy by subjectivity', possessed for Hegel the advantage that it was *not* a philosophy of reflection built on the principle of the identity of thought and being; it formulated, even if incompletely,[129] 'true' infinity (the uncaused; independent from an 'other'; the absolute) as the identity of producing and product (*natura naturans* and *natura naturata*). Before Hegel, the young Schelling[130] undertook a conscious attempt to unify Spinoza and Fichte, particularly in his work *On the I as a Principle of Philosophy*. Hegel reacted, beginning with the Jena writings and the *Phenomenology*, to Schelling's attempt at a unification of 'substance' and 'self-consciousness'[131] as a deeper conception of the 'identity of substance and subject'. In that sense one can agree with the Feuerbachian assessment to which – as it appears – Marx attached himself in *The Holy Family*.

> Spinoza is the real progenitor of modern speculative philosophy, Schelling its restorer, Hegel its completion . . . The philosophy of identity is distinguished from Spinozism in that it inspired the dead, phlegmatic image of substance with the spirit of idealism. Hegel in particular made autonomy, the power of self-distinction, the self-consciousness into an attribute of substance.[132]

The Marxian idea of Hegelian philosophy as the contradictory unity of Spinoza and Fichte is neither the conclusion nor the premiss of a deeper philosophical and historical analysis, and was obviously not intended as such. Though there is a certain simplification – for example, the distinction between the young Schelling and Hegel is not taken into consideration – this is simply an *aperçu* emphasizing, in connection with Marx's polemic against Bruno Bauer, one particular point: that Bauer's philosophy of man remains within a one-sided Hegelian philosophy and attempts to resolve the contradictions of speculation on the basis of speculation.

In *The Holy Family* Marx defines the concept of substance as 'metaphysically disguised nature separated from man'.[133] The universal empirical basis of the philosophical concept of substance – a metaphysical illusion – is nature, 'both as it exists outside man and as man's nature'.[134]

In *The German Ideology* emphasis in Marx's critique of 'substance' is placed on 'second nature' – objective social relations as the product of active men, fixed in the form of powers *opposed* to men, their views and their wishes. That is obviously connected with Marx's evaluation of Feuerbachian anthropology and its conception of 'human essence', that is, human nature as its natural organic qualities.[135] On Bauer's opposition of 'substance' and 'self-consciousness' we read in *The German Ideology*:

> Consequently, on the one hand, instead of real people and their real consciousness of their social relations which apparently confront them as something independent, he [Bruno Bauer – J.Z.] has the mere abstract phrase: *self-consciousness*, just as, instead of real production, he has the *activity, made independent, of this self-consciousness*. On the other hand, instead of real nature and the actually existing social relations, he has the philosophical summing-up of all the philosophical categories or names of these relations in the phrase: *substance*; for Bruno, along with all philosophers and ideologists, erroneously regards thoughts and ideas – the independent expression in thought of the existing world – as the basis of this existing world. It is obvious that with these two abstractions,[136] which have become senseless and empty, he can perform all kinds of tricks without knowing anything at all about actual people and their relationships.[137]

A striving to grasp praxis in its concrete historical forms replaces the speculative dispute between philosophies of substance and self-consciousness (the subject).[138] The metaphysical question of the relationship of substance and subject Marx considers not only completely unfruitful, superfluous and imaginary, but he criticizes it, and drops it; he replaces it with the question which states 'real conflicts',[139] the true 'problem', whose abstract, supra-earthly expression was the speculative problem of the relation of 'substance' and 'subject'. This 'real conflict' is recognized in *The German Ideology*, because under given relations, whose quintessence is Hegelian as well as Young Hegelian philosophy, products are made independent and are opposed to producers. These conflicts grow, and they compel – in the interests of human life and freedom – the communist reorganization of human society. Hegel's attempt to unify substance and self-consciousness must necessarily be contradictory and untenable, because he was the philosophical expression of the real conflicts just mentioned, but these real conflicts, real problems remain hidden and ungrasped. Hegel's identity of substance and subject, whether in the *Phenomenology*, which emphasizes *self-consciousness* as substance, or the system which emphasizes *substance* (absolute idea) as self-consciousness (subject), was an illusory conception, the intellectual transcendence and reconciliation of 'real conflicts'; it was in essence conservative and must therefore become the object of a powerful critique leading to the practical resolution of 'real conflicts'.

Marx employed a critique in principle of all kinds of metaphysics, in so far as it is a substantial ontology, that is, in so far as it fixes in thought an alienated objectivity which arises from the objectification of human activity under particular conditions. Hence *not every critique* of substantialist ontology, *not every* anti-substantial philosophy, meets with Marx's approval, as his polemic against Bruno Bauer and Max Stirner proves.

In Bauer's anti-substantial philosophy self-consciousness is transformed by real active men into something which is apparently *causa sui* and dependent on nothing else, the Spinozistic *'in se esse'* – hence real man is lost in this way in 'free' self-consciousness as *substance*.[140] Marx distances himself from Stirner's anti-substantial critique, as we have seen, because it is only apparently radical; it helps in reality to conserve a life with alienated products of human praxis, hence relations in which metaphysical illusions of 'substance' and the unconditioned 'subject' necessarily arise.

IT IS NOT SUFFICIENT TO MAKE FEUERBACH PRACTICAL

Besides Marx and Engels, Moses Hess was the communist theoretician who undertook in the 1840s the most important attempt to clarify the philosophical aspects of the communist critique of bourgeois society. His literary activity in that period developed in direct contact with Marx. The clarification of certain aspects of Marx's relation to Hess sheds light on the Marxian critique of Hegel, particularly during the years 1844–6.

In the *Economic and Philosophical Manuscripts* Marx names an article published by Hess in 1843 in the *Einundzwanzig Bogen aus der Schweiz*[141] as one of his sources, since he recognized in it an original contribution to a critique of political economy.[142]

In the critique of true socialism written in the spring of 1846 Marx modifies his assessment in that he also values the article by Hess for its time and place; hence the repetition of views expressed in the publications of 1845 would be a boring and reactionary rehearsal of 'antiquated' thoughts.[143]

Hess synthesizes – here he is close to the authors of *The German Ideology* – the development of French socialism and the development of German philosophy; he attempts to formulate in that sense a 'philosophical, scientifically grounded' socialism. Of that the true socialists took note: they attempted with the help of the German, particularly the Hegelian and Feuerbachian ideology,[144] to appropriate the ideas of foreign socialist and communist literature.

> They detach the communist systems, critical and polemical writings from the real movement, of which they are but the expression, and force them into an arbitrary connection with German philosophy. They detach the consciousness of certain historically conditioned spheres of life from these spheres and evaluate it in terms of true, absolute, i.e., German philosophical consciousness. With perfect consistency they transform the relations of these particular individuals into relations of 'Man'; they interpret the thoughts of these particular individuals concerning their own relations as thoughts about 'Man'. In so doing, they have abandoned the realm of real history and returned to the realm of ideology, and since they are ignorant of the real connection, they can without difficulty fabricate some fantastic relationship with the help of the 'absolute' or some other ideological method . . . The formation of this hybrid sect and the attempt to reconcile communism with the ideas prevailing at the time were necessary consequences of the actually existing conditions in Germany. The fact that a number of German communists, proceeding from a philosophical standpoint, should have arrived at communism by way of this transition was as necessary as the fact that others, unable to extricate themselves from this ideology, should go on preaching true socialism, to the bitter end.[145]

In order to clarify more basically what is original in the

Marxian critique of Hegel and in his conception of the end of philosophy, we must consider the philosophical grounding of communism and the communist critique of preceding philosophy mounted by Hess, its eventual influence of Marx, and its relation to the Marxian conception of the impossibility of a 'philosophical grounding' for communism.

In 1841 Hess sketched the idea of a new 'philosophy of action' in *The European Hierarchy*.[146] Hegel is the culmination of the philosophy of the past, but now the transition to the philosophy of action is the order of the day. The Young Hegelians found themselves in that transition, but their mistake was to limit themselves to 'spiritual freedom', that is, a critique of the religious conception of history and the world.[147] Their works are the *negation* of the philosophy of the past; the positive transition to the philosophy of action appears in the works of August von Cieszkowski and Hess.[148] Hegelian philosophy justifies and sanctions what was and is, but it is no philosophy of action for building the future. Hegel did not grasp what is truly an act.[149] Even the conception of nature as 'spirit alienated from itself' is incorrect: nature 'in and for itself' is absolute, just the same as history.[150]

The historical philosophical foundation of the philosophy of action, according to Hess, is Hegelian philosophy; that philosophy itself has Schelling's philosophy of nature as a presupposition, which itself rests on Spinozism.[151]

Among Hegel's works, the *Phenomenology of Mind* takes pride of place; it is 'the book of books', containing the whole Hegelian system in embryo.[152]

In an article of 1841 on the present crisis in German philosophy Hess recognizes in the Young Hegelianism represented by Ruge, Feuerbach and Bauer the philosophy of *praxis*. The Young Hegelianism overcomes, according to Hess, a contemplative conception of philosophy; it has its source in the Hegelian philosophy of self-consciousness and remains in essence true to Hegelianism.[153] Hegel recognizes nothing but the work of the spirit.[154] The Young Hegelians shattered Hegel's historicism in that they criticized the past and dedicated themselves to the positive construction of the future.

The passages in the *Einundzwanzig Bogen*, to which Marx draws attention in the Paris manuscripts, develop the philosophy of action as the philosophical foundation of communism still further. Only in Germany where philosophy has reached its peak can it overcome itself and move on to action.[155] Hess construes parallels between Fichte and Babeuf, Hegel and Fourier – between German philosophy of the autonomous spirit and French communist theories.[156] In both he sees – proceeding abstractly and speculatively – the manifestation and gradual development 'of the fundamental principle of the modern world', the 'absolute unity of all life'.[157] Here a Spinozistic motive appears: for Hess Spinoza is the 'true founder' of German philosophy, and Spinozism is also the basis of French social theory, particularly Fourierism.[158] When the 'principle of the times' is discovered in two separate but parallel forms, then it is a matter of realizing it in life. Hence the philosophy of action advances the unification of German philosophy and French communism.[159] The real obstacles to freedom are the state and church; one must grasp and abolish the basis of this dual phenomenon.[160] One of the main advantages of communism is that in it the antithesis of pleasure and labour disappears.[161] The communistic community is the practical realization of a philosophical ethic which recognizes true utility in free activity, the highest good. On the other hand in the society of isolated, egoistic owners 'free activity is negated, and it is degraded to the *labour* of slaves'.[162]

'The Philosophy of Action' by Hess specifies his conception of free (communist) activity through a critique of 'reflection' and 'dualism'. He begins with an ontological idea: 'Not being, but rather the *deed* is the first and last.'[163] That idea, however, is not original, but is a paraphrase of Fichte's exposition of the Cartesian 'cogito'. Ultimately Hess himself realizes that he wants to bring forward no new philosophical truths. He is conscious of the fact that he repeats the ideas of German transcendental philosophy,[164] for the goal of socialism is also that of idealism.[165]

In order to grasp the philosophical foundation of communism in Hess and a corresponding series of controversial ideas, we must clarify the principles which Hess uses in order to unite three motives in his philosophy of action: (a) German transcendental philosophy, (b) Spinozism and (c) the Feuerbachian critique of religion, extending to social and political life.[166]

For Hess, Spinozism is the historical and logical basis:

> The basis of the free action is the *ethics of Spinoza*, and the present *philosophy of action* ought to be merely a further development of it. Fichte has laid the cornerstone for that development; but German philosophy as such could not get beyond *idealism* . . . The value of negation for thought is recognized in Germany, but the value of activity is not.[167]

This appears obvious to Hess only because of his view that Fichte was the initiator of a new development in philosophy which rests on Spinoza's ethics; Fichte considered himself an antipode, a manipulator – not an expositor of Spinozism. Another difficult question crops up in connection with the genealogy of the communist 'philosophy of action': how is it that Spinoza's philosophy, overthrown by Jacobi[168] because it denied free human activity, and criticized by Bruno Bauer because it absorbed free men into substance, is elevated here above all other philosophies as the philosophical foundation of free communist activity?[169]

If we neglect a romantic aspect of pre-socialist pamphleteering, then we see that underlying communistic Spinozism is Fourier's absolute social harmony – any kind of pressure, necessity, determination from outside disappears and each individual is dealt with according to his own character and his preference treated as autonomous.[170] This idea was accepted by Hess; he found for it a philosophical counterpart and – as he thought – a basis in certain ideas of Spinoza which he drew rather one-sidedly from Spinoza's metaphysical conceptions.

Spinoza defines freedom in the *Ethics* as follows: 'That thing is called free, which exists solely by the necessity of its own nature, and of which the action is determined by itself alone.'[171] The 'good' for Spinoza is what strengthens our power or makes us happy.[172] Virtuous action is acting according to the laws of nature itself.[173] Hess based his view of free communist activity as the identity of labour and pleasure beyond virtue,[174] beyond the meaning of human life, on these ideas. Spinoza's philosophy of self-determination and human autonomy in society presents itself in that form for Hess.

The ethic of Spinoza was on the other hand the direct antipode to Jacobi's philosophy of self-determination. Jacobi contradicted Spinoza's view that *the* substance and the *sole* substance (that is, nature or God) is free, whereas the human will is not free, that everything which has happened and does happen takes place as determined by substance (nature, God).[175] Bruno Bauer also criticizes Spinozism in his anti-substantialist philosophy of self-consciousness.

The second source for the philosophical foundation of communism by Hess is German transcendental philosophy, particularly its conception of free thought (which is determined by nothing external, which determines only itself, creates itself). Hess formulates his conception of 'free activity', 'free praxis', by analogy. The concept of 'reflection', in a specific sense found in

German speculative philosophy, plays an important role here. Where there is a relation of reflection, non-identity, dualism, heteronomy, there is no freedom,[176] hence man – here there is a Feuerbachian motif – is fettered by theological consciousness. The two are characterized reciprocally: where there is reflection, there is theological consciousness, where there is theological consciousness there is reflection, dualism, heteronomy.[177] The two form the *root* of every form of servitude – religious, political and social. Here again we find idealism in the philosophy of Hess: he thinks that a particular intellectual principle – dualism, reflection – produces all evil and that theological consciousness is the *father* of political and social servitude, of all material powers and institutions which enslave men.[178]

Hess assimilates Hegel's idea that the freedom of an individual consists in an identification with the general, recognition and 'realization' of the identity of the particular and the general.[179] It appears that – at least in the additions to the *Einundzwanzig Bogen* – he considers the Hegelian 'unification' of individual freedom with the absolute character of the social totality to be philosophically tenable. In that evaluation he is different from the Young Hegelians, who see in the Hegelian philosophy of right the absorption of the real human individual by the abstract 'general'.

The 'philosophy of action' remains in the realm of speculative philosophy, particularly of the German sort, from whose different elements Hess, who is capable of original work at the highest levels of abstraction, creates his 'philosophical foundation' for communism.

Hess proceeds as arbitrarily with the Fichtean 'I', Hegelian 'Spirit', and Feuerbachian 'atheism', as he did with Spinoza's 'substance' (the unity of producers and product). On the basis of more or less superficial analogies he sees in those conceptions the philosophical basis or model for free activity understood in the spirit of Fourier's utopian communism.

Until now we have characterized the 'philosophy of action' in terms of publications by Hess in 1843 to which Marx refers in the Paris manuscripts. From our own standpoint the 1844 manuscripts written by Hess at about the same time as Marx's Paris manuscripts deserve particular attention.

The article 'Concerning Money', in which a theory of *economic alienation*[180] is formulated, is known to have been in Marx's hands as editor of the *Deutsch-Französische Jahrbücher* just before the demise of the paper. We do not know exactly what form it was in; hence we can draw no exact conclusions about the influence of that article on Marx. In general it is certain – and most new historical work lends support – that Hess had an effect on Marx's initiative to expand the theory of alienation to include a critique of social and economic relations.[181] Hess was concerned with the relationship of the communist critique of bourgeois society to classical German philosophy; his views, which were written down in May 1844, somewhat earlier than the Marxian *Economic and Philosophical Manuscripts*, were published in 1845 as 'On the socialist movement in Germany'. We shall take particular notice of a shift in his evaluation of the philosophies of Feuerbach and Hegel.

As opposed to the articles in the *Einundzwanzig Bogen*, the philosophical foundation of communism was divorced from an obvious dependence on Spinoza and German *speculative* philosophy, and founded instead on *Feuerbachian* anthropology:

> Feuerbach proves that the objective essence of the most highly developed religion, Christianity, is the alienated essence of man, and with that critique Feuerbach has destroyed the foundation of all theoretical errors and contradictions – although he does not work out systematically how *all* antitheses and contradictions develop from man alienating his essence.[182]

Feuerbach, according to Hess, is the German Proudhon. Just as Feuerbach's critique is the basis for understanding and superseding all *theoretical* conflicts, so Proudhon's critique of property – although Proudhon himself does not reach this conclusion – arrives at the basis for understanding and superseding all *practical* antitheses and conflicts in social life. Neither of the two is aware of the fact that they were working in parallel. 'But in fact one need only apply Feuerbachian humanism to social life in order to reach Proudhon's practical results.'[183] If we apply ourselves from the Feuerbachian standpoint just as critically to the practical God, money, if we apply Feuerbach's critique of the Christian religion to politics and social life, then the world of wage labour and property will be criticized at the roots.[184] Why was Feuerbach himself not driven to this practical result from his anthropological principle? Feuerbach's thesis that theology is anthropology is correct, but it is not the whole truth.

> The essence of man, it must be added, is social essence, co-operation of different individuals on the same goal from completely identical interests, and the true theory of man, the true

humanism is the theory of human socialization, i.e. anthropology is socialism.[185]

To the end Feuerbach clings to certain general defects in German philosophy. 'German philosophy as such founders on praxis, which it does not understand, *because it is merely theoretical.*'[186] [My emphasis – J.Z.] Feuerbach has in essence completed only a liberation in theory, but German philosophy, in particular Feuerbach, could never provide a programme for practical liberation.

In accord with that evaluation of Feuerbachian anthropology and with critical ideas on economic alienation, Hess modified his exposition and critique of *Hegelian* philosophy somewhat. His exposition of Fichtean subjective idealism was also altered: in it he no longer saw the beginning of communism in Germany, but only a philosophical justification for free thought and for free competition.[187] Liberation from the standpoint of subjective idealism and egoistic competition could not however be true to life: the misunderstood *social* nature of man makes itself apparent as an external power *against* the individual.[188] Parallel to that transition of revolutionary liberalism into despotism there arises in Germany a supra-naturalism and belief in authority: a reaction opposed to the subjective freedom of the isolated individual. But there can be no simple return to domination by alienated powers; real liberation of human individuals in their *social* dealings could not be won in that way. 'A terrible epoch of transition begins in which alienated communality, then individualistic liberalism takes over.'[189] This epoch of restoration and constitutionality produced – so Hess thought – Schelling and Hegel as its philosophical representatives. The first offers the speculative foundation for social theories and movements in which the alienated power of society is dominant and the individual subject is completely subordinated. Hegel, from Schelling, outlines a mediation through which free individual subjects are not robbed of every effective right. Hegel's philosophy became dominant, for it demonstrated scientifically the essence of the modern state and its presupposition, bourgeois society.[190] Hegel's logical dialectic, if we reduce it to its social basis, is the expression of a unification of opposites realized in the activity of capitalist society and the modern bourgeois state; in it there are the 'egoistic battles . . . the presupposition of state power, which for its part does not transcend the egoism of bourgeois society, but . . . takes shelter in it'.[191]

In the manuscripts of 1844 Hess succeeds with his independent communist critique of German philosophy, particularly Hegel's, in reaching a new stage by comparison with the 'philosophy of action'. At the same time in Marx's work in Paris and then in a collaboration in Brussels with Engels, there arose the communist critique of Hegel which we have traced in the preceding chapters. It is a critique which does not rest with making Feuerbachian anthropology practical, but advances to a new conception which agrees in part with Hess.

The development by Marx and Hess of a communist critique of German, particularly Hegelian philosophy may be characterized roughly as follows:

1. Hess was the first[192] person to concern himself with the relation of classical German philosophy to the communist critique of bourgeois society. When Marx as editor of the *Rheinische Zeitung* criticized utopian and eschatological elements in Hess,[193] his tendency to historical concreteness manifested itself, as distinct from a tendency to speculative constructions in Hess; at the same time one must be aware that in the eschatological utopianism of Hess Marx not only criticized *utopian* socialism but also utopian *socialism*.

2. Mutual residence in Paris and their manuscripts of 1844 signify the period of maximum similarity between Marx and Hess. Marx, too, thought that Feuerbachian anthropology forms the 'philosophical basis of communism'.[194] Mutual theoretical influence can be demonstrated. For example, Marxian considerations on 'crude communism' in the Paris manuscripts reveal in thought and expression the influence of Hess.[195] On the other hand, Hess cites Marx at times and links their works.[196] Theoretical differences during that period were mainly that Marx:

(a) criticized the 'principle of speculation' materialistically; hence he works from the standpoint of non-identity, and does not underpin Feuerbachian anthropology with a philosophical or speculative, anti-reflexive conception of reality;

(b) appeals positively to the empirical point of departure, while for Hess empiricism is a damnable sign of theological consciousness.[197]

3. *The German Ideology* signifies the principal theoretical break with the 'philosophy of action', the 'philosophical foundation' of communism, and the manuscripts of 1844 by Hess. Marx distances himself in principle from 'free communist activity' as the model for a 'free speculative thought' devoid of presuppositions,

from an attempt at a naturalistic and cosmological foundation for principles of communist life,[198] etc. The results of the theoretical work by Hess are by then regarded as antiquated.

4. Around the year 1847 there arises a new theoretical similarity in that Hess *accepts* Marxian theory, agrees in his publications[199] with Marx's materialist understanding of history, and capitulates theoretically. For Hess it is more an attempt than a real capacity to grasp Marx's standpoint, and there is a final break in February 1848.

MARX AND RUGE

At the beginning of 1845 – the time of the *Theses on Feuerbach* – Ruge subjected Hegel to a critique[200] and evaluated the controversies which Marx and Engels had taken up in *The German Ideology*. Ruge's panorama of the 'latest German philosophy' led to the idea that the completion of theoretical liberation is practical liberation reached only by a mass movement, practical humanism.

Let us attempt to clarify the relation of Ruge's to Marx's critique of Hegel. Ruge's essays contain a number of thoughts which appear to approach the Marxian standpoint. His principle, not merely for morality but for any theory and practice – so Ruge thinks – is to be real, living man.[201] German Protestantism and related philosophical systems, the philosophies of Kant and Hegel, remain religious, based on Christianity, that is, an old unfree conception. The recognition of atheism (the negation of God) is still not liberation. In place of atheism there must be man and a science of nature without presuppositions: in order to settle the religious problem in reality and not only in theory, there must be a social revolution, the overthrow of society.[202]

In Germany the critique of unfreedom must begin with the critique of Christianity, at the same time a critique of Hegelian philosophy, the completion of the Christian world.[203] Hegelianism is a philosophy with a dual character, containing in embryo a period of reaction as well as a principle for its liquidation.[204] It is a philosophical, theological theory divorced from life, but at the same time a theory of the contemporary world and in embryo its critique.[205] The essence of the Hegelian system is thus 'revolutionary criticism – freedom',[206] because in Hegelian philosophy a method of thought, the dialectical, is utterly basic – an incessant *critique*.

Dialectic as a method of critical thought which stops at

nothing is presented by Ruge, on the basis of the *Phenomenology of Mind*, in the following way.[207] If dialectic is explained through the formula thesis–antithesis–synthesis, it leads to false conceptions. The living process, of which Hegel's method is only a conscious expression, is a two-stage process of reflection peculiar to critical thought: we think of something particular, and then we make our thought of some content into an object of reflection – in so far as we are self-conscious men who arise out of animal spontaneity by means of culture – in that way we obtain a new object of reflection, a new synthetic object. Thought is the activity of reflection; through our free activity we apprehend the genesis and disappearance of content in thought.[208] In this way dialectical thought is the 'constitutive revolution'.[209]

Ruge, who takes method to be the secret of Hegel's whole system,[210] characterizes his *Science of Logic* as a great work which contains all the principles of previous philosophy, justifying as well as criticizing them. Independent principles – categories – do not work in isolation, but only as aspects of the thought process. Hegel has made the important discovery that every system is one-sided in so far as it is built on a single idea as principle; truth is but the intellect in motion.[211]

The sources of Hegelian theological logic are, according to the doctrine of being, inorganic nature and its movement; according to the doctrine of essence, they are chemical and physical processes, in which motion already has the appearance of autonomy. The subjective logic in the third book deals therefore with free thinking essence, which is true being or with self-consciousness, true being, self-determining freedom.[212] And when Hegel speaks of the supra-sensual incarnation of logical reality, it suffices to use nature and man – the hidden essence of his speculative theory. Just as Feuerbach had drawn theology back to its worldly, human basis, Hegelian logic must be explained and assessed as speculative logic.[213]

It is sufficient – so Ruge thinks – for us to take the Hegelian dialectic, correctly understood,[214] as the method of revolutionary criticism. Thus real historical man is brought to the foreground of philosophy, where he was in Hegelian philosophy, though hidden.[215]

We see that Ruge's conception of a critical relationship with Hegelian philosophy remains within the horizons of Feuerbach's humanized Hegelianism and is more a reform than a radical critique of it. Ruge's earlier works, published in the *Hallische Jahrbücher* and later in the *Deutsche Jahrbücher*, carry essentially the same relationship with Hegel. While Feuerbach narrowed his critique of Hegel to the problem of religion, Ruge among the Young Hegelians was the first to undertake a critical confrontation with Hegelian *legal* and political philosophy. In that way he had around 1843 a certain influence on Marx.

Ruge's articles on Hegel from 1840–1[216] give a critical characterization of the Young Hegelian relation to Hegel as the supersession of the master's accommodations and illogicalities through the reduction of Hegelian philosophy to its true essence;[217] hence they are linked to 'Fichtean activism' through a transition from inactive, contemplative Hegelianism.[218] The illogicalities of Hegelian philosophy which must be corrected are, for example, *absolute* knowledge, *absolute* art, *absolute* religion, the close of the history of philosophy, etc. By purifying Hegelian philosophy of unfreedom, accommodation and illogicalities there arises, according to Ruge, 'the new idealism' with 'a completely new relation to the external world'.[219] Its essence is his conviction that only self-conscious reflection on and acquisition of a content, hence philosophical criticism, shapes world history.[220]

It appears that under the influence of Feuerbach's critique of speculative philosophy in the *Preliminary Theses* and the *Foundations of the Philosophy of the Future* Ruge expressed a solution for the transition of liberalism to democracy together with a radical critique of Hegel.[221] After the separation of the revolutionary democratic and communist movements he turned back in 1844 to law-abiding views in the spirit of the articles from the *Hallische Jahrbücher* and the *Deutsche Jahrbücher*.

On the other hand during 1844–5 Marx moved to a new position in his critique of existing society, and with that went the radicalization of his critique of Hegel and speculative philosophy, his critical confrontation with Feuerbach, and his theoretical and political divorce from Ruge.

At that time the Marxian critique confronted speculative philosophy, in particular Hegelianism, with a new dimension in his critique of political economy. Ruge had never gone as far as that. A few sentences on the practical, social interpretation of man in Ruge's aphorisms remained unused.[222]

Ruge's evaluation of Feuerbach in 1845 remained the same as it was at the beginning of the 1840s.[223] While the Marxian conception of historicity in *The German Ideology* and the *Poverty of Philosophy* was developed in opposition to the Feuerbachian anthropological and teleological conception of history as the 'realization of the human essence' given 'in itself' at the beginning of history, hence realized 'for itself' – the speculative Hegelian origin of that procedure is obvious – Ruge stuck with the conception which brought him close[224] to Marx in the period of the *Deutsch-Französische Jahrbücher*. By then Marx had already distanced himself from Ruge's idealistic view of dialectic as self-consciousness and from Ruge's and Feuerbach's 'new religion'.[225]

Ruge's conclusion about the necessity for a transition from theoretical to practical freedom, reached only 'through mass movement gripped by theory'[226] has as a presupposition the view that history is 'rational', that this 'reason' (meaning) of history has been discovered theoretically through anthropology, and that the emancipation of man is a matter of a philosophical critique in connection with a mass movement. The theory to be realized is 'practical humanism', defined by Ruge rather indeterminately as the 'derivation of all order in human society from the demands of all individuals for a truly human existence'.[227] The similarity with the Marxian *Theses on Feuerbach* (in particular with Theses II, VIII and XI) is merely apparent.

CHAPTER 15

The *Poverty of Philosophy*

In the *Poverty of Philosophy* (1847) Marx concerns himself with Hegel in connection with a critique of Proudhon; he recognized analogies in their methods, and he wanted to show Proudhon's dependence on Hegel's dialectical idealism. Just as Hegel uses a metaphysical method, for example on law, and transforms legal philosophy into an expedient metaphysics, so Proudhon – according to Marx – treats political economy in a similar fashion. For Proudhon as for Hegel things and real social relations are incarnations of categories;[1] Proudhon's ideological system[2] yields a metaphysics of political economy.[3]

The *Poverty of Philosophy* presents a critique of Hegel's absolute method, even though the presentation is sometimes narrowly polemical.[4] To the metaphysician – says Marx, obviously meaning Hegelian speculative philosophy – logical categories appear as substances, and worldly things as mere embroidery:

Just as by dint of abstraction we have transformed everything into a logical category, so one has only to make an abstraction of every characteristic distinctive of different movements to attain movement in its abstract condition – purely formal movement, the purely logical formula of movement. If one finds in logical categories the substance of all things, one imagines one has found in the logical formula of movement the *absolute method*, which not only explains all things, but also implies the movement of things.

It is of this absolute method that Hegel speaks in these terms: 'Method is the absolute, unique, supreme, infinite force, which no object can resist; it is the tendency of reason to find itself again, to recognise itself in every object.' (*Logic*, Book III) . . . So what is this absolute method? The abstraction of movement. What is the abstraction of movement? Movement in abstract condition. What is movement in abstract condition? The purely logical formula of movement or the movement of pure reason. Wherein does the movement of pure reason consist? In posing itself, opposing itself, composing itself; in formulating itself as thesis, antithesis, synthesis; or, yet again, in affirming itself, negating itself and negating its negation.[5]

First, it must be explained what is meant here by 'motion' (*mouvement*). This is not mechanical motion and its abstract, formalized expression in mathematics. From the context we may conclude that Marx means the historical process and industrial labour, that is, the basic motion of human praxis.[6] Hence purely logical motion, that is, the purely logical formulas for history and the labour process in Hegel's 'concept', is the specific logical structure of mediation, the negation of the negation.

The *Economic and Philosophical Manuscripts* give a similar presentation of Hegel's negation of the negation, only differing in that Marx considered the primary source of the Hegelian negation of the negation to be the structure of world history understood in the spirit of Marxian–Feuerbachian communism of 1844, that is, communism as the negation of the negation, the rebirth of human species-being. History, beginning with the *Theses on Feuerbach* and *The German Ideology* and after the dissolution of teleological and eschatological elements of Hegelian–Feuerbachian origin,[7] is understood more deeply than in the Paris manuscripts: as individual and social human activity leading to new forms of life. Relations in history do not arise because it is the realization of the development of ideas, a (supratemporal) development of ideas within some kind of suprapersonal reason – as Proudhon thought when he was influenced by Hegel. When he understood historical movement in a Hegelian way, it was no longer history.[8] Proudhon, again in the footsteps of Hegel, could even maintain that 'it is not correct . . . to say that something *appears*, that something is *produced*: in civilisation as in the universe, everything has existed, has acted, from eternity'.

On the other hand for Marx no sort of action in history is predetermined by invariable external laws and principles; rather it develops when real, active, working men (*les hommes actifs et agissants*)[9] successively transform results reached by preceding generations.[10] Human activity in history creates new forms and contents which have not hitherto existed. Men, authors and actors of their own history, have the capacity to revolutionize 'themselves and things, in creating something that has never yet existed . . . '[11]

Though the *Poverty of Philosophy* goes further towards grasping history as the basis of Hegelian negativity than the Paris manuscripts, an attribute of Marx's Paris critique of Hegel's 'absolute method' is still an attempt to clarify its different uses in the *Phenomenology of Mind* and the *Science of Logic*. To that question – in the depth and breadth of the *Economic and Philosophical Manuscripts* – Marx never returned.

In so far as it deals with 'relations of consciousness', hence with categories and theoretical forms, Marx's critique of Proudhon's impoverished and degraded Hegelianism agrees completely with the position worked out in *The German Ideology*[12] and is then expressed in a few classical formulations. To explain why at a particular time, particular ideas and categories are dominant means to explain how men of this or that time lived:

> what were their respective needs, their productive forces, their mode of production, the raw materials of their production – in short, what were the relations between man and man which resulted from all these conditions of existence.[13]

The real point of departure for a rational understanding of history and categories could only be the practical activities of men.

From that there results not only the rejection of 'absolute method' in the Hegelian or Proudhonian sense, but also any supra-historical philosophy of history which was something other than a science built on the critical recognition of historical development.[14]

In the *Poverty of Philosophy* Marx clearly distinguishes (in contrast to Proudhon's Hegelianizing ideological conceptions) the starting point of the new, dialectical-materialist methods of scientific explanation of the origin and profane history of *economic* categories – the same method which directs the Marxian analysis and critique of bourgeois political economy in *Capital*. The question of an eventual distinction in historical character between economic categories and logical categories which do not so far appear to be historically transitory, for example the logical category of quantity, is not posed and explained;[15] what applies to economic categories is predicated, in certain formulations, of categories in general.

CHAPTER 16

Stages in the Marxian critique of Hegel

So far we have pursued Marx's critical confrontation with Hegel in his works of 1844–7, from the Paris manuscripts to the *Poverty of Philosophy*. We have attempted to divide the Marxian critique of Hegel into the decisive stages for the development of his basic theoretical conceptions.

Now we shall expand this analysis so that we locate this period within Marx's intellectual development and inquire from that point of view about stages in the Marxian critique of Hegel. Naturally, we shall devote more space to stages that have hitherto not concerned us. This does not mean that we shall omit the period 1844–7 – the most important, philosophically richest and most significant phase of the Marxian critique of Hegel.

1. If we leave aside Marx's letter to his father of 1837, which expresses his youthful infatuation with Hegel as philosophical mentor, since it shows no sign of an independent critical perspective, Marx's doctoral dissertation *Difference of the Democritean and Epicurean Philosophy of Nature* (1841) represents *the first step* in his critical confrontation with Hegelian philosophy.

At two points in particular the young Marx distances himself from Hegelian philosophy – though not sharply and explicitly, yet distinctive in content and radical: he encounters *atheism*, which is connected with a certain absolute view of free human self-consciousness[1] (similar to Bruno Bauer) and explicitly renounces the Hegelian 'principle of speculation'[2] (identity of subject and object) as the overall philosophical standpoint by which past thinkers are to be judged; in that way he distinguishes himself from Hegel in his evaluation of thinkers such as Epicurus.

Marx is interested then in 'the cycle of Greek philosophical self-consciousness' as the first break by self-conscious man from the chains of nature.[3] It is obvious that this problem – how life becomes the self-conscious life of human individuals – arises out of Hegelianism.[4] Moreover the evaluation of Epicurus as an 'enlightener' is similar in Hegel[5] and Marx. At certain points Marx breaks loose from Hegelian evaluations and takes the opposite view. Despite a positive evaluation of certain thoughts, Hegel considered Epicurus's work to be 'empty words';[6] Marx's evaluation is completely different. Epicurus is the philosopher of free human self-consciousness, even if this self-consciousness is only understood in the form of individuality.[7]

In the dissertation Marx adopts a *concrete* historicism, although it is conveyed idealistically and almost exclusively within the history of philosophy and the relationship of philosophy to the world.[8] A Fichtean motif appears throughout, in that the theoretical content of philosophy is dependent on the personality of the philosopher. The first presupposition of philosophical research is to be 'a bold, free spirit'.[9]

In the dissertation Marx traces how a particular understanding of nature proceeds hand in hand with a particular understanding of man, and the reverse.[10]

2. *The second stage* of the Marxian critique of Hegel is represented by the manuscript commentary of 1843 on the Hegelian *Philosophy of Right*.

In the doctoral dissertation Marx distanced himself from Hegel by wanting to correct his 'one-sidedness';[11] the comprehensive critique of speculative philosophy now begins. This demand occurs for the first time in Marx's contribution to Ruge's *Anekdota*, written at the beginning of 1842: one must free oneself from the concepts and judgements of speculative philosophy if one wants to reach things as they are, that is, reality; there is no other way to truth and freedom than through the 'brook of fire' [*Feuer Bach*] – through Feuerbach, the purifying medium of the present time.[12]

In the second stage Marx accepts the Feuerbachian method for a critique of Hegelian speculative philosophy formulated in the *Preliminary Theses on the Reform of Philosophy*:

> The method of the reforming critique of *speculative philosophy* in general is not distinguished on the whole from that already employed in the *philosophy of religion*. We need only make the *predicate* into the *subject*, and thus into the *object* and *principle* – hence merely *reverse* speculative philosophy so that we have the undisguised, pure, naked truth.[13]

Marx sees the secret of Hegelian philosophy in the fact that the activity of real men, the primary subjects of social activity – just like the activity (derived from the activity of individuals) of the real social subject – is interpreted by Hegel in a perverted way as the appearance, manifestation, mediating element of the activity of something else, namely the absolute idea. Thus Hegel's 'logical pantheistic mysticism'[14] arose. The different forms of *real mediation* through which human social life is formed – for example the interplay of circumstances and independent individuals, or arbitrary choice within certain limits – are represented as the self-mediation of the idea, a process which goes on behind the scenes. Reality is not revealed as what it is, but as another reality, the result of the self-creating activity of the idea.[15]

> The Idea is subjectivized and the *real* relationship of the family and civil society to the state is conceived as their *inner, imaginary* activity. The family and civil society are the preconditions of the state; they are the true agents; but in speculative philosophy it is the reverse. When the Idea is subjectivized the real subjects – civil society, the family, 'circumstances, caprice etc.' – are all transformed into *unreal*, objective moments of the Idea referring to different things.[16]

Hegel's logical pantheistic mysticism proceeds hand in hand with the deification of the state, a statist mysticism, because for him the idea made real (absolute reason) is constitutional monarchy.

> Hegel proceeds from the state and conceives of man as the subjectivized state; democracy proceeds from man and conceives of the state as objectified man. Just as religion does not make man, but rather man makes religion, so the constitution does not make the people, but the people make the constitution.[17]

Hegel is the interpreter of the modern state as derived from the anti-feudal revolution in France.[18] Marx values[19] Hegel's legal philosophy because it delves deeply into the essence of the modern bourgeois state; however it turns into a conservative apologetic for constitutional monarchy since the state is characterized as the embodiment of eternal reason.[20]

In so far as scientific method is discussed, Marx sees a *formalism* in Hegel's necessity: the necessary connections of all objects in 'scientific logic' is predestined.[21]

Whereas the doctoral dissertation demanded that a philosophical critique establish the individual existence of essence, the reality of the idea,[22] now Marx demands that reality be the criterion for the idea.[23]

Marx does not criticize the Hegelian idealization of constitutional monarchy in his 1843 commentary on the *Philosophy of Right* from the communist perspective. In 'democracy', the true form of the state, Marx sees the supersession of the *political* alienation which exists in all other forms of the state.

> Democracy is the solution to the *riddle* of every constitution. In it we find the constitution founded on its true ground: *real human beings* and the *real people*; not merely *implicitly* and in essence, but in *existence* and in reality. The constitution is thus posited as the people's *own* creation. The constitution is in appearance what it is in reality: the free creation of man.[24]

On the other hand in Marx's analysis of Hegelian philosophy the crucial concept of *economic* alienation is still not employed: it becomes the central critical motif at a further stage, to which his article in the *Deutsch-Französische Jahrbücher* marks the transition.

3. *The third stage* of the Marxian critique of Hegel is formulated in the *Economic and Philosophical Manuscripts*; *The German Ideology* and the *Poverty of Philosophy* represent a new, *fourth stage*. Those two stages have already been characterized in detail above.[25]

Our answer to the question whether there are any further stages in Marx's critical confrontation with Hegel must be negative. The relation of Marx to Hegel remains in essence as it was in *The German Ideology* and the *Poverty of Philosophy*. The considerations on the method of political economy in the *Introduction* of 1857, the *Grundrisse* and *Capital* were undertaken on that basis, as were the valuable characterizations of Hegel in Marx's letters.[26]

Let us compare our results with how Marx himself has assessed his intellectual development – even though the author's own evaluation is not always the best and cannot function as arbitrator in a scientific investigation.

Two of Marx's own characterizations are particularly relevant here; the assessments are almost identical.

(a) *The German Ideology* treats Marx's preceding theoretical development in the following critical way:

> Owing to the fact that Feuerbach showed the religious world as an illusion of the earthly world – a world which in his writings appears merely as a *phrase* – German theory too was confronted with the question which he left unanswered: how was it that people 'got into their heads' these illusions? Even for the German

theoreticians this question paved the way to the materialistic outlook on the world, an outlook which is *not without premises*, but
which empirically observes the actual material premises as such
and for that reason is, for the first time, *actually* a critical outlook on
the world. This path was already indicated in the *Deutsch-Französische Jahrbücher* – in the *Contribution to the Critique of Hegel's
Philosophy of Right. Introduction* and *On the Jewish Question*. But
since at that time this was done in philosophical phraseology, the
traditionally occurring philosophical expressions such as 'human
essence', 'genus', etc., gave the German theoreticians the desired
excuse for misunderstanding the real trend of thought and believ-
ing that here again it was a question merely of giving a new turn to
their worn-out theoretical garments . . . [27]

(b) The Preface to *A Contribution to the Critique of Political
Economy* gives a recapitulation of Marx's theoretical development:

in the spring of 1845 . . . we [Marx and Engels – J.Z.] resolved to
work out in common the opposition of our view to the ideological
view of German philosophy, in fact, to settle accounts with our
erstwhile philosophical conscience. The resolve was carried out in
the form of a criticism of post-Hegelian philosophy . . . We
abandoned the manuscript to the gnawing criticism of the mice all
the more willingly as we had achieved our main purpose – self-
clarification . . . The decisive points of our view were first scientifically, although only polemically, indicated in my work . . . the
Poverty of Philosophy . . . [28]

While Marx emphasizes continuity in the first self-evaluation,
it must be noted that he reacts immediately to Stirner's reproof
that his conception 'man' in the *Deutsch-Französische Jahrbücher* is
identical with Feuerbach's, that it represents philosophy inconsistent with *actual* men, and hence falls within Stirner's critique of
Feuerbachian anthropology. Marx was right when he remarked
that his sociological, political and historical conception of man in
the *Deutsch-Französische Jahrbücher*[29] – even if it was consciously
derived from Feuerbachian anthropology and leaned on it up to
the *Theses on Feuerbach* – had already outstripped Feuerbachian
philosophy and contained in embryo the practical materialism of
the *Theses on Feuerbach* and *The German Ideology*. A certain discontinuity in that development, which is expressed among other
things in a radical alteration in Marx's evaluation of Feuerbachian
anthropology and his modified relation to Hess and Proudhon,
appears indisputable. In that respect the second self-evaluation is

correct when it emphasizes this discontinuity and speaks of a 'settling of accounts with our erstwhile philosophical conscience' in *The German Ideology*. It does not follow that all Marx's works before *The German Ideology* must be subsumed in the same way under 'erstwhile philosophical conscience'. Traditional stages are not debarred; rather it is only claimed that in *The German Ideology* the first complete clarification took place and the philosophical, 'ideological' standpoint was finally abandoned.

If we interpret both self-evaluations in context, we conclude that they are not mutually exclusive and that they do not contradict our result – four stages in the Marxian critique of Hegel derived from an analysis of Marx's early writings.[30]

Even though the published literature on Marx has hitherto not addressed – so far as I know – the Marxian critique of Hegel in all its stages,[31] it does attempt to answer a few questions investigated here, and so it is useful for us to take it up.

Karl Löwith's[32] *From Hegel to Nietzsche*, though influential and valuable in many respects, suffers from not explaining the *stages* of the Marxian critique of Hegel. In that respect some of Löwith's criticisms of Marx and the Young Hegelians are anachronistic, for example when Löwith maintains that in opposition to Stirner's thesis on property and the ego Marx demands disappropriation 'in order to give man as "species-being" the world as his own'.[33] Here conceptions are transferred from a superseded stage to a later one, and the Marx–Stirner controversy appears confused.

J.-Y. Calvez conceives the stages of Marx's development as a gradual liberation from various 'alienations'.[34] One can certainly agree with Calvez when he says that the decisive clarification of Marx's dialectical method as the unity of theory and practice came in the years 1845–7, that it reached its full scope in that period, but that in essence his basic conception does not afterwards alter.[35] However Calvez, like many other Marxologues, does not explain the transition from the *Economic and Philosophical Manuscripts* to *The German Ideology*. That transition is the *experimentum crucis* for more recent literature on Marx and for the so-called humanistic and scientific, existential and essential tendencies in modern Marxism, since these controversies employ different interpretations of the young Marx.

The stages of the Marxian critique of Hegel are not analysed by Calvez,[36] and he does not even reflect on the problem, rather he limits himself to establishing that Marx's position on Hegel is more complicated than his view of Bauer, Stirner or Feuerbach, and then considers a few Marxian evaluations of Hegel from different periods. He thinks that Marx's critical orientation towards the Hegelian dialectic which appears, for example, in the Afterword to the second edition of *Capital* or in his letter of 1858 concerning the *Science of Logic* was formed during the years 1838–44 and that the Marxian critique of the *Phenomenology* in the Paris manuscripts is typical of Marx's whole critique of philosophy.[37] If our preceding analysis is correct, then we can say that Calvez reduces the fourth stage of the Marxian critique of Hegel to the third.

H. Popitz[38] proceeds in a similar way, though with the distinction that he attempts to analyse the stages of the Marxian critique of Hegel: (i) dissertation; (ii) criticism of Hegel's *Philosophy of Right* using the Feuerbachian method;[39] (iii) the Paris manuscripts, in which Marx, according to Popitz, conceives[40] the 'system of alienation' whose basis is the 'philosophy of labour'.[41] Here the philosophical bases of Marx's method are worked out – so Popitz thinks, as before him Marcuse – and these remain unaltered in *Capital*.

According to Popitz, Marx's *Economic and Philosophical Manuscripts* represent the focal point of his earlier development: 'The specifically Marxian character of his thought first comes to light here. On the basis of our interpretation of the Paris manuscripts Marx's development up to the *Communist Manifesto* can be demonstrated'.[42] Popitz calls the Paris manuscripts the 'most significant work of the young Marx'.[43] If this is intended to counteract a naturalistic and positivistic presentation of Marx, for example by Karl Kautsky, then the Paris manuscripts are in fact the most significant work in that they necessitated a revision of an interpretation usual at that time. However, Popitz's assessment of the theoretical significance of the Paris manuscripts obscures the fact that the young Marx made further advances in theory *immediately* after the *Economic and Philosophical Manuscripts*; for Popitz the theoretical efforts of the young Marx *culminate* in the Paris manuscripts, and the path from there to the *Theses on Feuerbach* and *The German Ideology* is not seen in terms of an improved logical clarification of the *same* problems in a way set out in the *Deutsch-Französische Jahrbücher* and the *Economic and Philosophical Manuscripts*; hence the contradiction between my interpretation and that of Popitz is obvious.

Popitz seems unacquainted with the works of Moses Hess and does not take into account the priority of his system of alienation over the Paris manuscripts. So some views which are taken over

from Hess on money as economic alienation, etc., are understood
as originating with Marx.

Though Popitz allows Marx's theoretical and philosophical
development to remain on the level of the *Economic and
Philosophical Manuscripts*, he has a certain foundation for recog-
nizing a humanistic eschatology[44] in Marx and for connecting a
secularized theory of alienation with the Christian myth of original sin and absolution.[45] But that does not prove that this is the
Marxian theoretical standpoint in the *Theses on Feuerbach*.

Lukács – if we limit ourselves to his post-war works *The
Young Hegel* and the 'Philosophical Development of the Young
Marx (1840–4)'[46] – has emphasized that in his critique of Hegel
and of all preceding philosophy Marx achieves a distinctive
theoretical advance, that he unites the critique of classical political economy with the critique of Hegelian philosophy.[47] Lukács
concentrates on the idealist dialectic of Hegel just as much as on
the Marxian critique of Hegel, including the problem of alienation.[48] Hence Lukács sees the fate of the – in his opinion –
central[49] philosophical conception of Hegelian idealist dialectic in
the anti-Hegelian critique of the 1840s, though in a simplified
perspective;[50] after Hegel comes Feuerbach, who executes the
'great return to materialism' but relates alienation to religion, and
then comes Marx, the Marx of the Paris manuscripts, in which
'for the first time since Hegel there arose in Germany a unification of economics and philosophy in the treatment of society and
philosophy itself'.[51] Any clarification of relations between Hess
and Marx with respect to social, historical and economic alienation is utterly lacking. Lukács takes everything as a simple
instance of a scientific clarification of the real economic facts of
objectification,[52] expressed by Marx in the Paris manuscripts on
the basis of his first acquaintance with classical political
economy. The further development of the Marxian conception
of alienation and its supersession, which he arrived at soon after
in *The German Ideology*, is not understood and interpreted. It
appears on the contrary that Lukács sees in the Paris manuscripts
the completion, the conclusion of Marx's theoretical,
philosophical development. According to Lukács, the Paris
manuscripts give the category of alienation a scientific sense.[53]
To be sure he mentions that the Paris manuscripts prepared 'that
pure, classical development of historical materialism' which took
place in *The German Ideology* and the *Poverty of Philosophy*.[54] But
the content of this 'maturity', whether it yields any distinction
between the *Economic and Philosophical Manuscripts* and the

'mature' formulation of the Marxian dialectic, is left by Lukács in complete darkness. Similarly his consideration of the differences between the Marxian and Feuerbachian critiques of Hegel[55] fixes the Marxian standpoint precisely at the level of the Paris manuscripts. Lukács has never understood *The German Ideology*.

In his biography of Marx and Engels, more valuable for its broad collection of material than for the theoretical depth of investigation, A. Cornu declares himself against a *general* treatment of Marx's relation to Hegel[56] and pursues his analysis of specific stages. Hence he fulfils this task only in part – only as the subordinate volume in a more comprehensive project; also he omits any interpretation of specialized philosophical problems, for example the last chapter of the Paris manuscripts; mere textual paraphrase rarely replaces a critical interpretation.

Hyppolite's charge against Cornu,[57] that he divorces the Marx of *Capital* from the young, philosophical Marx, does not take into account that the young Marx went through a process of intellectual development. Hyppolite is certainly right when he emphasizes that *Capital* connects in a positive way with the ideas of the young Marx – for example, *The German Ideology* – but it must be added that this is indisputably a work of the *young* Marx and the young Engels. If, however, Hyppolite's attack is to be taken against the thesis that 'Marx gradually gave up his early theoretical standpoint', that for example the relation of Marx to the Hegelian *Phenomenology* in *Capital* is the same as it was in the Paris manuscripts, then Hyppolite's analysis scarcely supports this, and from our point of view what has been said in connection with Calvez is true of Hyppolite.

Our analysis and conclusions contradict Lefebvre's contention in *Dialectical Materialism*[58] that Marx in *The German Ideology* and the *Poverty of Philosophy* is an empiricist without dialectic. In that period – so Lefebvre thinks – dialectical materialism does not exist and only after 1858 does Marx begin to appreciate Hegelian dialectic.[59] In our analysis of the stages of Marx's relation to Hegel we find in *The German Ideology* and the *Poverty of Philosophy*, as well as in Marx's methodological observations during 1857–8, a *common* philosophical and theoretical standpoint. The difference consists in that the manuscripts from the second half of the 1850s – the philosophical standpoint reached by Marx in the fourth stage of his critique of Hegel – reflect new problems, above all the method of analysis and the critique of the capitalist economy. Hence Marx comes to a positive valuation of certain Hegelian forms of thought (ascent from the abstract to the concrete, the concrete totality, etc.), which are not explicitly dealt with in *The German Ideology* and the *Poverty of Philosophy*. Hence there is no question of any alteration in principle on the Hegelian dialectic.

In France and Italy Althusser's interpretation of Marx has recently attracted attention.[60] As opposed to a mass of superficial literature – unscientifically grounded and lacking textual analysis – which is trying to surmount a dogmatic Marxism by reinterpreting Marx in the spirit of a Feuerbachian, existentialist anthropology, Althusser emphasizes the text and the intellectual development of the young Marx. When he insists that we have before us in the *Theses on Feuerbach* and *The German Ideology* a new stage of Marx's theoretical and philosophical development which transforms his preceding views, in particular the standpoint of the Paris manuscripts of 1844, we find that our results agree. But they are distinguished from Althusser on such questions as the content of those stages. Althusser characterizes the transition from the *Economic and Philosophical Manuscripts* to *The German Ideology* as a break or cleavage ('*rupture*; *coupure épistémologique*') which corresponds to a transition from humanism to *anti-humanism*; in that sense Marx utterly rejects his old problems and concepts, and appropriates radically new ones and a radically new method.[61]

Our analysis[62] is the foundation for the view that the theoretical, philosophical standpoint of the *Theses on Feuerbach* and *The German Ideology* represents *a new form of humanism*. In the Paris manuscripts and in *The German Ideology* Marx deals above all with 'real' men. In both cases he takes on the task of explaining social and historical reality solely from the life process of 'real' men. If from the standpoint of *The German Ideology*, from that conception of 'real' men and history as introduced in the Paris manuscripts, Marx appears 'ideological', then we are dealing in *The German Ideology* – following our preceding analysis – with the *radicalization* of humanism, the creation of *a new form* of humanism.

Althusser's error in connection with humanism can be illustrated in his citation of one of Marx's comments on his method in *Capital*:[63]

[Wagner] who has not once noticed that my *analytic* method, which does not start out from *man*, but from the economically-given social period, has nothing in common with the academic German method of connecting concepts . . . [64]

The concept 'economically-given social period' was not understood by Marx as objective, divorced from the activity of human individuals. This Marxian observation does not prove his anti-humanism, but rather refutes the ideological concept 'men in general' ('Man') and advances a theory based on 'real' men in the sense of practical materialism. He wants to say only what he had already said about the starting point for economic theory in the *Introduction* of 1857: 'Individuals producing in society – hence the starting point is naturally the socially determined production [carried on] by individuals.'[65]

CHAPTER 17

A new type of rationality and the supersession of traditional ontology

When we inquire into the relationship of the Marxian critique of political economy with the Marxian critique of Hegelian philosophy, two aspects of this problem must be distinguished:

1. First, the critique of bourgeois political economy, although conceived in an extraordinarily sketchy way, made possible for Marx a deep, critical view of Hegelian philosophy as the completion of traditional metaphysics and a break with the whole of traditional 'ideological' philosophy (in particular, Young Hegelian and Feuerbachian anthropology). In other words: the beginnings of the ontopraxeological supersession of traditional philosophy, as sketched in the *Theses on Feuerbach* and *The German Ideology*, presuppose a critical perspective on political economy and a grasp of the connection between bourgeois forms of individual and social life – and metaphysics.

2. In Marx's analysis of capitalism pursued by means of structural-genetic analysis, forms of thought are used which are close to a materialist, 'inverted' Hegelian dialectic, the high point of metaphysical philosophy. This approach develops out of the last system of traditional metaphysics (Hegel) and the first negation of metaphysics and break with traditional 'ideological' philosophy (Marx) which took place within corresponding forms of praxis. But in the first instance we have an apologetic, and in the second instance a critique in principle.

In the letter to Engels of 14 January 1858 Marx notes: 'In the *method* of treatment the fact that by mere accident I again glanced through Hegel's *Logic* has been of great service to me . . . '[1]

When in his fifteen years work on the methodological problems involved in the critique of classical political economy Marx makes use of Hegel's logic and, we might add: Hegel's *Philosophy of Right*[2] – this does not mean that the radical critique of Hegel's speculative philosophy, as taken up in *The German Ideology* and the *Poverty of Philosophy*, has been abandoned. Marx thinks – at bottom, and with respect to a specific methodological problem – that what he had laid bare as the secret of Hegelian speculative dialectic in the middle of the 1840s (the 'rationale' of Hegelian dialectic) is a speculative absolutizing and eternalizing of post-revolutionary bourgeois forms of individual and social life. Hence it is no wonder that in the critique of those forms of life as in the critique of their 'mystification', that is, their absolute and eternal forms, we encounter certain formulations which – after a materialist inversion – embody elements of Hegelian method.

The inversion, which makes up materialist demystification – with reference to the methods of the Marxian critique of bourgeois political economy, as treated in the *Introduction* of 1857 – consists above all in this: for Marx's theoretical standpoint bourgeois society exists as the given substratum of knowledge and the given subject outside the intellect – independent of theory (that is, independent of the intellectual reproduction of capitalism through the ascent from the abstract to the concrete).[3]

It would be unjustified to extrapolate this methodological excursus, which is addressed to specific questions in the critique of classical political economy – even if it is at times formulated in general terms – and to see in it a consideration of the general problem of rationality from the standpoint of practical materialism.

In its logical structure *Capital* traces the activity of bourgeois society. The subject of the proceedings in *Capital* is not men, just as in bourgeois society they are not the sovereign subject, men who enter into this or that relationship; the subject is capital as a social relation, which rules over men in that society and is realized through their mediation. Capital as the specific object of investigation, as substance and subject at the same time, is alterable in form, but inalterable in essence. We have seen that for his presentation of bourgeois society Marx uses logical means different from traditional, pre-Marxist science, and advances to the completely new 'paradigm' of the critique of political economy and bourgeois reality, a 'paradigm' whose objective correlative is revolutionary negation.

Today we can represent historical forms in theory which are essentially different from the theoretical analysis in *Capital*; that analysis has given a specific imprint to the logical structure of

Capital. For example in the history of communism social relations are no longer the subject, but men and human activity itself.
And if in the intellectual appropriation of those new forms
logical procedures are used which derive from *Capital* – we can
then say that they are in each case a base and point of departure
for new dimensions contained implicitly in *Capital*. The dialectic
of communist society will undoubtedly grow richer and more
complicated.[4] In that respect *Capital* is only a beginning. In the
concluding chapters we shall draw together our results from the
first and second parts of this work, so that Marx's theoretical
initiative is set in its historical and theoretical context.

PART III

Some theoretical conclusions: being, praxis and reason

CHAPTER 18

Kant and Marx

Taking into account our results in this work we shall attempt to broaden our view of Marx's practical materialism, and inquire into whether it is something new in philosophy, or a new theoretical and practical position.

There are certain arguments for examining the relationship of Kant and Marx. This is not a matter of revitalizing an attempt by certain neo-Kantian Marxists of the Second International to extend Marxism through the Kantian theory of perception and to reinterpret Marx's scientific method in the spirit of Kantianism. After the publication of Marx's Paris manuscripts of 1844 and the preparatory material of 1857–8 for *Capital* the untenability of that attempt is obvious.

Marx was not a critic of reason in the specifically Kantian sense. In another sense, as a critic of all speculative philosophy and Hegel's philosophy of reason in particular, Marx was without doubt a 'critic of reason'. In the critique of Hegelian reason Marx formulated his conception of the supersession of all traditional metaphysics and ontology, not only pre-Kantian ontology, but also transcendental philosophy derived from Kant.

Kant suspected he had initiated a revolution in the conception and resolution of metaphilosophical problems. In that way Kant established – before Feuerbach and Marx – that traditional metaphysics was at an end. However in response to Kant's views on the destruction of pre-critical ontology there arose philosophical systems in which Feuerbach and Marx recognized the culminating defence of metaphysics. For post-Hegelian thinkers the end of metaphysics means the end of speculative philosophy.

In that respect it seems justified to ask: is Marx's break with philosophical tradition, in so far as scientific thought is concerned, a return to pre-critical thought, to ontology of the pre-Kantian type or to aphilosophical pre-Kantian empiricism – or is it a departure from Kant in theoretical work or is it an attempt to solve in a new way the problems of a critique of pre-Kantian metaphysics, a critique begun by Kant?

If it is the last possibility, can one then see in Marx's critique of Hegelian speculative reason the use and a certain advancement of Kant's principles?

Marx, however, did more than just contribute to philosophy. He saw the solution of the social – and as one of its aspects: theoretical – problems of his time in a practical revolutionary movement striving to replace bourgeois forms of human activity with new communist forms of life. An integrating aspect – not to be neglected – of that revolutionary process is scientific activity, above all the 'conception of praxis'[1] as positive science – the science of practical activity, the practical process of development of men ('positive science' – 'the presentation of practical activity, the practical process of development of men').[2] The critique of political economy and bourgeois society in general, which he undertook in his later works, was considered by Marx to be the starting point for positive, critical science, in principle open-ended, just as in 'practical materialism' human praxis creates new contents and forms.

How is a positive science which 'grasps praxis' possible? With Marx there is no question of founding such a science – in the sense of a Kantian critique of reason – since Marx would consider the very question of a standpoint for practical materialism to be uncritical, a return to speculative philosophizing.

Since Marx, as far as is known, did not get to grips explicitly with the Kantian 'critique of pure reason', we might reconstruct, for example on the basis of *The German Ideology*, Marxian arguments which depart in principle from the Kantian form of putting the question. Human knowledge – and there is no other sort of knowledge – is a specific activity of real men, conditioned by the division of labour, men as they produce under particular presuppositions and conditions both material and intellectual. Thought, in particular scientific thought, is an aspect of the practical, social and individual life process of men.

Since there can be no investigation of the problem of the foundation of science in abstract (Marx's sense), speculative 'ideological' form, we must note at the outset that human consciousness and thought are *just* those specific forms of being; they exist only as aspects of the practical process of human life. Because Kant does not take this into consideration from the beginning, we must reject the form in which he puts the question of the foundations of science.

For Marx the analysis of the real practical process of life in bourgeois society is the basis for the analysis and critique of the forms of scientific thought peculiar to the capitalist era, and this is the basis for an understanding of corresponding types of rationality. In that respect the Marxian conception of the foundations of knowledge is the negation and rejection in principle not only of Kant's solution but also of his way of putting the question.

Let us now clarify in what respect Marx's conception of science advances along lines begun by Kant.

In our previous work on the distinction between Marx on the one hand, and Feuerbach, Hess and Stirner on the other, we find proof that Marx is more radical in theoretical initiative and more deeply linked with a philosophical revolution initiated by Kant. If this is correct, then the result is that Kroner's conclusion – that philosophical development from Kant to Hegel forms a totality, 'a coherent chapter in thought, to be taken on its own terms, which does not lead us beyond its boundaries' – must be sharpened up. 'In the direction set by Kant there can be no further progress', Kroner says, 'if there is to be a successor to Hegel, a new beginning must be made.'[3] What concerns us here is the character of Marx's new beginning, its relationship to the work begun by Kant.

When Marx in his first thesis on Feuerbach contrasts his understanding of reality with Feuerbach's, he announces his departure from transcendental philosophy and at the same time his assessment of its theoretical contribution. The main defect of materialism up to then, according to Marx, consists in

that the thing, reality, sensuousness, is conceived only in the form of the *object or of contemplation*, but not as *sensuous human activity, practice*, not subjectively. Hence, in contradistinction to materialism, the *active* side was developed abstractly by idealism – which, of course, does not know real, sensuous activity as such.[4]

The fragmentary character of the first thesis on Feuerbach allows at least two interpretations. Does Marx want to say that the object, reality must be grasped not only as the perception of objects *but also* as human activity, praxis? (Then further questions about this 'not only – but also' arise.) Or, is the Marxian critique of Feuerbach and previous materialism to be understood in this way: that reality is to be grasped exclusively as human activity, and that there exists no reality in the form of objects?

From the second section of this work I conclude that the first thesis on Feuerbach is not to be interpreted as a reduction of all reality to practical human activity – as the young Lukács was prone to do, for example in his influential work *History and Class Consciousness*.[5] Hence we take the first interpretation as our starting point. According to Marx, Feuerbach's mistake is not that the existence of objects, distinct from objects of thought and from intellectual activity, is not recognized but that it is recognized in a 'very narrow', that is unhistorical mode.[6] Since Feuerbach generally works with social relations and history, he attempts to clarify everything in terms of the realization 'of the human essence', which he understands unhistorically as merely the natural qualities of the species.

Disagreeing with that, Marx emphasizes that 'human essence' is at all times 'historical production'. History is neither produced by the world spirit nor by '*man*', but by men as they really are, which means, according to Marx: as they work materially and intellectually. In history we find at every stage a historically created relation to nature and a reciprocal relationship of individuals to one another; these reciprocal relations are expressed in terms of particular powers of production and relations of production, and every generation inherits them from their predecessors. The inherited circumstances and powers of production are modified by new generations, but they also prescribe their conditions of life. One can therefore say that 'circumstances make men just as much as men make circumstances'.[7] In that way Marx arrives at his most fundamental apothegm: the alteration of circumstances and human activity (or their self-alteration) coincide and 'can be conceived and rationally understood only as *revolutionary praxis*'.[8]

For Marx the 'essence of man' is real human activity in definite and sometimes adaptable historical forms of self-alteration, in an individual, social unity of 'making circumstances' and 'situations made by circumstances', and it has its real basis in the social objectivity produced by preceding generations.[9] The difference between bourgeois and non-bourgeois society consists, according to Marx, in that for the former the past rules over the present, for the latter the present rules over the past.[10]

From the standpoint of practical materialism the traditional contraposition of consciousness and object, thought and being, appears too simple and abstract. ('Abstract' in Marx's sense is related to the Feuerbachian concept 'divorced from real men'. In any case Marx replaces the Feuerbachian, 'ideological' understanding of man with his own conception; hence 'abstract–concrete' takes on another meaning. Also, for Marx

Feuerbach is abstract in all his philosophical conceptions because he lacks historical, practical understanding of man and of reality.)

Feuerbach grasps the unity of consciousness and object, thought and being, either dualistically in a contemplative way, or he reaches at best an unhistorical, reciprocal interaction between consciousness and object, thought and being, a unity of the two conceived naturalistically. 'The true relation of thought to being is this: being is the subject, thought is the predicate. Thought is derived from being, but being is not derived from thought.'[11]

For Marx, thought is a moment of being[12] and by 'being' Marx means his practical conception of reality. On the basis of 'being' understood in that way Marx distinguishes different forms of objectivity: (i) objectivity, created by men through mutual interaction of individuals according to different social conditions, appears opposed to active individuals as an alien power, or is not an alienated objectivity, but an aspect of the conscious self-realization of man; (ii) objectivity not mediated by the activity of men, something present without human agency,[13] and according to historical conditions does or does not become the material substratum for human labour and life; (iii) an objectivity for human subjectivity, as an aspect of praxis, among other things. Marx is not satisfied with the relationship of thought and being, thought and different forms of objectivity, the subject–predicate relationship used by Feuerbach. This presupposes a substantial-attributive structure which we do want to characterize in terms of 'subject and predicate'. For Marx, however, the relationship of 'thought' to 'reality understood practically' has a different structure, and hence for him Feuerbach's characterization is unsuitable.

The scientific task of 'grasping praxis' is in any case not fulfilled by Marx in the *Theses on Feuerbach* and *The German Ideology* in the sense of a practical materialism, since general definitions of a new, non-objectivistic and non-subjectivistic conception of reality are not worked out. Also the relationship of the general and particular, like all other traditional metaphilosophical questions, is grasped anew in Marx's practical materialism.

If we understand these general definitions (subjectivity–objectivity, 'essence' of man, etc.) as supra-historical abstractions, generalities, if we are not aware that they fail in their abstraction to conceive praxis in a particular historical form, we would – according to Marx – abandon our historical foundation and find ourselves again in the realm of ideology.[14] In themselves, divorced from real history, these abstractions have no value.[15] If, however, they are conceived as historical abstractions, they have – as Marx sought to demonstrate in his polemic against Stirner – great philosophical and methodological significance. They are an aspect of real knowledge and are indispensable for 'grasping praxis', hence for real revolutionary praxis.

Marx's economic analysis, with its explicit or implicit conceptions of different sorts of being, the relationship of subjectivity and objectivity, spontaneity and receptivity, autonomy and heteronomy, nature and history, etc., is in my opinion relevant to metaphilosophy not as the mere concretization of supra-historical generalities, but as a theory characterizing and bearing his new metaphilosophical view.

Feuerbach's post-Hegelian anthropology sees in the development from Kant to Hegel only a rationalization of theology and hence a certain closing of the gap between the absolute and man, and then a transition from theism as a gross form of the alienation of the human essence to anthropological philosophy as a retrieval of human species-being. In that sense German speculative philosophy has great historical significance.[16]

From the standpoint of practical materialism Marx reveals the apparent radicalism of Feuerbach and Stirner and then shows how the two remain in the realm of tradition. On the other hand, he emphasizes the significance ignored by Feuerbach, of German transcendental philosophy for the development of a science capable of 'grasping praxis'.

A detailed interpretation of the connection between Marx's new materialism and the development 'of the active side' in German idealism could proceed from Kant's 'transcendental deduction of the concept of pure understanding', in which experience and experiential reality are understood in essence as intellectual activity and the product of intellectual activity, hence as a certain form of *activity*. We would have to continue with Fichte's radicalization of Kantian transcendentalism by dropping 'the thing in itself' and freeing us to understand the subject–object relationship, and being as production; with Schelling's expansion of the Kantian idea of an 'intellectual archetype' and enrichment of transcendentalism through a social, historical dimension; with Hegel's concern to give a more consistent theory of the whole of experience and a more consistent theory of freedom, theories of the self-reproduction of spirit on the basis of transcendentalism, than Kant, Fichte and Schelling. Marx criticized Hegel's philosophy of the self-generation of spirit in the *Economic and Philosophical Manuscripts* when he put forward the philosophical presuppositions of his critique of political economy and his Feuerbachian theory of communism. The self-reproduction of philosophical self-consciousness as depicted in Hegel's *Phenomenology* is explained as a speculative expression for the historical self-generation of man; this conception is then recast in *The German Ideology*, after Marx's rejection of eschatological and 'ideological' elements of Feuerbachian and Hegelian provenance, in a more advanced critical and practical understanding of reality – the new materialism.

The practical, social background for the most important conceptions of German classical philosophy, including Hegel, is formed by the historical relations (a specific historical relationship between individual and society) and forms of dependence on nature, and the rule of nature by man which accompany the bourgeois era, in particular the epoch of the French Revolution; every practical problem obtains its expression, in theoretical and metaphilosophical terms, in a new formulation of the problem of determination and self-determination.

Kant's central question, on which the opening question of the *Critique of Pure Reason* concerning the possibility of synthetic judgements *a priori* is derivative, can be formulated in the following way:

If autonomous being cannot be reconciled with Newtonian reality, which has an unshakeable place in natural science, and if there is no doubt about the existence of autonomous being (primarily the conscious moral agent), what philosophical first principles would be capable of grasping that state of affairs and comprehending their coexistence, their unity?

This is a matter of the relationship between the natural and the human, their unity, which Kant understands as 'natural' and 'human' in a specific sense. *The Natural* is 'appearance', is only scientifically accessible within the limits of Newtonian natural science.

Human in the proper sense is existence not determined in time and space, not 'apparently caused', hence not an object of scientific knowledge because it is beyond natural mechanisms: it is the moral agent who determines his own will through a moral law of man as the ultimate purpose (in Kantian terminology: the will which acts 'freely'). For this self-determining reality, for an understanding of this type of being, one must not use definitions which apply to appearances. The subject acting through 'free causality' is 'real' in a particular way, different from natural phenomena, and this reality *sui generis* opens up new possibilities for knowledge – not scientific knowledge, but knowledge which at least partly, at least in a limited realm discloses 'being in itself'.

This raises the problem of the relations and unity of one such understanding of the natural and the human, nature and man. Kant solves the problem in terms of a dualistic coexistence: natural mechanisms apply in the realm of 'appearances', 'freedom' exists in the realm of the intellect. If appearances and things in themselves could not be distinguished, then Spinozism would be the inescapable alternative, that is a philosophical system, which – according to Kant – knows no self-determination in the proper sense and lets freedom sink into a fatalistic concept of necessity.

For Kant the concept of freedom is the keystone in the whole structure of pure reason:[17] hence he begins with philosophical first principles in which self-determining structures, analogous to the autonomous I, have primacy, so other structures have a derivative role. In that way, Kant clears a place in philosophy for the problem of self-determination as shown in human action (choice under moral law); he is responsible for a significant development in philosophical first principles: he humanizes the problem of creation, whereas previously Christian metaphysics had put this in an alienated form, which gave pride of place to the problem of the divine creation and man's relationship to it.

The central problem for the philosophical epoch from Kant to Marx is the problem of human freedom, how to make men free. The burden of Kant's thought is his striving 'to make the concept of nature and the concept of freedom coincide', so that he is primarily concerned with *human* freedom as linked with bourgeois forms of social and individual life – with the free individual as bourgeois (the juridical 'agent') and with the *Rechtsstaat*.

If we consider the central problem in Marx's critique of Hegel and the Young Hegelians, to which in essence all other problems can be reduced, we find that this is also the problem of the relation of human freedom to natural necessity, the relation and unity of man with nature, which includes his *second* nature, objective human works.

The central conception in the philosophical standpoint attained by Marx in the *Theses on Feuerbach* and *The German Ideology* is neither the relation of 'substance' and 'subject', nor the concept 'man in general', nor 'matter in general',[18] nor even a principle as understood in previous ontologies, but the practical understanding of reality and truth. Pre-critical ontology is replaced by the investigation and clarification of ontopraxeo-logical problems, which are necessarily renewed in the develop-ment of human material, intellectual praxis, that is the problems sketched in the *Theses on Feuerbach*.

In that sense one can see in Marx's practical understanding of reality a new answer to the question put by traditional ontology and German transcendental philosophy. This answer presup-poses the destruction of pre-Kantian 'dogmatic' ontology and arises out of transcendental philosophy.

Marx's ontopraxeological standpoint is related to Kant's transcendentalism in that Marx, as before him Kant, understands objectivity, reality, not simply as something given which can be appropriated intellectually and truthfully known by man as a mere receptor. Both inquire into the human mediation of reality and truth. There is obviously a great difference in the way that Kant and Marx answer these questions. Marx's practical, histori-cal 'criticism' has new dimensions: the historical connection with Kant's critique of reason is, however, essential.

Marx appears to stand closer to Kant than to the idealist fulfilment of transcendental philosophy in Hegel's dialectic of reason in three respects:

(a) In Hegel's eyes it was a deficiency of Kantian criticism that the 'absolute standpoint' had been only 'man and humanity'. 'Thus it is not recognized that philosophy can only proceed from God, but rather, as is said, from man.'[19] In that sense Marx returned at a new level to Kant, since he saw the alpha and omega of all theory in men, how they are active in particular, historically alterable, social and natural relations.

(b) We can say of Marx's relation to mathematics that it is a departure from the Hegelian critique of Leibniz and Kant, and establishes a certain reapproach to Kant. Even though Marx departs from mathematics as an absolute, he does not consider, as Hegel did, mathematical knowledge to be subordinate and second-rank, with no expectation of being 'truly scientific'. He replaces this with a potentially increasing use of mathematics, to be sure in relation to the dialectic, as is shown, for example, by his letter to Engels of May 1873 on the possibility of a mathematical account of the laws of economic crises. In *The German Ideology* Marx abruptly rejects 'belletristic philippics, derived from the Hegelian tradition, against quantification'.[20]

(c) In his recognition of the limitations of human reason Marx seems to stand closer to Kant than Hegel, even though human knowledge is understood differently by the two thinkers – with Kant, a supra-historical distinction between experiential knowledge and 'thing in itself'; with Marx, a result from his practical, historical understanding of reality.

Hence in certain conceptions Marx approaches the starting point of German transcendental philosophy albeit at a new level; he reacts to post-Kantian developments in transcendental philosophy and takes them as preparation for his theory.

CHAPTER 19

The supersession of
traditional ontology

Fichte succeeded in working out a more consistent philosophy of freedom than Kant, the first logical ontological conceptions which broke with traditional ontology not only in disputing objective truth and counterposing to it 'the critique', but also in content and principle.

The decisive step consists in the exclusion of the 'thing in itself' as a residue of 'dogmatism',[1] so that with the transformation of Kantian transcendentalism this became for Fichte the problem of being and 'praxis', in the sense that all reality appeared as an aspect of consciousness, an aspect of the self-reproduction of the absolute I, 'reason'.

Fichte is aware that he introduced new ideas into the domain of ontology which are incompatible with tradition, and he wrestled with a diction which led to misunderstandings. The sole absolute, according to him, is 'pure activity',[2] the 'activity of the I'. It has a subject–object structure in which both poles are identical – they are the I, 'reason'.[3] The I is at the same time its own act and the product of reason.[4] To grasp the identity of activity and production means, according to Fichte, to grasp the pure I and to rise to the standpoint of transcendental philosophy.[5] From the activity of the absolute I or intelligence must be derived all determinations of consciousness, all conceptions which we find in consciousness, for example the conception of the material world which we find in consciousness, and the conception of the external material world which exists without our agency.[6] The action of the I is thus 'free', and complete freedom is only possible as the action of the I.

Thus through the transformation of Kant's synthetic unity of apperception, and through an examination of the Kantian postulate of the unity of speculative and practical reason which is directed against traditional ontology, there arises a new metaphysical conception 'absolute action', from which Fichte

('I', 'reason, 'intelligence'), Schelling ('absolute I', 'intelligence') and Hegel ('self-consciousness', 'spirit', 'reason') proceeded. Being, action and reason are therefore unified in the post-Kantian development of German transcendentalism by these metaphysical conceptions.

As we have indicated above, Kant was concerned in the *Critique of Pure Reason* not only with the possibility of theoretical knowledge but also with the possibility of practical freedom. He establishes the possibility of their coexistence and formulates in the *Fundamental Principles of the Metaphysics of Morals* a programme for the unification of theoretical and practical reason.[7] In the *Critique of Practical Reason* he understands the unity of speculative and practical reason dualistically, coexistence in parallel.

As a rule 'practical' means this for Kant: concerning conscious action brought by reason to consciousness.[8] The will is nothing but 'practical reason'.[9] The investigation of practical reason is the theory of (moral) duty as a special sort of action. There is a difference between what is technically and morally practical, between practice and praxis.[10] In a later work, the *Metaphysics of Morals*, Kant distinguishes between the theoretical and practical points of view, and in the latter he recognizes the pragmatic, moral standpoint.[11]

The primacy of praxis is understood by Kant as the primacy of moral problems.[12] The science of praxis is something other than a theory of how to choose the best means for reaching the best goals, and something other than technology.[13] In ethics as in the science of praxis it is a matter of making intelligible the moral relation of men to one another.[14]

Kant's thesis on the unity of theory and praxis[15] makes plain that his standpoint was analogous to that of English political economy. It is an attempt to explain and sanction the rationality which corresponds to bourgeois society. In an ideological inversion the result is that the principles of bourgeois society are revealed as the realization of pure, *a priori* 'reason', and 'morally' free action is what bourgeois law not only locates in legality itself but also pursues in terms of supra-historical 'moral' laws.

In the Kantian conception of practical reason and freedom there is expressed – according to the practical, materialist offspring of classical German philosophy – an impotent conception of freedom and praxis. Material praxis is carried out, according to Kant, wholly in accord with the laws of natural necessity. Man can develop initiative, but he must relate this to what is wholly determined in the world of experience by natural necessity. Historical science establishes that the most powerful force in history is human foresight; our projects have no influence on the course of history.[16]

How has Fichte fulfilled the Kantian postulate[17] of the unification of theoretical and practical reason, theoretical and practical philosophy? It must first of all be explained why from the standpoint of Kantian transcendentalism the unification of theoretical and practical reason is logical and necessary. Kant wants his 'critics' to answer three questions: What can one know? What ought one to do? What may one hope for?[18] He wants to give a scientific answer, which means, under the prevailing conception of science, that it is general and necessary. Because there are no two generalities and necessities, one must postulate in the end a 'reason' to answer these questions, *if* a scientific answer may be given. Kant is convinced that it can be.

Fichte's postulates are these: reason is in essence 'practical', because it is self-determining, identical with the absolute I, freely acting self-consciousness.[19] 'Practical' reason as explained in, for example, the *System of Morals*,[20] is never anything but theoretical reason. To define one's own activity is identical with being practical. In a certain way, Fichte adds, it was always recognized that reason ought to be practical, in the sense that it helps to find the means to realize goals determined from outside, for example by biological need or by our will. In that sense reason is technical and practical. But Fichte had something else in mind: reason is a self-determining activity and an end in itself, in so far as it is 'purely practical'.[21]

'Absolute action' has a specific structure: it is 'self-positing as antithesis' and antithesis as self-posited, or 'actively returning into itself',[22] identity of subject and object. Negation and the negation of the negation are aspects of the absolute activity of the I.[23] It is activity returning to its starting point; it has a structure analogous to organic process, with the teleology investigated by Kant in the *Critique of Judgement*.

According to Fichte it is possible and necessary to distinguish theoretical and practical activity from one another ('practical' here in a narrow sense). Practical activity – biological human activity and conscious material labour – is in that sense primary; it is the condition for this – that the theoretical I can be conscious of itself.[24] The primacy of practical, free activity of the 'rational essence' over purely noetic activity was established by Fichte in the *Foundations of Right* in that the theoretical activity of the I ('the world view') does not suffice to posit rational essence as such,[25] that is, it cannot be sufficient that independent, free, autonomous man merely thinks. With Fichte we are also dealing with a contemplative theoretical view of 'action': rational essence must posit itself as perceiving. From the standpoint of transcendental philosophy theoretical perception is nothing but the 'I returning to itself', and the world is nothing but the I, considered in its proper limits. Then however – Fichte thinks – the autonomous I must be ready to have something ascribed to it. He puts the question how the independent, autonomous I arose originally, and *that is not to be explained* from a contemplative perception of the world ('the world view').

Both the activity of the I in contemplative perception and the activity of the I in the practical appropriation and supersession of contradictions established by the not-I are activity, but the first form of activity is 'free activity under certain conditions',[26] that is a certain dependence on subjects, while only the second sort is free, completely autonomous action. Fichte concludes that the rational essence could not be independent, freely reasoning essence, I, intelligence, if there were no *practical* essence. Will and practical activity are the roots of the I.[27]

In his works of 1794 Fichte explains why practical activity is necessary, when the free I is already contained in praxis: hence the autonomous I is maintained and is thus independently and autonomously renewed.[28] This conception depends on Fichte's views on the highest goal of man, which consists 'in the complete coincidence of man with himself and – as a condition of that – the coincidence of all things outside him with his practical concepts, the concepts which determine how every circumstance *is to be*'. The final goal is to overthrow everything 'unreasonable' that is, what is incompatible with the autonomous, self-positing I, and to appropriate this freely, according to its own laws.[29]

Let us consider how Fichte's writings on science view the relation of theoretical and practical activity (and reason).

It must be emphasized that *before* his presentation of the foundations of theoretical knowledge and the 'foundations of practical science', Fichte puts his exposition of the principles of *all* scientific doctrines. In these principles of science there is a complete unification of theoretical and practical philosophy. It is relevant here that the 'praxeological' part of the doctrine of science is 'by far the most important' for Fichte's assessment; it offers the only firm basis for the theoretical part.[30]

With his presentation of the basis of theory Fichte in essence does nothing but reflect the forms and structures used in the Kantian transcendental deduction of categories, after the exclusion of the 'thing in itself' as a residue of dogmatism. Fichte wants to be more critical and more fundamental than Kant. He thinks that he has only expressed comprehensively and consciously what Kant did in actuality when he formulated this proposition:

> The I posits (posits itself) as determined by the not-I in order to consider whether and in what aspects this principle is conceivable. It wants to consolidate the Kantian conception and to move beyond it in principle, to open up the way to new metaphilosophical conceptions in which the absolute I, practical reason, is the sole principle above all others.

Fichte's work on the problems of society and law was significant for the transcendence of traditional ontology and for post-Fichtean conceptions of the unity and identity of theoretical and practical philosophy.

The concept of the individual and the concept of law are conditions of self-consciousness, says Fichte in the *Foundations of Natural Law*.[31] How is this to be interpreted? It is not a matter of using general truths revealed in his earlier works on social and legal relations. In Fichte's writings on natural law and morals (*The System of Moral Philosophy*) we see a further development and deepening of his view of the primacy of praxis. While in the *Foundations of the Doctrine of Science* practical activity is characterized and analysed, preferably in connection with struggle, desire and feeling, in the *Foundations of Natural Law* and in the *System of Moral Philosophy* praxis in a wide range of social and legal forms is Fichte's object. He integrates social and legal problems into his metaphilosophical investigations.

Traditional ontology is transformed by Fichte into a metaphysics of practical reason. The fundamental problems of logic (the theoretical position) are inseparably united here with particular – one could say today – existential, practical activities which cannot be theoretically deduced and cannot be reduced to any kind of theoretical activity. The primacy of the extra-rational[32] practical relation proclaimed by Fichte, is straight away – one could say prenatally – rationalized, transformed into conditions in which absolute reason, positing itself, creates itself.

Fichte's unification of praxis and reason into 'practical reason', whose primary form is 'absolute activity' (through the self-positing of the contradiction) is the key to understanding a further development in German transcendental philosophy, and the Marxian supersession of traditional ontology in his critique of speculative philosophy, that is, the metaphysics of practical reason.

Marx's new method of putting and investigating the problems of science, praxis and nature which we have called his ontopraxeological procedure, takes critical account of the move towards practicality in the first principles of German transcendental philosophy, whose central difficulty is the reduction of human praxis to an absolute 'practical reason'.

CHAPTER 20

Praxis and reason

After Fichte reached the view that the concept of the individual and the concept of right are conditions of self-consciousness, it was for Schelling, who considered his 'system of transcendental idealism' to be an improvement on the philosophical discoveries of Fichte, to add: *history* is therefore the basis of self-consciousness.[1] It is the explication of the absolute I; its 'cell' is 'absolute action' (self-positing through contraposition, the negation of the negation). History with its structure of thesis–antithesis–synthesis is something derivative and subordinate; it is the means to the self-realization of the absolute I, which is itself not temporally defined.[2]

For Schelling the I ('Intelligence') is in essence practical. It arises through an original act of self-determination (freedom); the self-determination of intelligence is 'wanting' in the most general sense of the word, transcendental, free (practical) process.[3] The theory of right and the theory of history are integrated by Schelling into the metaphilosophical system of transcendental idealism, necessarily paralleled by a new philosophy of nature. Hence he deepens that unification of theoretical and practical philosophy by which Fichte had enlarged traditional ontology and added a new dimension.[4]

Hegel went further when he developed the idea of 'absolute activity' and the principle of 'practical reason' into a comprehensive philosophical system.[5] Everything which is or which we want to be free, reasonable and autonomous must have the structure of 'absolute activity', self-positing through antitheses, the negation of the negation. And everything which possesses an analogous structure is 'reasonable' (for example, the bourgeois constitutional state, love, and in an incomplete form – natural organisms).

Hegel is conscious of the fact that he advances along lines laid down by others who made first principles practical. In the Jena writings on legal philosophy he agrees that Kant and Fichte have already established the absolute in practical philosophy.[6] They have however not brought it consistently to its end in the construction of a whole system of philosophy based on 'absolute activity', and this must necessarily be corrected.

The unification of theoretical and practical philosophy is detailed in Hegel's new conception of speculation and consequently in his conception of scientific theory (philosophy). True science must correspond in object and content to the absolute (infinity, freedom). Kant and Fichte were more preoccupied with infinity[7] (that is, unlimitedness, unconditionedness, independence, autonomy, freedom) than preceding philosophers, but their conception of the unconditioned and freedom remains unliberating. This is because it is based on the autonomy of the individual and the contract theory of the state. Such an understanding of freedom, Hegel thinks, leads to damnation. Fichte considered thinking (theoretical activity), to be limited, while he took man to be unlimited in his wants (free behaviour); Hegel turned these characteristics around: man is only unlimited in thought, in theory, while in free activity only a people organized into a *political state* is free, hence the sovereign state. Making bourgeois forms of life absolute in the legal terms which reflect them is the secret of the Hegelian unification of theoretical and practical philosophy.

Kant's idea of freedom as the keystone of the whole structure of philosophy is realized here with the fulfilment of the Kantian postulate of the unification of theoretical and practical reason as a higher principle, 'reason', which is the essence of absolute spirit.

Traditional pre-Kantian metaphysics are transformed in the *Phenomenology of Mind* and the *Science of Logic*, but this logic is the theory of 'absolute action' – 'practical reason' – it is mystified praxeology and therefore ontotheology.

Only within an ontotheological unification of theoretical and practical philosophy do Hegel's views on the distinction and relationship between theoretical and practical activity in *the sphere of consciousness* (the sphere of 'ultimate subjective spirit')[8] retain an authentic sense, as does Hegel's analysis of human labour.

If with Fichte, Schelling and Hegel legal philosophy has a particular place in metaphilosophical considerations, in *Marx's* explanation of basic philosophical and theoretical problems the critique of political economy takes on a particular role, that is, the theoretical analysis of capitalist economic praxis as the 'basic form' of praxis under given historical conditions.

Historically the conception of rationality in Marx's economic work may be characterized as corresponding to the first phase of communist (theoretical and practical) criticism of bourgeois society, in which the revolutionary negation of bourgeois life and forms of thought take place within forms created by capital, the most powerful 'subject' in history.

At the same time one of the results from Marx's new conception is that when the practical process of life has a character different from classical capitalism, it will be necessary to include new relations in explaining ontopraxeological problems (that is, the foundations of our knowledge of human praxis and nature) and to reflect on this.

Marx does not return to a pre-Kantian ontology which considered knowledge to be the reflection of the objective world unmediated by praxis. This amounts to the formulation of the aporia of that attempt. German transcendental philosophy proceeds in the opposite direction. It wants the unity of subject and object, the possibility of knowledge to be explained by considering objective being to be the product of consciousness. Here there arises new aporia, as the being to be 'deduced' stands in free praxis outside consciousness. Without prior acknowledgement, at the very least in the form of the Fichtean impulse, the free practical I cannot be 'deduced'. The aporia of that sort of transcendental, idealist attempt began to be revealed and criticized by Feuerbach when he pointed out that transcendental idealism knows no real 'unmediated being' outside the mind, that it is therefore bewitched by consciousness. Marx considers the relation of being, praxis and reason with respect to the consequences of these two attempts and offers a new solution. He refers to transcendental philosophy in so far as it was reflected in the theory of freedom as self-reproduction, the coincidence of spontaneity and receptivity in certain structures analogous to the structures of human praxis. At the same time Marx broke through transcendental philosophy, gave up consciousness as a standard, and turned back to *empiricism*. This – from the high point of classical German philosophy – was a return to something which was essentially unphilosophical and unscientific. It was, however, a new empiricism conceived as the non-identity of theory and praxis on the basis of a newly understood (and lived) unification of theory and praxis. This is an empiricism which conceives experience as praxis, which means that the pre-Kantian contraposition of *a posteriori* and *a priori* now loses its original meaning.

For Descartes the sole starting point for absolute certainty was the *cogito, ergo sum*; Fichte was the first to modify that subjective starting point into subjective-free, subjective-practical – though at the same time he relied on metaphysical principles of idealist speculation. From the standpoint of practical materialism the starting point is never the *cogito, ergo sum*, and never the Fichtean self-creating, theoretical and practical I am I, but the life and knowledge of practical, active, individual men in which the existence, the non-identity and the relationship of my conscious being to my extra-conscious *objective* (natural, social) being are posited. The indeterminacy of that starting point is undeniable, because it is merely the starting point, not a 'principle' of philosophy – which alters nothing, since it is the sole *fundamentum inconcussum* for the explanation of ontopraxeological problems from the standpoint of practical materialism.[9]

In Marxism we find a new type of theory. In the ancient type, expressed classically by Aristotle, we find a contemplative conception of theory as the focal point of human behaviour, which has meaning and is an end in itself. In the bourgeois epoch, the basic conception of the relationship of theory to praxis is utilitarian and technical; it gains ground through the illusions of the primacy of purely supra-historical theory ('reason', including 'practical reason', in classical German philosophy). In that type of theory, theory itself is not grasped as an aspect of praxis which is transformed historically. This was expressed in philosophy, since the thinkers of classical German philosophy, who formulated the unification of theoretical and practical philosophy, assigned to these forms of thought an absolute and eternal character which the bourgeois world took as reasonable. That applies not only to Hegel, but also to Kant and Fichte and others. In that sense Marx notes in the eleventh thesis on Feuerbach: the philosophers have only interpreted the world, the point is to change it. The contemplative quality which Marx has in mind here is not the Aristotelian type, for the typical philosophers of the bourgeois era were interested in practical things. Marx wants to say only that philosophers, that is, the bearers of inverted views concerning the role of pure 'reasonable' theory, do not grasp the relation of theory and praxis in its practical, materialist sense, that is, contemporary Marxian terminology; they are prisoners of 'ideology'. Hence all their critiques of the existing world and their programmes for its alteration remain within the bounds of bourgeois forms of life; they are only platitudes, different interpretations of what already is. A critique which presupposes

supra-historical reason over praxis can give no realizable programme for the alteration of the bourgeois world.

There are arguments for the view – these are beyond the scope
of this work – that the present struggle for the solution of
contemporary economic, political, technical, emotional and
moral problems takes place under conditions – thanks to the
results of revolutionary workers' movements, among other
things – different from those conditions determined by capital
and from the revolutionary negation of those conditions, with
the *retention* of old basic forms of material praxis. Hence there is
pressure to clarify the basic questions of a new type of rationality
corresponding to the opening of the second phase in revolutionary criticism of bourgeois forms of social praxis. If this
investigation is pursued by means of the logical, dialectical-
materialist procedure discovered by Marx, then this implies a
recognition of the historical coherence of the Marxian conception of rationality as a consideration of historically transitory
forms of thought in the critique of political economy.[10]

At the same time the essence of the Marxian method – the
practical materialist conception of reality and theory – has
become topical, as worked out in the critique of bourgeois political economy and speculative philosophy, in particular Hegel.
Only by referring to these elements and to the methodological
essence of Marxian theory is it possible to make any progress
with ontopraxeological problems in the second half of the twentieth century.

Notes

INTRODUCTION

1. For a critical discussion of this literature see Jindřich Zelený, 'K problému logiky Marxova "Kapitálu" ', *Filosofický časopis*, 2/1960.
2. See V. I. Lenin, 'Philosophical Notebooks', in *Collected Works*, vol. 38, Foreign Languages Publishing House, Moscow, 1961, pp. 352–3. (Hereafter referred to as 'Philosophical Notebooks'.)
3. Ibid., p. 372.
4. See V. Filkorn, *Predhegelovská logika*, Bratislava, 1953, pp. 22, 45, 53. (Hereafter referred to as Filkorn, *Predhegelovská*.) And see below, p. 98.
5. See the definition in A. Tarski, 'Über den Begriff der logischen Folgerung', in *Actes du Congrès International de Philosophie Scientifique*, fasc. VII (Logique), Paris, 1936, pp. 1–11, or E. W. Beth, *Semantic Entailment and Formal Derivability*, Amsterdam, 1955. (Hereafter referred to as Tarski, 'Folgerung', and Beth, *Semantic Entailment*, respectively.)
6. See for example H. Scholz, *In der Geschichte der Logik*, Berlin, 1931, pp. 15–16.
7. See below, pp. 109–10.
8. See Engels to Mehring, 14 July 1893, in Karl Marx and Frederick Engels, *Selected Correspondence*, 2nd edn, Progress, Moscow, 1965, pp. 458–62. (Hereafter referred to as *Selected Correspondence*.)

PART I, CHAPTER 1

1. Karl Marx, *Capital*, vol. 3, Progress, Moscow, 1971, pp. 267, 837. (Hereafter referred to as *Capital*, vol. 3.)
2. Karl Marx, *Capital*, vol. 1, Allen & Unwin, London, 1957, p. xix. (Hereafter referred to as *Capital*, vol. 1.)
3. Ibid., p. 102.
4. *Capital*, vol. 3, p. 143.
5. See Adam Smith, *Essays on Philosophical Subjects*, Basel, 1799. (Hereafter referred to as Smith, *Essays*.)
6. See V. Filkorn, in *Metoda vědy*, Bratislava, 1956, pp. 6, 60, 139, 142, 160, etc.; and R. Lenoble, 'Types d'explication et types logiques au cours de l'histoire des sciences', in *Actes du XIième Congrès International de Philosophie*, Amsterdam and Louvain, 1953, pp. 10–15; and see below, Part III, Chapter 18.
7. David Ricardo, *Principles of Political Economy and Taxation*, 3rd edn, ed. R. M. Hartwell, Penguin, Harmondsworth, p. 49. (Hereafter referred to as Ricardo, *Principles*.)
8. Ibid., p. 57, and see also pp. 55–71, *passim*.

9. Ricardo's one-sided quantitative standpoint is distinguished from positivism, which excludes the relationship of appearance and essence from scientific explanation and reduces scientific knowledge to mathematical relationships at the level of appearances.
10. See Ricardo's presentation of 'the nature of capital' and the 'nature of rent' in *Principles, passim*.

PART I, CHAPTER 2

1. See Karl Marx, *Theories of Surplus Value*, vol. 2, Progress, Moscow, 1968, p. 504. (Hereafter referred to as *Theories of Surplus Value*, vol. 2.) See also *Theories of Surplus Value*, vol. 3, Lawrence and Wishart, London, 1972, p. 131. (Hereafter referred to as *Theories of Surplus Value*, vol. 3.)
2. *Capital*, vol. 1, p. 47.
3. Ibid., pp. 8, 21 ff.
4. Ricardo, *Principles*, pp. 67–71.
5. *Capital*, vol. 1, Penguin, Harmondsworth, 1976, pp. 144–6. (Hereafter referred to as *Capital*, vol. 1, Penguin.)
6. Today it would be possible to present Marx's condensed exposition in an even briefer mathematical form.
7. See Smith, *Essays*, p. 154.
8. *Capital*, vol. 1, pp. xxx–xxxi.
9. See 'Philosophical Notebooks', pp. 253–4.
10. Ricardo, *Principles*, p. 118.
11. See Karl Marx, *Grundrisse*, Penguin, Harmondsworth, 1974, p. 560. (Hereafter referred to as *Grundrisse*.)
12. Ricardo, *Principles*, p. 49.
13. See Karl Marx, *Introduction* to the *Grundrisse*, in *Texts on Method*, Blackwell, Oxford, 1975, pp. 64–5. (Hereafter referred to as *Introduction*, 1857, *Texts on Method*.) See also *Capital*, vol. 3, pp. 877 ff.

PART I, CHAPTER 3

1. See below Part I, Chapter 9.
2. L. A. Mankovsky, 'Kategorii "veshch' " i "otnoshchenie" v Kapitale Marksa', *Voprosui filosofii*, 5/1956. (Hereafter referred to as Mankovsky, 'Kategorii'.)
3. *Capital*, vol. 1, p. 26.
4. Mankovsky, 'Kategorii', p. 47.
5. Ibid., p. 59.
6. Ibid., p. 49.
7. *Capital*, vol. 1, p. 30.
8. See Karl Marx, *Notes on Adolph Wagner*, in *Texts on Method*, pp. 206–7. (Hereafter referred to as *Notes on Wagner, Texts on Method*.)
9. *Capital*, vol. 1, p. 55; see also *Theories of Surplus Value*, vol. 2, pp. 170–3; and see also *Grundrisse*, p. 560.
10. See Dušan Machovec, *Dvě studie o Aristotelově filosofii*, Prague, 1959.
11. René Descartes, *Philosophical Writings*, eds E. Anscombe and P. T. Geach, Nelson, Edinburgh and London, 1954, p. 216.
12. John Locke, *An Essay Concerning Human Understanding*, Book II, Chapters 14, 23.

13. Christian Wolff, *Philosophia rationalis, sive logica*, Frankfurt and Leipzig, 1732; §§64, 65, 66, 67, 69. (Hereafter referred to as Wolff, *Philosophia rationalis*.) idem, *Philosophia prima, sive ontologia*, Frankfurt, 1730, §143.
14. See *Capital*, vol. 1, Part Three ('The Production of Absolute Surplus-value').
15. Karl Marx, *A Contribution to the Critique of Political Economy*, Lawrence and Wishart, London, 1971, p. 52. (Hereafter referred to as *A Contribution to the Critique of Political Economy*.)
16. This can be a matter of substantial properties and relations as well as surface phenomena.
17. Karl Marx, *Capital*, vol. 2, Lawrence and Wishart, London, 1970, pp. 385–386. (Hereafter referred to as *Capital*, vol. 2.) See also ibid., pp. 204–5, 375, 389 ff.; and *Introduction*, 1857, *Texts on Method*, p. 206.
18. *Grundrisse*, p. 514.
19. See *Theories of Surplus Value*, vol. 3, pp. 145–6.
20. E. W. Beth, 'Critical Epochs in the Development of the Theory of Science', *British Journal for the Philosophy of Science*, 1/1950; and his 'Fundamental Features of Contemporary Theory of Science', idem, no. 4.
21. Since Mankovsky, at the conclusion of his article, also mentions that essences are relative and alterable (p. 54), he finds himself in contradiction with his previous remarks, and this affirmation is itself finally weakened by the priority accorded to a reduction to quantitative relationality and alterability.
22. G. W. F. Hegel, *The Phenomenology of Mind*, 2nd edn, Allen and Unwin, London, 1966, pp. 80–1, 84–5, 113–15. (Hereafter referred to as *Phenomenology*.) See also his *Encyclopaedia*, §§27–33.
23. *Phenomenology*, p. 80.
24. Ibid., p. 84. See also Hegel's *System der Philosophie*, Part I, Stuttgart, 1929, p. 105, §31 addition.
25. *Phenomenology*, p. 81.
26. Ibid.
27. Filkorn, *Predhegelovská*, p. 182.
28. Ibid., p. 199.
29. Ibid., p. 201.
30. See L. Infeld, 'Neskol'ka zamechany o teorii otnositel'nosti', *Voprosui filosofii*, 5/1954; and A. Kolman, 'Současné spory kolem filosofických problémů teorie relativity', *Pokroky matematiky, fyziky a astronomie*, 5/1960; and F. Enriques, *La théorie de la connaissance scientifique de Kant à nos jours*, Paris, 1938, Chapters 6 and 7.
31. It is difficult to avoid misunderstanding on these problems, that is, conceiving something in the spirit of pre-dialectical conceptions, here, conceptions of the object and its properties, which are only a rough image of the ontological structure of small portions of a few real forms. Hegel has emphasized in this connection that the principle of the identity of opposites cannot be formulated except through inexact, somewhat misleading verbal expressions.

PART I, CHAPTER 4

1. See *Capital*, vol. 1, pp. xxix–xxxi.
2. Ibid.

3. *Introduction*, 1857, *Texts on Method*, p. 73.
4. See E. V. Ilenkov, *Dialektika abstraktnogo i konkretnogo v 'Kapitale' Marksa*, Moscow, 1960, pp. 15–18. (Hereafter referred to as Ilenkov, 'Dialektika'.)
5. See *Introduction*, 1857, *Texts on Method*, p. 72.
6. See Karl Marx and Frederick Engels, *The German Ideology*, Progress, Moscow, 1968, p. 38. (Hereafter referred to as *The German Ideology*.) See below, Part I, Chapter 9.
7. See *Introduction*, 1857, *Texts on Method*, pp. 71 ff.
8. *Theories of Surplus Value*, vol. 2, pp. 164–9.
9. *Introduction*, 1857, *Texts on Method*, p. 72; see also *A Contribution to the Critique of Political Economy*, pp. 57–8.
10. See below, Part I, Chapter 9.
11. See F. Behrens, *Zur Methode der politischen Ökonomie*, Berlin, 1952, especially Chapter 3.
12. Frederick Engels, 'Karl Marx, *A Contribution to the Critique of Political Economy*' [Review], in *A Contribution to the Critique of Political Economy*, p. 225. (Hereafter referred to as *Review*, 1859.)
13. 'Philosophical Notebooks', pp. 360–1.
14. See *Grundrisse*, p. 259; see also below, Part I, Chapters 5 and 6.
15. See Karl Marx, *Grundrisse der Kritik der politischen Ökonomie*, [East] Berlin, 1953, p. 907. (Hereafter referred to as *Grundrisse der Kritik der politischen Ökonomie*.)
16. See *Phenomenology*, pp. 99–101.
17. See G. W. F. Hegel, *Science of Logic*, Allen and Unwin, London, 1969, p. 71. (Hereafter referred to as *Science of Logic*.)
18. *Science of Logic*, p. 81.
19. Ibid., p. 73.
20. *Notes on Wagner*, *Texts on Method*, pp. 198–9.
21. *Introduction*, 1857, *Texts on Method*, pp. 72–4.

PART I, CHAPTER 5

1. *Review*, 1859, p. 225.
2. See *Introduction*, 1857, *Texts on Method*, pp. 74–5, 81.
3. Actually it proceeds on three levels. But here we abstract from the fact that Marx also pursues the development of the literature of political economy.
4. This is not a matter of a derivation in the sense of deduction from an axiomatic system, or at least not predominantly so. See below, Part I, Chapter 8.
5. Cf. *Capital*, vol. 1, pp. xxix–xxx.
6. *Introduction*, 1857, *Texts on Method*, p. 73.
7. See *Capital*, vol. 3, p. 87; and *Capital*, vol. 1, Chapter 15 ('Machinery and Modern Industry').
8. See *Grundrisse*, p. 459.
9. Ibid. See also pp. 460–1.
10. See, for example, *Capital*, vol. 3, Chapters 8, 10, 12, 16 and 37.
11. *Introduction*, 1857, *Texts on Method*, p. 81.
12. Sometimes only the narrow sense of the *development* of a particular form, the *becoming* of a particular form, has been ascribed to the term 'genetic'; hence it would be more exact to call the Marxian analysis an analysis of a 'structure-in-process'.

13. See Nicolas Bourbaki (pseudonym of a group of French mathematicians), 'Architektura matematiky', *Pokroky matematiky, fyziky a astronomie*, 5/1960; see also K. Strubecken, 'Einige neuere Entwicklungslinien in der Mathematik', *Scientia*, 1/1970.
14. See the collective volume *Notion de structure et notion de la connaisance*, Paris, 1956.
15. *Introduction*, 1857, *Texts on Method*, p. 73.
16. *A Contribution to the Critique of Political Economy*, pp. 51–2.
17. *Capital*, vol. 1, p. 15.
18. *A Contribution to the Critique of Political Economy*, pp. 64, 100.
19. See *Grundrisse der Kritik der politischen Ökonomie*, p. 880.
20. See *Capital*, vol. 3, pp. 267 ff.
21. When we speak of Marx's analysis as logical and historical, 'logical' is understood in the sense of the specific logical form 'conceptual knowledge', not in the sense of an axiomatic, deductive or inductive derivation.
22. Cf. *Capital*, vol. 1, p. 311; see also *Capital*, vol. 3, pp. 13–14, 177, 242–3; see also *Grundrisse*, p. 710.
23. *Capital*, vol. 3, pp. 287–8.
24. B. A. Grushin, 'Logicheskie i istoricheskie priemui issledovaniya v "Kapitale" Marksa', *Voprosui filosofii*, 4/1955. (Hereafter referred to as Grushin, 'Logicheskie'.) See also V. Ruml, 'Jednota logického a historického v materialistické dialecktice', *Filosofický časopis*, 3/1955; and Otto Morf, *Das Verhältnis von Wirtschaftstheorie und Wirtschaftsgeschichte bei K. Marx*, Basel, 1951; see also Grushin's *Ocherki logiki istoricheskogo issledovaniya*, Moscow, 1961, especially Chapter 7.
25. Grushin, 'Logicheskie', p. 47.
26. Ibid., p. 47.
27. Ibid., p. 48.
28. Ibid.
29. Ibid., p. 49.
30. Ibid., p. 50.
31. Ibid., p. 48.
32. Ibid., pp. 45, 46.
33. See ibid., p. 70.
34. See *Grundrisse*, p. 459.
35. Grushin, 'Logicheskie', p. 48.
36. *Capital*, vol. 1, Chapter 10 ('The Working Day').
37. Ibid., p. 344.
38. Ibid., p. 382.
39. Grushin, 'Logicheskie', p. 48; *Capital*, vol. 1, pp. 123–4.
40. *Capital*, vol. 1, p. 123.
41. See above, p. 40.
42. See Grushin, 'Logicheskie', p. 48.

PART I, CHAPTER 6

1. See below, Part I, Chapter 8.
2. See Wolff, *Philosophia rationalis. Discursus praeliminaris*, §§30, 139; *Logica*, §792.
3. See Immanuel Kant, *Critique of Pure Reason*, trans. N. K. Smith, Macmil-

lan, London, 1933, repr. 1970, pp. 575–6. (Hereafter referred to as *Critique of Pure Reason*.)
4. *Capital*, vol. 1, pp. 16–41.
5. Ibid., p. 15.
6. Cf. ibid., pp. 139–40.
7. Ibid., pp. 15–17.
8. See Karl Marx, *Das Kapital*, vol. 1, Hamburg, 1867, pp. 15, 19. (Hereafter referred to as *Kapital*, 1867.)
9. *Capital*, vol. 1, pp. 31–2.
10. Ibid., pp. 34–5.
11. Ibid., p. 40.
12. Ibid., p. 59; see also *A Contribution to the Critique of Political Economy*, p. 50.
13. See above, Part I, Chapter 3, and below, Part I, Chapter 7.
14. See *Capital*, vol. 1, p. 40.
15. H. Grossman, *Das Akkumulations- und Zusammenbruchsgesetz des kapitalistischen Systems*, Leipzig, 1929, p. vi.
16. *Capital*, vol. 3, pp. 895–6.
17. See *Kapital*, 1867, p. 34; see also *Grundrisse*, p. 310.
18. Marx to Engels, 2 March 1858, in *Selected Correspondence*, p. 105.
19. Friedrich Engels, 'Konspekt über das "Kapital" von Karl Marx. Erster Band' [1868], in Karl Marx and Friedrich Engels, *Werke*, [East] Berlin, 1956 etc., vol. 16, p. 248. (The series is hereafter referred to as *Werke*.)
20. *Capital*, vol. 1, p. 59.
21. Ibid., pp. 60–1.
22. *Grundrisse*, p. 151.
23. *A Contribution to the Critique of Political Economy*, pp. 50–1; see also *Kapital*, 1867, p. 44.
24. *Theories of Surplus Value*, vol. 3, p. 130; see also *Grundrisse*, pp. 146–8.
25. *Capital*, vol. 2, pp. 16–17.
26. See Engels to Marx, 16 June 1867, in *Selected Correspondence*, pp. 186–7; and Marx to Engels, 22 June 1867, ibid., pp. 188–9.
27. See *Kapital* 1867, p. 34; and *Capital*, vol. 1, p. 41.
28. Ibid., pp. 33–4.
29. *A Contribution to the Critique of Political Economy*, pp. 50–1.
30. See ibid., p. 48.
31. Engels to Marx, 16 June 1867, in *Selected Correspondence*, p. 187; and Marx to Kugelmann, 13 October 1866, in *Werke*, vol. 31, p. 534.
32. See Engels to Marx, 16 June 1867, in *Selected Correspondence*, p. 187; and *Capital*, vol. 3, pp. 891 ff.
33. See Marx to Engels, 1 February 1858, in *Selected Correspondence*, p. 101; and Marx to Engels, 25 February 1859, in *Werke*, vol. 29, p. 404; and Marx to Engels, 9 December 1861, in *Werke*, vol. 30, p. 207; see also *Introduction*, 1857, *Texts on Method*, p. 81.
34. *Grundrisse der Kritik der politischen Ökonomie*, p. 945.
35. See above, pp. 36–7.
36. See *Introduction*, 1857, *Texts on Method*, p. 78.
37. *Theories of Surplus Value*, vol. 3, pp. 498–501.
38. See S. B. Tsereteli, 'O prirode svyazi osnovaniya i sledstviya', *Voprosui filosofii*, 1/1957, p. 97.
39. See *Critique of Pure Reason*, pp. 212–13.

40. Hegel's philosophical work is an unbroken polemic with Kant. But Hegel also saw the service Kant had done in dismantling the old mathematical, mechanical natural science (particular in the *Critique of Judgement*, though also in the *Critique of Pure Reason*), even though Kant was still very much of the old school.
41. *Phenomenology*, pp. 67–130.
42. See *Science of Logic*, pp. 48 f.
43. *Phenomenology*, pp. 70–1.
44. *Science of Logic*, pp. 48, 63–4.
45. *Phenomenology*, p. 68.
46. Ibid., p. 72.
47. Ibid., pp. 101–3.
48. *Science of Logic*, pp. 53–4 f.
49. *Phenomenology*, p. 103.
50. Ibid., p. 105.
51. Ibid., p. 111.
52. Ibid., pp. 112–13; see also pp. 111, 117, and *Science of Logic*, pp. 28–9.
53. *Phenomenology*, pp. 137–8.
54. *Capital*, vol. 1, p. xxx.
55. *Introduction*, 1857, *Texts on Method*, pp. 72–3; see also Ilenkov, 'Dialektika'.
56. *Phenomenology*, pp. 107–8, 110.
57. See Karl Marx, *Critique of Hegel's Doctrine of the State*, in *Early Writings*, Penguin, Harmondsworth, 1975, p. 159. (Hereafter referred to as *Critique of Hegel* and *Early Writings*, respectively.)
58. Ibid., p. 109.
59. See above, 'Grushin's interpretation', pp. 42–3.
60. See Grushin, 'Logicheskie', p. 68.
61. Ibid., pp. 51–2.
62. Ibid., p. 52.
63. Ibid., p. 51.
64. *Texts on Method*, p. 36.
65. Marx to Meyer, 30 April 1867, in *Selected Correspondence*, p. 186.
66. *Texts on Method*, p. 35.
67. Karl Marx, *Theories of Surplus Value*, vol. 1, Lawrence and Wishart, London, 1969, p. 345.
68. At this point it is obvious that Marx's conception is critically related to the Hegelian view of the relation between the most developed philosophical systems and the preceding philosophical literature.
69. *Review*, 1868, p. 225.
70. *Grundrisse*, p. 460.
71. Ibid., p. 673.
72. A particular theme, which does not concern us here, is the investigation of the logical character and structure of Marxian historiography.

PART I, CHAPTER 7

1. In particular his article 'Marxovo pojetí vnitřní rozpornosti společenských zákonů, *Filosofický časopis*, 6/1958. (Hereafter referred to as Cibulka, 'Marxovo'.)
2. Il'enkov, 'Dialektika', pp. 87–100 ff.

3. V. Sós, 'Problémy teorie kausality v Marxově "Kapitálu" ', *Filosofický časopis*, 5/1960. (Hereafter referred to as Sós, 'Problémy'.) V. Filkorn, *Úvod do methodologie vied*, Bratislava, 1960, pp. 196 ff., 292 ff., 337 ff. (Hereafter referred to as Filkorn, *Úvod*.) O. Lange, *Ekonomia polityczna*, Warsaw, 1959, pp. 85 ff. (Hereafter referred to as Lange, *Ekonomia*.) L. Tondl, 'Kauzální analýza a kauzální explikace', in Zich, Málek and Tondl, *K metodologii experimentálních věd*, Prague, 1959.

4. Cibulka, 'Marxovo', p. 872.

5. Ibid., p. 900.

6. Ibid., pp. 900–2.

7. Ibid., pp. 872–4.

8. Ibid., p. 888.

9. *Capital*, vol. 3, p. 182.

10. *A Contribution to the Critique of Political Economy*, p. 186. See also *Grundrisse*, pp. 297–8, 870; and *Capital*, vol. 2, pp. 345–6; and see also *Grundrisse*, pp. 130–1.

11. *Grundrisse*, p. 118; see also *Capital*, vol. 2, pp. 501–2; and *Capital*, vol. 3, pp. 494–5.

12. *Capital*, p. 638; and see ibid., p. 649; see also *Grundrisse*, p. 358.

13. *Capital*, vol. 3, p. 807.

14. *Grundrisse*, pp. 122–3.

15. *Grundrisse*, pp. 608–9; see also *Capital*, vol. 3, p. 236.

16. *Capital*, vol. 3, p. 422.

17. Sós, 'Problémy', p. 717.

18. See Galileo Galilei, *Le opere*, Florence, 1929–39, vol. 4, p. 22; vol. 7, pp. 443, 469, 471; vol. 10, p. 248. See also the thesis by Zd. Pokorný, *Determinismus klasické fyziky*, Prague, 1958.

19. Ricardo, *Principles, passim*.

20. Ibid., p. 114.

21. This 'absolute' can only be grasped correctly as the unity of antitheses; relative rest, relative stability is an aspect. Without the presence of these antithetical aspects the 'absolute' character of the self-development breaks up and is transformed into its opposite.

22. Motion in the sense of alteration. If Marx formulates the goal of his investigation as laying bare the 'law of motion' of capitalism, and if for example for Newton the goal is laying bare the laws of motion, then there is obviously an essential difference here.

23. See *Capital*, vol. 3, p. 755; see also *Capital*, vol. 2, p. 144; and *Capital*, vol. 1, p. 635.

24. See *Grundrisse*, p. 358.

25. Ibid., p. 459.

26. *Capital*, vol. 3, p. 237.

27. *Grundrisse*, p. 414.

28. Ibid., p. 459.

29. Ibid., p. 460.

30. See Chapter 6 above.

31. See F. H. Jacobi, *Werke*, 1812 ff., vol. 4, part II, p. 93.

32. See 'Philosophical Notebooks', pp. 160–1.

33. Ibid., pp. 162–3.

34. Ibid., pp. 163–4.

35. See below, pp. 101–2.

36. See B. F. Enriques, *Probleme der Wissenschaft*, vol. 2, Leipzig and Berlin, 1910, pp. 458 ff.
37. *Capital*, vol. 1, pp. xxx–xxxi; *Grundrisse*, pp. 279 ff.
38. Marx to Engels, 22 June 1867, in *Selected Correspondence*, p. 188.
39. *Grundrisse*, p. 519; *Capital*, vol. 1, p. 21.
40. See Cibulka, 'Marxovo', Chapter 1; see also G. Stiehler, *Hegel und der Marxismus über den Widerspruch*, Berlin, 1960.
41. See Cibulka, 'Marxovo', p. 895.
42. See Ricardo, *Principles*, pp. 316–18.
43. Ibid., p. 55.
44. See *Theories of Surplus Value*, vol. 2, p. 507; see ibid., p. 501.
45. See *Capital*, vol. 1, pp. 1–21; *A Contribution to a Critique of Political Economy*, pp. 27–41; *Kapital*, 1867, pp. 1–19. See also *Capital*, vol. 3, p. 249.
46. *Capital*, vol. 1, p. 8.
47. See L. Szánto, 'Dielo, ktoré znamenalo revolúciu vo viede', *Vybrané state*, Bratislava, 1958.
48. *Theories of Surplus Value*, vol. 2, p. 166. See also *Grundrisse*, pp. 596, 754.
49. *Theories of Surplus Value*, vol. 3, pp. 55–6; see also pp. 54–5.
50. Ibid., p. 84.
51. Ibid., pp. 55–6.
52. Ibid., pp. 84–5. See below, p. 84.
53. Ibid., p. 88.
54. Ibid., pp. 501–2.
55. Ibid., pp. 503–4.
56. Ibid., p. 57.
57. With a dialectical identity of antitheses the antithesis itself is retained; there is no 'immediate identity of antitheses', as was mentioned in connection with James Mill, for in that conception the antithesis itself *is missing*.
58. Wolff, *Philosophia rationalis*, §518, §519. See also *Critique of Pure Reason*, pp. 625–6.
59. See *Capital*, vol. 1, p. 608 n. Marx uses the term 'contradiction' in a number of senses, without consistently distinguishing 'contradiction' in a specifically dialectical sense from 'contradiction' in the traditional sense of inconsistent, incongruent, etc. To illustrate, the following uses of the term 'contradiction' in Marx can be cited:
    (a) In the sense of 'inconsistency in thought'. See *Theories of Surplus Value*, vol. 3, pp. 14 ff. In some cases these contradictions or inconsistencies can be the expression of misunderstood dialectical contradictions in a perceived reality, as for example with Ricardo; see *Theories of Surplus Value*, vol. 3, p. 84. Others are simple 'nonsense'; see *Capital*, vol. 3, pp. 779, 816.
    (b) In the sense of non-agreement between the theories of different thinkers ('theoretical contradiction'). See *Theories of Surplus Value*, vol. 3, pp. 84–5.
    (c) In the sense of the interpenetration of opposing forces and of mechanical opposition. See *Capital*, vol. 3, pp. 189–90; and *Grundrisse*, pp. 413 f.
    (d) In the sense of an objective non-agreement of the contradiction, the incongruence of phenomena, for example in capitalism the determination of the value of a commodity through the amount of necessary labour and the effect of the average rate of profit. See

Theories of Surplus Value, vol. 3, pp. 29, 70–1. This contradiction is resolved 'through mediation'. See ibid., pp. 87–9.

(e) In the sense of inner contradiction whose expression can be an external contradiction. See *Capital*, vol. 1, Chapters 1 and 2; and *Capital*, vol. 3, pp. 256–7.

The terms 'contradiction' and 'antithesis' are used interchangeably by Marx. See for example, *Theories of Surplus Value*, vol. 2, pp. 500–1, See also B. A. Grushin, 'Protsess obnaruzheniya protiverechiya obekta', *Voprosui filosofii*, 1/1960; and I. I. Mochalov, 'Ob odnom momente bor'bui protivopolozhnostei', idem, 9/1960. On the concept of 'contradiction' see Fr. Gregoire's *Études hégéliennes*, Louvain, 1958.

60. See *Kapital*, 1867, p. 19.
61. *Grundrisse*, p. 414; see also *Capital*, vol. 1, p. 432; see also *Grundrisse*, pp. 146–7.
62. *Capital*, vol. 1, p. 37; see also ibid., p. 791.
63. See Chapter 9 below.
64. See *A Contribution to a Critique of Political Economy*, pp. 50–1.
65. See *Theories of Surplus Value*, vol. 3, pp. 163–4.
66. *Capital*, vol. 1, p. 494.
67. See Lenin's formulation in *Collected Works*, vol. 4, Foreign Languages Publishing House, Moscow, 1960, p. 61.
68. *Capital*, vol. 1, p. 512.
69. Ibid., p. xvii.
70. Ibid., p. xix.
71. *Werke*, vol. 32, p. 540.
72. See *Theories of Surplus Value*, vol. 3, pp. 160–1.
73. See *Grundrisse*, pp. 146–8.
74. See 'Philosophical Notebooks', pp. 355–63. See also B. S. Ukraintsev, 'Formui dialekticheskogo edinstva v obshchestvennom razvitii', *Voprosui filosofii*, 7/1961.
75. See *Capital*, vol. 1, p. 608.
76. Ibid., pp. xxx–xxxi.
77. Ibid., p. xxxi.
78. See 'Philosophical Notebooks', pp. 359–60.
79. See *Capital*, vol. 1, pp. 76–7.
80. See *Grundrisse*, pp. 405–6; see also *Capital*, vol. 1, p. 494.
81. See *Grundrisse*, pp. 646–7, 705–7; *Capital*, vol. 1, pp. 321–2, 543–4; *Capital*, vol. 3, pp. 355–6; and *Grundrisse*, pp. 541–2.

PART I, CHAPTER 8

1. See K. Schröter, 'Die Tragweite und die Grenzen der axiomatischen Methode', *Deutsche Zeitschrift für Philosophie*, 4/1957; see also P. S. Novikov, *Elementui matematicheskoi logiki*, Moscow, 1959, pp. 11–37. (Hereafter referred to as Novikov, *Elementui*.)
2. See for example I. Butaev, 'Matematika v dialekticheskom analize v "Kapitale" Marska', *Pod znamenem marksizma*, 9–10/1928. See also Lange, *Ekonomia*, pp. 123 ff.
3. *Capital*, vol. 3, p. 49.
4. Ibid., p. 53.

5. Ibid., p. 69.
6. See for example Novikov, *Elementui*, Chapter 5.
7. Ibid., p. 16.
8. Derivation is a process undertaken by the researcher; logical consequence is an objective relation independent of whether any researcher is conscious of it; it is formulated in theory (in the 'derivation').
9. Hilbert and Ackermann, *Osnovui teoreticheskoi logiki*, Moscow, 1947, pp. 247 ff. (Hereafter referred to as Hilbert/Ackermann, *Osnovui*.)
10. The material implication is defined by this truth table:

p	q	$p \rightarrow q$
1	1	1
1	0	0
0	1	1
0	0	1

11. Hilbert/Ackermann, *Osnovui*, p. 249.
12. K. Ajdukiewicz, *Abriss der Logik*, Berlin, 1958, p. 158. [A translation of *Zarys logiki*.] (Hereafter referred to as Ajdukiewicz, *Abriss*.)
13. Ibid., p. 148.
14. Ibid.
15. Beth, *Semantic Entailment*, *passim*.
16. Tarski, 'Folgerung', pp. 1–11.
17. Beth, *Semantic Entailment*, p. 2.
18. Ibid.
19. After the formulation by K. Berka and M. Mleziva, *Co je logika?* Prague, 1962.
20. See A. Tarski, 'Undecidable Theories', in *Studies in Logic and the Foundations of Mathematics*, 1953, p. 6. See also John G. Kemeny, 'A New Approach to Semantics', *Journal of Symbolic Logic*, 1–2/1956.
21. *Capital*, vol. 1, Penguin, p. 94; *Notes on Wagner, Texts on Method*, p. 200.
22. See K. Ajdukiewicz, *Język i poznanie*, vol. 1, Warsaw, 1960, p. 62.
23. I have adopted certain ideas from P. Materna which were formulated in 'Zu Marxens Auffassung der Begründung eines Satzes', prepared by us for the international colloquiuum on methodology in Warsaw in 1961.
24. 'Philosophical Notebooks', pp. 220–2.
25. See A. Grzegorczyk, *Zarys logiki matematycznej*, Warsaw, 1961, p. 91.
26. R. Carnap and W. Stegmüller, *Induktive Logik and Wahrscheinlichkeit*, Vienna, 1958, p. 30. [Based on Carnap's *Logical Foundations of Probability*, Chicago, 1950.] (Hereafter referred to as Carnap/Stegmüller, *Induktive Logik*.)
27. Our critique does not destroy the value of Carnap's investigation of the 'logical implication'. It is directed against Carnap's ordering of his investigations within a more comprehensive view of logical investigation and against his conception of the logical.
28. *Science of Logic*, pp. 33–49. See also *Kapital*, 1867, p. 21; and *Notes on Wagner, Texts on Method*, pp. 205–7.
29. The concept 'form' is generally used in economic analysis in *Capital* in a sense closer to Aristotle than to Kant. With Marx we find 'form' used mainly in the sense of 'specific essence'. Marx distinguishes for example

inner (immanent) and external (contingent, alien) forms (see *Grundrisse*, pp. 359–60) from original and derived 'secondary' forms (see ibid., p. 595).

30. See O. Zich, *Moderní logika*, p. 225.
31. The relativity of the type of logical relations which we have designated 'traditional deductive derivation' is formulated so that the relative independence of the 'theory of logical consequences' is justified.
32. Mathematical proof as the science of deductive systems (in the sense of the modern axiomatic method) can be considered as a small, but relatively well-developed section of the general theory of dialectical materialism as a theory of ontology and logic.
33. The apparent independence of logical procedures and definitions in Ajdukiewicz rests on the fact that these problems are pushed aside and are hidden in the concept of the logical constant and its definition.
34. See O. Zich, *K metodologii experimentalních věd*, Prague, 1960, p. 84.
35. See Carnap/Stegmüller, *Induktive Logik*, p. 8. See also G. H. von Wright, *The Logical Problem of Induction*, Oxford, 1957, pp. 12 f. (Hereafter referred to as Wright, *Induction*.)
36. Wright, *Induction*, p. 172.
37. *Capital*, vol. 1, p. xxix.
38. See *Theories of Surplus Value*, vol. 3, pp. 500–1.
39. See *Capital*, vol. 1, p. 516.
40. René Descartes, *Discourse on Method*, in *The Method, Meditations, and Selections from the Principles*, 16th edn, Blackwood, Edinburgh and London, 1925, pp. 19–20.
41. See above, Chapter 6.
42. See for example Marx to Engels, 31 May 1873, in *Werke*, vol. 33, p. 82.
43. See *Capital*, vol. 1, pp. 3, 76–7.
44. See Marx to Engels, 10 May 1870, in *Werke*, vol. 32, p. 504.
45. See Marx's mathematical manuscripts in the edition by S. A. Yanovskaya, *Matematicheskie rukopisi*, Moscow, 1968.
46. I would say: the concept of reality, if this term did not have for Hegel a specific, narrow meaning.
47. E. Meyerson, *De l'explication dans les sciences*, Paris, 1921, particularly vol. 2, Chapter 40; see also A. Kojève, *Introduction à la lecture de Hegel*, Paris, 1947; and J. Hyppolite, *Genese et structure de la Phenomenologie de Hegel*, Paris, 1947.
48. *Encyclopaedia*, §267.
49. Ibid.
50. Ibid., §270.
51. *Science of Logic*, p. 216.
52. *Encyclopaedia*, §246; see also ibid., §9, §12.

PART I, CHAPTER 9

1. See *Theories of Surplus Value*, vol. 2, pp. 165 ff.
2. See *Capital*, vol. 1 pp. 1–2.
3. See *Kapital*, 1867, pp. 13–15, 766–8; and *Capital*, vol. 1, pp. 17–18.
4. See *Capital*, vol. 3, p. 25; and Marx to Engels, 27 June 1867, in *Selected Correspondence*, pp. 190–1.
5. See *Capital*, vol. 2, p. 25.
6. *Capital*, vol. 1, pp. xvi–xvii.

7. *Theories of Surplus Value*, vol. 2, pp. 166 ff.
8. *Capital*, vol. 1, p. 156.
9. Ibid., p. 88.
10. Ibid., pp. 135–7; see also *Grundrisse der Kritik der politischen Ökonomie*, pp. 880 f.
11. See *Grundrisse*, p. 310; see also *Capital*, vol. 3, p. 110; and *Grundrisse*, pp. 450, 649, 850–1.
12. See Marx to Engels, 24 August 1867, in *Selected Correspondence*, pp. 192–3; see also *Capital*, vol. 1, p. 315; *Capital*, vol. 3, pp. 47–8, 51; *Theories of Surplus Value*, vol. 2, pp. 215–16, 373 ff.
13. *Theories of Surplus Value*, vol. 2, pp. 105–6, 174; see also *Capital*, vol. 1, p. 576; *Capital*, vol. 2, pp. 461–2; *Capital*, vol. 3, pp. 624–5; and *Capital*, vol. 1, pp. 125–6; and *Capital*, vol. 2, p. 25.
14. Marx to Engels, 27 June 1867, in *Selected Correspondence*, pp. 190–1.
15. D. P. Gorsky, *O sposobakh obobshcheniya i abstragirovaniya*, Moscow, 1961.

PART I, CHAPTER 10

1. See E. de Condillac, *La Logique*, Paris, 1780, vol. 1, Chapter 2, §6, and vol. 2, Chapter 6, §50.
2. M. K. Mamardashvili, 'Protsessui analiza i synteza', *Voprosui filosofii*, 2/1958.
3. Ibid., p. 58.
4. Ibid.
5. Ibid., p. 59.
6. *Encyclopaedia*, §§227, 228, 238, 239.
7. Aristotle, *Nicomachean Ethics*, 1095a. See also C. Prantl, *Geschichte der Logik im Abendlande*, vol. 2, Leipzig, 1927, pp. 322–3.
8. In modern conceptions the axiomatic method abandons these distinctions and uses different forms of analytical procedure.
9. See I. Kant, *Prolegomena to any future Metaphysics*, §5.
10. Ibid., vol. 3, p. 33.
11. *Science of Logic*, pp. 456–69.
12. Ibid.; see also G. W. F. Hegel, *Werke*, ed. H. Glockner, 3rd edn, vol. 8, Stuttgart, 1955, pp. 449–50.
13. Hegel, *Werke*, ed. Glockner, vol. 8, pp. 441 f.; see also J. G. Fichte, *Werke*, ed. F. Medicus, vol. 3, p. 33. (Hereafter referred to as Fichte, *Werke*.)
14. See Hegel, *Werke*, ed. Glockner, vol. 8, p. 449.
15. See *Theories of Surplus Value*, vol. 3, pp. 501–2; see also *Notes on Wagner, Texts on Method*, pp. 198–9.
16. *Capital*, vol. 2, pp. 99–100, 396.
17. This question becomes still more complicated if we remember that, apart from the different sorts of whole in the actual structure of capitalism, it is necessary to distinguish different sorts of wholes in a dialectical-materialist 'intellectual reproduction of reality' for capitalism. At different stages of the 'intellectual reproduction of reality' under particular abstract presuppositions (and other presuppositions) we encounter 'wholes' and 'unities' which are the mirror image of particular totalities and unities of capitalist reality and are distinct from the real, 'primary' totalities whose image they are.
18. See René Descartes, *Discourse on Method*, part two, rule three; and G. W.

Leibniz, *Nouveaux essays*, in *Die philosophischen Schriften*, ed. C. J. Gerhardt, vol. 5, Berlin, 1882, part 4, Chapter 2. See also Ajdukiewicz, *Logik*, p. 192.
19. See R. O. Gropp, *Zu Fragen der Geschichte der Philosophie and des dialektischen Materialismus*, Berlin, 1958, pp. 14 f.
20. See above, p. 103.

PART I, CHAPTER 11

1. See for example S. Yanovskaya's attempt 'O tak nazuivaemuikh "opredeleniyakh cherez abstraktsiyu"', in *Pod znamenem marksizma*, 4/1935.

PART II, CHAPTER 12

1. Karl Marx, *Economic and Philosophical Manuscripts*, in *Early Writings*, pp. 279–400. (Hereafter referred to as *Manuscripts*, 1844.)
2. Ibid., p. 379.
3. *The German Ideology*, p. 24.
4. *Manuscripts*, 1844, pp. 381–2.
5. Ibid., p. 382.
6. Ibid., p. 358.
7. Ibid., p. 357.
8. Ibid., p. 348.
9. Ibid., p. 386.
10. Ibid., p. 344.
11. Ibid.
12. Ibid., p. 349.
13. See Hegel's *Erste Druckschriften*, ed. G. Lasson, Leipzig, 1928, p. 14.
14. *Manuscripts*, 1844, p. 386.
15. Ibid.
16. Ibid.
17. See *Encyclopaedia*, §13.
18. See L. Feuerbach, *Das Wesen des Christentums*, Berlin, 1956, pp. 39, 75. (Hereafter referred to as *Das Wesen des Christentums*.)
19. *Manuscripts* 1844, p. 386.
20. Ibid., pp. 353–4.
21. Ibid., p. 384.
22. Ibid., p. 324.
23. Ibid., p. 386.
24. Ibid., p. 281.
25. See Hegel, *Werke*, ed. Glockner, vol. 8, pp. 94 ff.
26. *Manuscripts*, 1844, p. 381.
27. Ibid.
28. Ibid., p. 386.
29. Cf. Ibid., p. 384.
30. Ibid.
31. Ibid., p. 385.
32. Ibid.
33. Ibid.
34. Ibid., p. 386.
35. Cf. Ibid., p. 392.

36. Ibid., p. 386.
37. Ibid., p. 393.
38. Ibid., p. 386.
39. Ibid.
40. Ibid., p. 379.
41. Ibid., pp. 379, 382–3.
42. Ibid., pp. 382–3.
43. Ibid., p. 388.
44. L. Feuerbach, *Zur Kritik der Hegelschen Philosophie*, Berlin, 1955, p. 48. (Hereafter referred to as *Zur Kritik der Hegelschen Philosophie*.)
45. Ibid., p. 390.
46. See *Das Wesen des Christentums*, p. 54.
47. *Manuscripts*, 1844, p. 389.
48. Ibid.
49. See *Das Wesen des Christentums*, pp. 39–40.
50. See ibid., pp. 39, 269; see also *Zur Kritik der Hegelschen Philosophie*, pp. 136, 144.
51. See *Das Wesen des Christentums*, p. 96.
52. *Manuscripts*, 1844, p. 396.
53. Ibid., p. 395.
54. See *Das Wesen des Christentums*, pp. 34–6, 40; and *Manuscripts*, 1844, pp. 328–9, 390–1.
55. *Manuscripts*, 1844, p. 384.
56. Ibid.
57. Karl Marx and Friedrich Engels, *Gesamtausgabe*, ed. D. Ryazanov *et al.*, Frankfurt, Berlin, Moscow, and Leningrad, Series I, vol. 3, p. 154. (Hereafter referred to as MEGA.)
58. Cf. *Manuscripts*, 1844, pp. 392–5.
59. Ibid., pp. 396–7.
60. Ibid., pp. 387, 392, 396–7.
61. Ibid., pp. 396–7.
62. Cf. Ibid., pp. 395–6.
63. See *The German Ideology*, p. 671.
64. Ibid., p. 548.
65. Ibid.
66. Ibid., p. 29.
67. Karl Marx, *Theses on Feuerbach*, in *German Ideology*, p. 660. (Hereafter referred to as *Theses on Feuerbach*.)
68. *German Ideology*, pp. 101–2, 163, 210.
69. Ibid., p. 259.
70. *Critique of Pure Reason*, pp. 129, 160 ff.
71. *Manuscripts*, 1844, p. 384.

PART II, CHAPTER 13

1. Karl Marx and Frederick Engels, *The Holy Family, or Critique of Critical Criticism*, 2nd edn, Progress, Moscow, 1975, p. 11. (Hereafter referred to as *The Holy Family*.)
2. Ibid., pp. 225–6.
3. Ibid.
4. Ibid.

5. Ibid., p. 226.
6. Ibid., p. 227.
7. Ibid., p. 166.
8. Ibid., p. 100.
9. Ibid., p. 166.
10. Ibid., p. 164.
11. Ibid., pp. 68–9.
12. See Marx's doctoral dissertation, in Karl Marx and Frederick Engels, *Collected Works*, Lawrence & Wishart, London, 1975 ff, vol. 1, pp. 29–30. (Hereafter referred to as *Collected Works* and *Dissertation*, respectively.)
13. *The German Ideology*, p. 668.
14. See *The Holy Family*, pp. 72, 97–8.
15. Ibid., p. 164.
16. *The German Ideology*, pp. 101, 284 ff.

PART II, CHAPTER 14

1. See above, pp. 130 ff.
2. See *The German Ideology*, pp. 43–6.
3. Ibid., pp. 164–5.
4. Ibid., p. 190.
5. See Marx to Ruge, 13 March 1843, in *Werke*, vol. 27, p. 417.
6. 'Letters from the *Franco-German Yearbooks*', in *Early Writings*, p. 207. (Hereafter referred to as 'Letters'.)
7. Ibid., p. 208.
8. Ibid., p. 209.
9. Ibid., p. 208.
10. Ibid., p. 209.
11. *Critique of Hegel, Introduction*, pp. 243–4.
12. Ibid., p. 244.
13. Ibid., pp. 244–5, 251.
14. Ibid., *passim*; see also *Zur Kritik der Hegelschen Philosophie*, pp. 53, 70; and *Das Wesen des Christentums*, pp. 61, 70, 118.
15. *Critique of Hegel*, pp. 158–9.
16. In the *Deutsch-Französische Jahrbücher* and throughout the article 'On the Jewish Question' the boundaries of the programmatic conception of the critique are over-ridden, since religious and political 'dehumanization' are displaced by the more fundamental *economic* alienation.
17. *The German Ideology*, pp. 43–5.
18. Ibid., pp. 45–6.
19. Ibid., pp. 82–5.
20. Ibid., p. 86.
21. See *Das Wesen des Christentums*, p. 6.
22. *Manuscripts*, 1844, p. 312.
23. Ibid., pp. 367–8.
24. 'Letters', p. 208.
25. *Critique of Hegel*, p. 89; see also *Manuscripts*, 1844, p. 333, and MEGA, Series I, vol. 3, p. 545.
26. *The German Ideology*, p. 51, etc.
27. *Manuscripts*, 1844, p. 348.
28. *The German Ideology*, pp. 540–1.

29. Ibid., p. 38.
30. Karl Marx, *Poverty of Philosophy*, Progress, Moscow, 1976, p. 110. (Hereafter referred to as *Poverty of Philosophy*.)
31. See *Vorläufige Thesen*, in *Zur Kritik der Hegelschen Philosophie*, pp. 73, 84, 85, 86; *Grundsätze der Philosophie der Zukunft*, in *idem*, pp. 123, 166; and *Das Wesen des Christentums*, p. 17.
32. Hegel, *Werke* ed. Glockner, vol. 6, p. 38.
33. Moses Hess, *Philosophische und sozialistische Schriften*, Berlin, 1961, p. 384.
34. See *The German Ideology*, p. 260.
35. Ibid., p. 38.
36. Ibid., p. 259.
37. See *Dissertation*, pp. 84–5; and *Collected Works*, vol. 1, pp. 195–6.
38. See above, pp. 139–40.
39. *Critique of Hegel*, p. 250.
40. Ibid.
41. Ibid., pp. 250–1.
42. Ibid., p. 251.
43. Ibid., p. 257.
44. See *Zur Kritik der Hegelschen Philosophie*, p. 123; see also *Critique of Hegel*, p. 250.
45. *Manuscripts*, 1844, p. 381.
46. *Zur Kritik der Hegelschen Philosophie*, pp. 85–9, 93, 147, 149, 160, 166.
47. *The Holy Family*, p. 11.
48. *Theses on Feuerbach*, p. 661.
49. *The German Ideology*, p. 38.
50. See Marx to Engels, 19 November 1844, and 20 January 1845, in *Selected Correspondence*, pp. 23–4, 25–7.
51. See Stirner's 'Das unwahre Prinzip unserer Erziehung oder der Humanismus und Realismus' in the *Rheinische Zeitung* (April 1842), in Max Stirner, *Kleinere Schriften*, ed. von Mackay, Berlin, 1898.
52. See above, p. 143.
53. *Zur Kritik der Hegelschen Philosophie*, p. 123.
54. Max Stirner, *Der Einzige und sein Eigentum*, 2nd edn, Leipzig, 1882, p. 50. (Hereafter referred to as Stirner, *Der Einzige*.)
55. Ibid., pp. 34–5, 59–60, 179.
56. Ibid., p. 97.
57. Ibid., p. 98.
58. Ibid., p. 108.
59. Ibid., p. 99.
60. Ibid., p. 351.
61. Ibid., p. 373; see also p. 186.
62. Ibid., pp. 127, 257.
63. Ibid., p. 155.
64. Ibid., pp. 121–2.
65. Ibid., p. 264.
66. Ibid., p. 280.
67. Ibid., pp. 125–6.
68. Ibid., p. 280.
69. Ibid., p. 179.
70. *The German Ideology*, pp. 258–9.
71. Ibid., p. 260.

72. Stirner, *Der Einzige*, p. 35.
73. *The German Ideology*, pp. 137–8.
74. Ibid.
75. Ibid., pp. 136–7.
76. Stirner, *Der Einzige*, p. 33.
77. *The German Ideology*, pp. 134–5.
78. Ibid., p. 134.
79. Ibid.
80. Stirner, *Der Einzige*, p. 15.
81. *The German Ideology*, pp. 143–4.
82. Ibid., p. 405.
83. *Critique of Hegel*, p. 98.
84. Ibid., pp. 77–8.
85. *Manuscripts*, 1844, p. 350.
86. *The Holy Family*, p. 28.
87. Ibid., p. 226; see also *The German Ideology*, pp. 101–2.
88. Ibid., pp. 514–15.
89. Ibid., pp. 45–6, 88–9; see also *Grundrisse*, pp. 704–6.
90. *Grundrisse*, pp. 491–2.
91. See Marx to Annenkov, 28 December 1846, in *Werke*, vol. 4, pp. 547–57. See also *The German Ideology*, pp. 272–3.
92. *The German Ideology*, pp. 493–4.
93. *Grundrisse*, pp. 196–7.
94. *The German Ideology*, pp. 494–5.
95. Ibid., pp. 81–7.
96. Ibid., p. 495.
97. Ibid., pp. 233–4.
98. Ibid., pp. 86–7. See also *Poverty of Philosophy*, pp. 134–5.
99. Ibid., p. 153.
100. Ibid., p. 144.
101. Ibid., pp. 461–2.
102. Ibid., p. 367.
103. Ibid., p. 291.
104. Ibid., pp. 315–16.
105. Ibid.
106. Ibid., p. 290, and see also pp. 275–6.
107. Ibid., pp. 259–60.
108. See *Das Wesen des Christentums*, pp. 22, 26, 287; and *idem, Kleine philosophische Schriften*, Leipzig, 1950, pp. 42, 183.
109. *The German Ideology*, p. 270.
110. Ibid., p. 38, and see also pp. 188–9.
111. See *Capital*, vol. 1, p. 367 n.
112. *The Holy Family*, pp. 67–8; see above, pp. 140–1.
113. *The German Ideology*, p. 101.
114. *The Holy Family*, p. 68.
115. Ibid., p. 71.
116. Bruno Bauer, *Die Posaune des jüngsten Gerichts über Hegel den Atheisten und Antichristen. Ein Ultimatum*, Leipzig, 1841, pp. 50, 63. (Hereafter referred to as Bauer, *Posaune*.) See also MEGA. Series I, vol. 1/1, p. 103.
117. Bauer, *Posaune*, p. 53.
118. See ibid., p. 69.

119. Ibid., p. 65; see also *Werke*, vol. 1, p. 436.
120. Bauer, *Posaune*, p. 70.
121. See Bruno Bauer, *Das endeckte Christentum*, Barnikols edn, Leipzig, 1927, p. 155. (Hereafter referred to as Bauer, *Christentum*.)
122. Bauer, *Posaune*, p. 177.
123. Hegel, *Werke*, ed. Glockner, 3rd edn, vol. 19, Stuttgart, 1959, pp. 374, 376.
124. Ibid., p. 379.
125. Ibid., p. 375; see also *Science of Logic*, pp. 536–7.
126. Hegel, *Werke*, ed. Glockner, vol. 19, p. 370.
127. *Science of Logic*, pp. 538–9.
128. Ibid., pp. 580–1.
129. Hegel, *Werke*, ed. Glockner, vol. 19, p. 375.
130. See the introduction to the first edition.
131. See Hegel, *Werke*, ed. Glockner, vol. 19, p. 665.
132. *Zur Kritik der Hegelschen Philosophie*, p. 70.
133. *The Holy Family*, p. 164.
134. Ibid., p. 167.
135. Bauer, *Christentum*, p. 162.
136. See *The German Ideology*, p. 102; and *The Holy Family*, pp. 130–1.
137. *The German Ideology*, p. 102; and see also ibid., pp. 258–60.
138. Ibid., pp. 58–9.
139. Ibid., p. 101.
140. Ibid., pp. 104–5.
141. In Moses Hess, *Philosophische und sozialistische Schriften 1837–1850*, eds A. Cornu and W. Mönke, Berlin, 1961, pp. 197–320. (Hereafter referred to as Hess, *Schriften*.)
142. See *Manuscripts*, 1844, pp. 281–2; and MEGA, Series I, vol. 3, p. 34.
143. *The German Ideology*, pp. 551–3. See also Hess, *Schriften*, pp. 281–307, 311–26, 329–48.
144. *The German Ideology*, p. 514.
145. Ibid., pp. 514–15.
146. Hess, *Schriften*, pp. 77 ff.
147. Ibid., pp. 77, 82–3, 86.
148. Ibid., pp. 85–6, 89.
149. Ibid., pp. 82–6, 89; see also ibid., p. 79.
150. Ibid., pp. 80–4.
151. Ibid., p. 78.
152. Ibid., pp. 79–80.
153. Ibid., p. 169.
154. Ibid., p. 170.
155. Ibid., p. 198.
156. Ibid., p. 199.
157. Ibid., pp. 198, 199, 200, 201, 202.
158. Ibid., p. 200.
159. Ibid., p. 202.
160. Ibid., p. 198.
161. Ibid., p. 204.
162. Ibid., pp. 204, 206.
163. Ibid., p. 210.
164. Ibid., p. 212.
165. Ibid., p. 219.

166. See ibid., p. 213.
167. Ibid., p. 221.
168. See F. H. Jacobi, *Werke*, 1812 ff, vol. 4, pp. 26, 223. (Hereafter referred to as Jacobi, *Werke*.)
169. Hess, *Schriften*, pp. 220, 325, 363.
170. See ibid., pp. 201, 206; and see also ibid., p. 202. See also *Werke*, vol. 1, p. 483.
171. Benedict de Spinoza, *The Ethics*, in *The Chief Works*, trans. R. H. M. Elwes, Bell, London, 1884, vol. 2, p. 46. (Hereafter referred to as Spinoza, *Ethics*.)
172. Ibid., p. 242.
173. Ibid., p. 253.
174. See Hess, *Schriften*, p. 325.
175. Spinoza, *Ethics*, Propositions xxix/ xxxii/ xxxiii.
176. See Hess, *Schriften*, pp. 213 ff.
177. See ibid., pp. 212–13.
178. See ibid., pp. 213, 216.
179. See ibid., pp. 215, 216 ff.
180. See ibid., pp. 334–5.
181. See ibid., p. xlvi.
182. Ibid., p. 293.
183. Ibid.
184. See ibid., p. 293.
185. Ibid.
186. See ibid., p. 295; see also ibid., pp. 287, 294.
187. Ibid., p. 287.
188. Ibid., p. 288.
189. Ibid.
190. Ibid., pp. 288–9.
191. Ibid.
192. See *Werke*, vol. 1, p. 494.
193. See *Collected Works*, vol. 1, p. 183.
194. See Marx to Feuerbach, 11 August 1844, in *Probleme des Friedens und des Sozialismus*, 2/1958.
195. Hess, *Schriften*, p. 214.
196. Ibid., pp. 187 ff.
197. Ibid.
198. See ibid., pp. 334, 349.
199. See for example ibid., pp. 420, 439, 442.
200. Arnold Ruge, *Werke*, 3rd edn, Leipzig, 1850, vol. 6, pp. 1–134. (Hereafter referred to as Ruge, *Werke*.)
201. Ibid., p. 5.
202. Ibid., p. 4.
203. Ibid., p. 17.
204. Ibid., p. 19.
205. Ibid., p. 27.
206. Ibid., p. 31; see also ibid., pp. 122–3.
207. Ibid., pp. 29–33.
208. Ibid., pp. 31–2; see also ibid., vol. 4, p. 49.
209. Ibid., p. 32.
210. Ibid., p. 29.

211. Ibid., pp. 23–4.
212. Ibid., p. 34.
213. Ibid., p. 36.
214. Ibid., p. 33.
215. See ibid., p. 41.
216. See ibid., vol. 2, pp. 288, 290; vol. 4, pp. 397–433; vol. 4, pp. 254–97; vol. 4, pp. 246–53; vol. 2, pp. 287–8.
217. Ibid., vol. 2, p. 291; see also ibid., vol. 4, pp. 407, 413.
218. Ibid., vol. 4, p. 404; see also ibid., p. 273.
219. Ibid., p. 47.
220. Ibid., p. 49.
221. See ibid., vol. 2, pp. 316–17.
222. See ibid., vol. 6, pp. 364, 367, 374.
223. See ibid., p. 57; vol. 4, pp. 56, 77.
224. Ibid., vol. 6, p. 355.
225. See ibid., vol. 4, p. 248.
226. See ibid., vol. 6, p. 134.
227. Ibid., p. 65.

PART II, CHAPTER 15

1. *Poverty of Philosophy*, pp. 91–3.
2. Ibid., pp. 92–3.
3. Ibid., pp. 94–5.
4. Ibid.
5. Ibid., pp. 93–4.
6. Ibid.; see also ibid., pp. 101–3.
7. See above, pp. 138–9.
8. *Poverty of Philosophy*, p. 100; see also Marx to Annenkov, December 1846, in *Selected Correspondence*, p. 36.
9. *Poverty of Philosophy*, p. 101.
10. Ibid., pp. 95–6; see also Marx to Annenkov, December 1846, in *Selected Correspondence*, p. 35.
11. Karl Marx, *The Eighteenth Brumaire of Louis Bonaparte*, in Karl Marx and Frederick Engels, *Selected Works* in one volume, Lawrence and Wishart, London, 1973, p. 96. (Hereafter referred to as *Selected Works*.)
12. See above, Part II, Chapter 14.
13. *Poverty of Philosophy*, p. 100.
14. Marx to *Otechestvennie Zapiski*, November 1877, in *Selected Correspondence*, p. 313.
15. *Poverty of Philosophy*, pp. 92–3.

PART II, CHAPTER 16

1. See *Dissertation*, pp. 30–1.
2. See Hegel, *Werke*, ed. H. Glockner, 3rd edn, vol. 6, Stuttgart, 1956, §35.
3. *Dissertation*, pp. 52–3.
4. See Hegel's exposition in the *Phenomenology* on the classical philosophy of self-consciousness.
5. Hegel, *Werke*, ed. Glockner, 3rd edn, vol. 18, Stuttgart, 1959, p. 498.

6. Ibid., p. 500.
7. *Dissertation*, pp. 72–3.
8. Ibid., pp. 35–6; *Collected Works*, vol. 1, pp. 113–14, 144, 307; see also MEGA, Series I, vol. 1/1, pp. 131, 133.
9. *Dissertation*, pp. 36–7, 42; and MEGA, Series I, vol 1/1, p. 122.
10. *Dissertation*, pp. 42, 52–3, 65–6, and MEGA, Series I, vol. 1/1, p. 92.
11. *Dissertation*, pp. 29–30.
12. MEGA, Series I, vol. 1/1, p. 175.
13. *Zur Kritik der Hegelschen Philosophie*, p. 70.
14. *Critique of Hegel*, pp. 61–2.
15. Ibid., pp. 64–6; see also ibid., pp. 84–5, 98–9.
16. Ibid., pp. 61–2.
17. Ibid., pp. 87–8.
18. Ibid., pp. 150–1.
19. Ibid., pp. 116–17 ff.
20. Ibid., p. 100.
21. Ibid., pp. 69–70.
22. *Dissertation*, p. 43.
23. *Critique of Hegel*, pp. 143–4.
24. Ibid., p. 87–8.
25. See ibid., pp. 69–70 ff.
26. See for example, *Werke*, vol. 29, pp. 260, 274; vol. 30, p. 207; vol. 31, pp. 234, 306; vol. 32, p. 52; and *Selected Correspondence*, pp. 123–4, 199–200, 240.
27. *The German Ideology*, p. 259.
28. Karl Marx, Preface to *A Contribution to the Critique of Political Economy*, in *Selected Works*, pp. 182–3.
29. See *Early Writings*, p. 244.
30. See J. Habermas, *Theorie und Praxis*, Neuwied, 1963, p. 288.
31. See G. Lukács, 'Die philosophische Entwicklung des jungen Marx (1840–1844)', *Deutsche Zeitschrift für Philosophie*, 2/1954, p. 288. (Hereafter referred to as Lukács, 'Marx (1840–4.)'
32. K. Löwith, *Von Hegel zu Neitzsche. Der revolutionäre Bruch im Denken des neunzehnten Jahrhunderts*, 5th edn, Stuttgart, 1964, p. 295.
33. Ibid., p. 120.
34. J.-Y. Calvez, *La pensée de Karl Marx*, Paris, 1956.
35. Ibid., p. 36.
36. Ibid., pp. 121–2, 320, 338–45.
37. Ibid., p. 122.
38. H. Popitz, *Der entfremdete Mensch*, Basel, 1953.
39. Ibid., p. 69.
40. Ibid., p. 113.
41. Ibid., p. 115.
42. Ibid., p. 3.
43. Ibid.
44. Ibid., pp. 12–13.
45. Ibid., p. 21.
46. G. Lukács, *Der junge Hegel und die Probleme der kapitalistischen Gesellschaft*, Berlin, 1954, pp. 622–39. (Hereafter referred to as Lukács, *Hegel*.) Lukács, 'Marx (1840–4)', pp. 288–343.
47. Lukács, 'Marx (1840–4)', p. 331.

48. Lukács, *Hegel*, pp. 623–4.
49. Ibid., p. 624.
50. Ibid., pp. 623–4.
51. Ibid., p. 623.
52. Ibid., p. 627.
53. See Lukács, 'Marx (1840–4)', pp. 335–6.
54. Ibid., p. 339.
55. Lukács, *Hegel*, p. 636.
56. A. Cornu, *Karl Marx und Friedrich Engels*, Berlin, 1962, vol. 2, p. 204.
57. J. Hyppolite, *Étude sur Marx et Hegel*, Paris, 1955, p. 172.
58. H. Lefebvre, *Le Matérialisme dialectique*, Paris, 1949, pp. 62–3.
59. See ibid.
60. L. Althusser, *Pour Marx*, Paris, 1965; *idem*, *Lire le Capital*, Paris, 1966. (Hereafter referred to as Althusser, *Marx*, and Althusser, *Capital*, respectively.)
61. Althusser, *Marx*, pp. 233, 235–6.
62. See above, Part II, Chapter 15.
63. Althusser, *Marx*, p. 225.
64. *Notes on Wagner*, *Texts on Method*, p. 201.
65. *Introduction*, 1857, *Texts on Method*, p. 47.

PART II, CHAPTER 17

1. *Werke*, vol. 29, p. 260.
2. See *Introduction*, 1857, *Texts on Method*, pp. 73–82; and see also Hegel's *Philosophy of Right*, §31, §32.
3. See Hegel, *Werke*, ed. Glockner, vol. 6, §35; and see also *Introduction*, 1857, *Texts on Method*, p. 73.
4. See R. Richta *et al.*, *Civilizace na rozcesti*, Prague, 1966.

PART III, CHAPTER 18

1. Cf. *Theses on Feuerbach*, p. 661.
2. *The German Ideology*, pp. 38–9.
3. R. Kroner, *Von Kant bis Hegel*, 2nd edn, Tübingen, 1961, p. 6.
4. *Theses on Feuerbach*, p. 659.
5. See G. Lukács, *Geschichte und Klassenbewusstsein*, Berlin, 1923, pp. 28, 160.
6. *The German Ideology*, pp. 58–9.
7. Ibid., pp. 50–1.
8. *Theses on Feuerbach*, p. 666; see also *The German Ideology*, pp. 233–4.
9. Ibid., p. 59.
10. See Karl Marx and Frederick Engels, *Communist Manifesto*, in *Selected Works*, pp. 47–8.
11. *Zur Kritik der Hegelschen Philosophie*, p. 84.
12. *The German Ideology*, pp. 288–90.
13. *Capital*, vol. 1, p. 157.
14. See *The German Ideology*, pp. 41–2 f., 670.
15. Ibid., pp. 38–9.
16. *Zur Kritik der Hegelschen Philosophie*, pp. 96 ff.
17. Immanuel Kant, *Critique of Practical Reason*, trans. T. K. Abbott, 6th edn, London, 1909, p. 87. (Hereafter referred to as *Critique of Practical Reason*.)

18. *The German Ideology*, p. 101.
19. Hegel, *Werke*, ed. H. Glockner, 3rd edn, vol. 1, Stuttgart, 1958, p. 291.
20. Cf. *The German Ideology*, p. 577.

PART III, CHAPTER 19

1. Fichte, *Werke*, vol. 2, p. 27; vol. 3, p. 15.
2. Ibid., vol. 2, p. 406.
3. See ibid., p. 5; and vol. 3, p. 24.
4. Ibid., vol. 3, p. 26.
5. Ibid., p. 27.
6. Ibid., vol. 3, p. 24.
7. Kant, *Werke*, vol. 4, Berlin, 1903, p. 391.
8. Ibid., pp. 396 ff.
9. Ibid., p. 412.
10. Kant, *Werke*, ed. E. Cassirer, vol. 6, Berlin, 1923, p. 460.
11. Ibid., vol. 7, p. 161.
12. *Critique of Pure Reason*, p. 632.
13. Kant, *Werke*, ed. Cassirer, vol. 7, Berlin, 1922, pp. 18, 456.
14. Ibid., vol. 7, p. 302.
15. Idem, *Werke*, ed. Cassirer, vol. 6, p. 357.
16. Ibid., p. 395.
17. *Critique of Practical Reason*, p. 105.
18. *Critique of Pure Reason*, pp. 635–6.
19. Fichte, *Werke*, vol. 1, p. 290; see also vol. 2, p. 28.
20. Ibid., vol. 2, p. 451.
21. Ibid., pp. 451–2.
22. Ibid., p. 21; see also vol. 1, p. 296.
23. Ibid., vol. 1, pp. 296, 299, 325, 328, 330, 332, 346, 379, 399, 419.
24. See M. Sobotka, *Člověk a práce v německé klasické filosofie*, Prague, 1964, pp. 61 ff.
25. Fichte, *Werke*, vol. 2, p. 22.
26. Ibid., p. 23.
27. Ibid., p. 25.
28. Ibid., vol. 1, p. 226.
29. Ibid., p. 227.
30. Ibid., p. 213; see also ibid., pp. 317, 321, 411, 478, 486, 511; and see vol. 2, p. 397.
31. Ibid., pp. 56–7.
32. The primacy of the extra-rational here – as Fichte says – means the primacy of 'will and desire'. This is not, as in Pascal, the primacy of passive, timid religious feeling.

PART III, CHAPTER 20

1. See F. W. J. Schelling, *System des tranzendentalen Idealismus*, Tübingen, 1800, p. 417.
2. Ibid., pp. 246, 296.
3. Ibid., pp. 324–5.
4. Ibid., p. 327.
5. See Fichte, *Werke*, vol. 2, pp. 451, 453.

6. Hegel, *Werke*, ed. Lasson, 2nd edn, vol. 7, Leipzig, 1923, p. 331.
7. Ibid., p. 361.
8. Ibid., vol. 3, pp. 25, 34, 38; vol. 7, §4.
9. See *The German Ideology*, p. 507.
10. When we recognize the merely apparent anti-dogmatism of ontologizing Marx's theory of commodity fetishism and making it absolute, then we see that these theoretical efforts are a superseded phase, even if they are important for the destruction of dogmatic conceptions in other areas.

Bibliography

Adorno, T. W. *Drei Studien zu Hegel*. Frankfurt, 1963.

Alekseev, M. N. *Dialekticheskaya logika*. Moscow, 1960.

Althusser, L. *Pour Marx*. Paris, 1965. See also the discussion in *La Nouvelle Critique*, nos. 165 ff., and *Les Temps Modernes*, no. 240, May 1966.

——. 'Du "Capital" à la philosophie de Marx', in *Lire le Capital*, vol. 1. Paris, 1966.

Badaloni, N. *Marxismo come storicismo*. Milan, 1962.

Baer, R. *Hegel und die Mathematik; Verhandlungen des 2. Hegel-Kongresses*. Tübingen, 1932.

Bakuradze, O. M. *K voprosu o formirovanii filosofskikh vzglyadov K. Marksa*. Tblisi, 1956.

Balibar, E. 'Sur les concepts fondamentaux du matérialisme historique', in *Lire le Capital*, vol. 2. Paris, 1966.

Barbon, A. 'La dialectique du "Capital" ', *Revue Internationale*, September 1946.

Barion, J. *Hegel und die marxistische Staatslehre*. Bonn, 1963.

Bartoš, J. 'Pojem "náhoda" u Hegela a u zakladatelů marixsmu', *Sborník prací filosofické fakulty brněnské university, rada sociálně-vědná*, 3/1959.

Bauer, O. 'Die Geschichte eines Buches', *Neue Zeit*, 1907–1908, I.

Bednář, J. 'Hegelova kritika "bürgerliche Gesellschaft" ve Fenomenologii ducha a ve Filosofii práva', *Filosofický časopis*, 4/1964.

Bekker, K. *Marx' philosophische Entwicklung, sein Verhältnis zu Hegel*. Zürich and New York, 1940.

Berka, K. and Mleziva, M. *Co je logika?* Prague, 1962.

Beth, E. W. *Semantic Entailment and Formal Derivability*. Amsterdam, 1955.

——. *The Foundations of Mathematics, A Study in the Philosophy of Science*, Amsterdam, 1959.

Beyer, W. R. *Hegel-Bilder. Kritik der Hegel-Deutungen*. Berlin, 1964.

——. 'Hegels Begriff der Praxis', *Deutsche Zeitschrift für Philosophie*, 5/1958.

Bigo, P. *Marxisme et humanisme*. Paris, 1953.

Bollhagen, P. 'Die Spezifik der Einheit des Logischen und Historischen in der Geschichtswissenschaft', *Deutsche Zeitschrift für Philosophie*, 1/1964.

——. *Soziologie und Geschichte*. Berlin, 1966.

Bonnel, P. 'Hegel et Marx', *La Revue socialiste*, no. 111, November 1957.

Bošnjak, B. 'Ime i pojam "praxis" ', *Praxis*, 1/1964.

Brus, W. *Niektóre zagadnienia metody dialektycznej w świetle Kapitala Marksa*. Warsaw, 1952.

Buhr, M. *Der Übergang von Fichte zu Hegel*. Berlin, 1965.

——. 'Entfremdung – philosophische Anthropolgie – Marx-Kritik', *Deutsche Zeitschrift für Philosophie*, 7/1966.

——. (ed.) *Wissen und Gewissen. Beiträge zum 200. Geburtstag Johann Gottlieb Fichtes*. Berlin, 1962.

Butaev, I. 'Matematika v dialekticheskom analize v "Kapitale" Marksa', *Pod znamenem marksizma*, 9–10/1928.

Cahiers Internationaux de Sociologie, no. 4, 1948. (Special number on Marx.)

Calvez, J.-Y. *La pensée de K. Marx*. Paris, 1956.

Černík, V., and Karásek, J. 'K otázke jednoty historického a logického', *Slovenský filozofický časopis*, 1/1959.

Černíková, V. 'K otázke hodnotenia Heglovej dialektiky', *Slovenský filozofický časopis*, 4/1959.

Chatelet, F. *Logos et praxos. Recherches sur la signification theorique du marxisme*. Paris, 1962.

Cibulka, J. 'Marxovo pojetí vnitřní rozpornosti společenských zákonů', *Filosofický časopis*, 6/1958.

——. 'Přinos Marxova Kapitálu k poznáni společenských zákonů', *Rozpravy ČSAV*, 1962.

Cornu, A. *Karl Marx und Friedrich Engels. Leben und Werk*, vol. 1. Berlin, 1954; vol. 2. Berlin, 1962.

Cunow, H. 'Zum Verständnis der Marxschen Forschungsmethode', *Neue Zeit*, 1909–1910, II.

Dawydow, J. N. *Freiheit und Entfremdung*. Berlin, 1964.

Deborin, A. 'Marks i Gegel'', *Pod znamenem marksizma*, 8–9/1923, 10/1923, 3/1924.

Derbolav, J. 'Hegels Theorie der Handlung', *Hegel-Studien*, vol. 3, Bonn, 1965.

——. 'Die kritische Hegelrezeption des jungen Marx und das Problem der Emanzipation des Menschen', *Studium Generale*, 1962.

Desanti, J.-T. 'Le jeune Marx et la métaphysique', *Revue de Métaphysique et de Morale*, 3–4/1947.

Dubský, I. *Hegels Arbeitsbegriff und die idealistische Dialektik*. Prague, 1961.

——. *Raná tvorba Karla Marxe a Bedřicha Engelse*. Prague, 1958.

——, and Sobotka, M. 'Pomer marxismu k filosofii Hegelove', *Nová mysl*, 11/1956.

Eichhorn, W. 'Das Problem des Menschen im historischen Materialismus', *Deutsche Zeitschrift für Philosophie*, 7/1966.

Establet, R. 'Présentation du plan du "Capital" ', in *Lire le Capital*, vol. 2, Paris, 1966.

Feuerbach, L. *Sämtliche Werke*. Leipzig, 1846 ff.

Filkorn, V. *Úvod do metodológie vied*. Bratislava, 1960.

Fleischmann, E. J. 'Die Wirklichkeit in Hegels Logik. Ideengeschichtliche Beziehungen zu Spinoza', *Zeitschrift für philosophische Forschung*, 1/1964.

Fritzhand, M. *Myśl etyczna mlodego Marksa*. Warsaw, 1961.

Fromm, E. *Marx's Concept of Man*. New York, 1961.

Garaudy, R. *Dieu est mort. Étude sur Hegel*. Paris, 1962.

——. 'A propos des manuscrits de 1844', *Cahiers du communisme*, March 1963.

——. *Karl Marx*. Paris, 1964.

Gokieli, L. P. *O prirode logicheskogo*. Tblisi, 1958.

Goldman, L. *Recherches dialectiques*. Paris, 1959.

Gorsky, D. P. *Voprosui abstraktsii i obrazovanie ponyaty*. Moscow, 1961.

Grégoire, Fr. *Études hegéliennes*. Louvain and Paris, 1958.

Grib, V. 'Dialektika i logika kak nauchnaya metodologiya', *Pod znamenem marksizma*, 6/1928.

Gropp, R. O. *Zu Fragen der Geschichte der Philosophie und des dialektischen Materialismus*. Berlin, 1958.

Grossmann, H. 'Die Änderungen des Aufbauplans des Marxschen Kapitals und ihre Ursachen', *Archiv für die Geschichte des Sozialismus und der Arbeiterbewegung*, XIV, 2/1929.

——. *Das Akkumulations- und Zusammenbruchsgesetz des kapitalistischen Systems.* Leipzig, 1939.

Grushin, B. A. 'Logicheskie i istoricheskie priemui issledovaniya v Kapitale Marksa', *Voprosui filosofii*, 4/1955.

——. *Ocherki logiki istoricheskogo issledovaniya.* Moscow, 1961.

——. 'Protsess obnaruzheniya protivorechiya obekta', *Voprosui filosofii*, 1/1960.

Gulian, K. I. *Metod i sistema Gegelya*, 2 vols. Moscow, 1963.

Habermas, J. *Theorie und Praxis.* Neuwied, 1963.

Hegel-Jahrbuch. Ed. W. R. Beyer. Vol. 1, Munich, 1961; vol. 2, Munich, 1964.

Hegel-Studien, vol. 1, Bonn, 1961; vol. 3, Bonn, 1965.

Heintel, E. 'Der Begriff des Menschen und der "spekulative" Satz', *Hegel-Studien*, vol. 1, Bonn, 1961.

Heise, W. 'Über die Entfremdung und ihre Überwindung', *Deutsche Zeitschrift für Philosophie*, 6/1965.

Heiss, R. 'Hegel und Marx', *Symposium* I, Freiburg, 1949.

Hess, M. *Philosophische und sozialistische Schriften 1837–1850.* Eds A. Cornu and W. Mönke. Berlin, 1961.

Hommes, J. *Der technische Eros.* Freiburg, 1955.

Hook, S. *From Hegel to Marx. Studies in the intellectual development of Karl Marx.* Ann Arbor and Toronto, 1962.

Horn, J. H. *Widerspiegelung und Begriff.* Berlin, 1958.

Hyppolite, J. *Études sur Marx et Hegel.* Paris, 1955.

Ilenkov, E. V. *Dialektika abstraktnogo i konkretnogo v Kapitale Marksa.* Moscow, 1960.

——. 'K istorii voprosa o predmete logiki kak nauki', *Voprosui filosofii*, 1/1966.

Joja, A. 'Marx et la logique moderne', *Acta logica*, 1/1958.

Kempski, J. 'Über Bruno Bauer. Eine Studie zum Ausgang des Hegelianismus', *Archiv für Philosophie*, 11/3–4.

Keseleva, V. 'Rannie proizvedeniya Marksa i ikh sovremennuie falsifikatorui, *Kommunist* (Moskva), 6/1965.

Klaus, G. 'Hegel und die Dialektik in der formalen Logik', *Deutsche Zeitschrift für Philosophie*, 12/1963.

——, and Wittich, D. 'Zu einigen Fragen des Verhältnisses von Praxis und Erkenntnis', *Deutsche Zeitschrift für Philosophie*, 11/1961.

Kojève, A. *Introduction à la lecture de Hegel.* Paris, 1947.

Korsch, K. *Marxismus und Philosophie.* 2nd edn. Leipzig, 1930.

Kosík, K. *Dialektika konkrétního.* Prague, 1963.

Kroner, R. *Von Kant bis Hegel.* 2nd edn. Tübingen, 1961.

Kroński, T. *Rozwazania wokól Hegla.* Warsaw, 1960.

——. *Hegel.* Warsaw, 1962.

Kuderowicz, Zb. *Doktryna moralna mlodego Hegla.* Warsaw, 1962.

——. 'Logika heglowska a idea odpowiedzialności moralnej', *Studia filozoficzne*, 3–4/1963.

Kudrna, J. 'O významu Heglova pojetí činnosti pro základní problematiku jeho filosofie', *Filosofický časopis*, 4/1959.

——. *Studie k Hegelovu pojetí historie.* Prague, 1964.

Kushin, I. *Dialekticheskoe stroenie Kapitala Marksa.* Moscow, 1928.

Lakebrink, B. 'Geist und Arbeit im Denken Hegels', *Philosophisches Jahrbuch*, Munich, 1962.
Lapin, N. I. 'O vremeni rabotui Marksa nad rukopis'yu "K kritike gegelevskoi filosofii prava" ', *Voprosui filosofii*, 9/1960.
Lefebvre, H. *Les problèmes actuels de marxisme*. Paris, 1958.
———. *Marx philosophe*. Paris, 1963.
———. *Métaphilosophie*. Paris, 1965.
Lenin, W. I. 'Philosophische Hefte', in *Werke*, vol. 38, Berlin, 1964.
Lim Sok-Zin. *Der Begriff der Arbeit bei Hegel*. Bonn, 1963.
Löwith, K. *Von Hegel zu Nietzsche*. 5th edn. Stuttgart, 1964.
———. *Die Hegelsche Linke*. Stuttgart–Bad Canstatt, 1962.
Lübbe, H. *Politische Philosophie in Deutschland*. Bern, 1963.
Lukács, G. *Geschichte und Klassenbewusstsein*. Berlin, 1923.
———. *Der junge Hegel und die Probleme der kapitalistischen Gesellschaft*. Berlin, 1954.
———. 'Zur philosophischen Entwicklung des jungen Marx (1840–1844)', *Deutsche Zeitschrift für Philosophie*, 2/1954.
Lunau, H. *Karl Marx und die Wirklichkeit. Untersuchung über den Realitätsgehalt der wissenschaftlichen Ansichten von Marx auf Grund seines Werkes, 'Das Kapital'*. Brussels, 1937.
Macherey, P. 'A propos du processus d'exposition du "Capital" ', in *Lire le Capital*, vol. 1, Paris, 1966.
Major, L. 'K Hegelově filosofii náboženství', *Filosofický časopis*, 4/1964.
———. K historii sporu o politický profil Hegelovy filosofie práva', *Filosofický časopis*, 4/1966.
Makarov, A. 'K. Marks i ego kritika "Filosofii prava" Gegelya', *Pod znamenem marksizma*, 4/1938.
Mamardashvili, M. K. 'Protsessui analiza i sinteza', *Voprosui filosofii*, 2/1958.
Mankovsky, L. A. 'Kategorii "veshch" i "otnoshenie" v Kapitale Marksa', *Voprosui filosofii*, 5/1956.
———. *Logicheskie kategorii v 'Kapitale' K. Marksa*. Moscow, 1962.
Marcuse, H. *Reason and Revolution*. New York, 1941.
'Marxisme ouvert contre marxisme scolastique'. Special number of *Esprit*, May–June, 1948.
Marxismusstudien, vol. 1, Tübingen, 1954; vol. 2, 1957; vol. 3, 1960; vol. 4, 1962.
Materna, P. 'Zu einigen Fragen der modernen Definitionslehre', *Rozpravy ČSAV*. Prague, 1959.
Mende, G. *Karl Marx' Entwicklung vom revolutionären Demokraten zum Kommunisten*. 3rd edn. Berlin, 1960.
Menzel, L. Několik poznámek k problému dialektiky v Kantově filosofii', *Filosofický časopis*, 5/1964.
Merker, N. *Le origini della logica hegeliana*. Milan, 1961.
Michaud, J. C. *Teoria e storia nel 'Capitale' di Marx*. Milan, 1960.
Michňák, K. *Individuum a společnost*. Prague, 1966.
Moenke, W. *Neue Quellen zur Hess-Forschung*. Berlin, 1964.
Morf, O. *Das Verhältnis von Wirtschaftstheorie und Wirtschaftsgeschichte bei K. Marx*. Bern, 1951.
Münz, Th. 'K otázke vzt'ahu marxismu k Hegelovi a Hegelovo odkazu dnešku', *Slovenský filozofický časopis*, 2/1957.
Narsky, J. S. *Voprosui dialektiki poznaniya v Kapitale Marksa*. Moscow, 1959.
Naville, P. *Le nouveau Leviathan I. De l'aliénation à la jouissance*. Paris, 1957.

Nersesyants, V. S. 'Marksova kritika gegelevskoi filosofii prava', *Vestnik moskovskogo universiteta*, 1/1965.
Oizerman, T. I. *Formirovanie filosofii marksizma*. Moscow, 1962.
——. *Die Entfremdung als historische Kategorie*. Berlin, 1965.
Orudzhev, G. M. 'Nachalnuy etap formirovaniya vzglyadov K. Marksa i F. Engel'sa i ikh otnoshenie k Gegelyu', *Izvestiya Akad. nauk Azerbaydzhanskoi SSR*, 1/1958, seriya obshchestvennuikh nauk.
Ovsyannikov, M. F. *Filosofiya Gegelya*, Moscow, 1959.
Patočka, J. 'Descartes a Hegel', in *Aristotles, jeho předchůdci a dědicová*. Prague, 1964.
——. 'K vývoji Hegelových estetických názorů', *Filosofický časopis*, 2/1965.
Pazhitnov, L. N. *U istokov revolyutsionnogo prerevorota v filosofii. Ekonomichesko-filosofiskie rukopisi 1844 Karla Marksa*. Moscow, 1960.
Petrashik, A. P. 'Put' molodogo Marksa k materializmu i kommunizmu', *Voprosui filosofii*, 3/1958.
Petrović, G. *Filozofija i marksizam*. Zagreb, 1965.
Pietranere, G. 'La struttura logica del Capitale', *Società*, 1956.
Popelová, J. *K filosofické problematice Marxova Kapitálu*. Prague, 1954.
——. 'Die Suspension der moralischen Persönlichkeit in Hegels Philosophie des Rechts und die von ihr hervorgerufenen Dialoge', *Filosofický časopis*, 4/1966.
Popitz, H. *Der entfremdete Mensch. Zeitkritik und Geschichtsphilosophie des jungen Marx*. Basel, 1953.
Průcha, M. 'Cogito a první filosofie v marxismu', *Filosofický časopis*, 3/1965.
Rancière, J. 'Le concept de critique et la critique de l'économie politique des "Manuscrits" de 1844 au "Capital" ', in *Lire le Capital*, vol. 1, Paris, 1966.
Revue internationale de philosophie, nos. 45–6, Brussels 1958. (Special number on Marxism.)
Richta, R., *et al. Civilizace na rozcestí*. Prague, 1966.
Riedel, G. *Ludvík Feuerbach a mladý Marx*. Prague, 1962.
Riedel, M. *Theorie und Praxis im Denken Hegels*. Stuttgart, 1965.
——. 'Grundzüge einer Theorie des Lebendigen bei Hegel und Marx', *Zeitschrift für philosophische Forschung*, 4/1965.
Ritter, J. *Hegel und die französische Revolution*. Cologne, 1957.
Rosenberg, D. I. *Die Entwicklung der ökonomischen Lehre von Marx und Engels in den vierziger Jahren des 19. Jahrhunderts*. Berlin, 1958.
Rosenzweig, F. *Hegel und der Staat*. Nachdruck der Ausgabe von 1920. Aalen, 1962.
Rossi, M. 'Marx, la sinistra hegeliane e l'ideologia tedesca I–II', *Società* 5, 6/1958.
——. *Marx e la dialettica hegeliana*. 1. *Hegel e lo Stato*. Rome, 1960.
Röttcher, F. 'Theorie und Praxis in den Frühschriften von Karl Marx', *Archiv für Philosophie*, 11/3–4.
Rozenblyum, O. 'K voprosu o logike Kapitala Marksa', *Pod znamenem marksizma*, 2/1935.
Rozental, M. M. *Voprosui dialektiki v Kapitale Marksa*. Moscow, 1955.
Rubel, M. *Karl Marx, essai de biographie intellectuelle*. Paris, 1957.
Rubin, I. 'Dialekticheskoe razvitie kategory v ekonomicheskoi sisteme Marksa', *Pod znamenem marksizma* 4,5/1929.
Ruge, A. *Sämtliche Werke*. 3rd edn. Leipzig, 1850.
Ruml, V. 'Jednota logického a historického v materialistické dialektice', *Filosofický časopis*, 3/1955.

Rutkewitsch, M. N. 'Für eine dialektische Auffassung der Praxis', *Deutsche Zeitschrift für Philosophie*, 11/1962.
Ryazanov, D. B. 'Siebzig Jahre "Zur Kritik der politischen Ökonomie" ', *Archiv für die Geschichte des Sozialismus und der Arbeiterbewegung*, Leipzig, 1930.
Sabetti, A. 'La "Deutsche Ideologie" e il problema della filosofia come ideologia', *Società*, 4/1958.
Sagacky, A. *Teoriya stoimosti Marksa (k izucheniyu metodologii Marksa)*. Moscow, 1931.
Sakhaltuev, A. 'Za leninsky put' issledovaniya dialektiki Kapitala Marksa', *Pod znamenem marksizma*, 6/1931.
Sanis, S. *Dialektika kategory Marksovoi ekonomicheskoi sistemui*. Kiev, 1931.
Sarcević, A. 'Neke mysli o metodi Marksova Kapitala', *Pogledi*, 8/1953.
Sartre, J.-P. *Critique de la raison dialectique*. Paris, 1960.
Schaff, A. *Marksizm a egzystencjalizm*. Warsaw, 1961.
——. *Filozofia człowieka*. Warsaw, 1962.
——. *Marksizm a jednostka ludzka*. Warsaw, 1965.
Schmidt, A. *Der Begriff der Natur in der Lehre von Marx*. Frankfurt, 1962.
Shinkaruk, V. I. *Logika, dialektika i teoriya poznaniya Gegelya*. Kiev, 1964.
Sichirollo, L. 'Hegel und die griechische Welt', *Hegel-Studien*, Bonn, 1961.
Sobotka, M. 'Hranice a problémy Hegelovy dialektiky', *Filosofický časopis*, 5/1956
——. *Člověk a práce v německé klasické filosofii*. Prague, 1964.
——. 'Poznání a předmětná činnost v Hegelově filosofii', *Filosofický časopis*, 4/1964.
——. *Die idealistische Dialektik der Praxis bei Hegel*. Prague, 1965.
Sochor, L. 'Filosofie a ekonomie', in *Sedmkrát o smyslu filosofie*. Prague, 1964.
Sós, V. 'Problémy teorie kauzality v Marxově Kapitálu', *Filosofický časopis*, 5/1960.
Steussloff, H. 'Bruno Bauer als Junghegelianer und Kritiker der christlichen Religion', *Deutsche Zeitschrift für Philosophie*, 9/1963.
Stiehler, G. *Hegel und der Marxismus über den Widerspruch*. Berlin, 1960.
Stirner, M. *Der Einzige und sein Eigentum*. 2nd edn. Leipzig, 1882.
——. *Kleine Schriften*. Ed. J. H. Mackay. Berlin, 1898.
Struik, D. 'Marx and Mathematics', *Science and Society*, 1/1948.
Stuke, H. *Philosophie der Tat. Studien zur 'Verwirklichung der Philosophie' beiden Junghegelianern und den wahren Sozialisten*. Stuttgart, 1963.
Svoboda, J. 'K otáce logických a mimologických konstant'. (Thesis). Prague, 1961.
Szántó, L. *Vybrané state*. Bratislava, 1958.
Thier, E. 'Die Anthropologie des jungen Marx nach den Pariser ökonomisch-philosophischen Manuskripten'. (Foreword to an edition of Marx's Paris manuscripts.) Cologne, 1950.
Togliatti, P. 'Da Hegel al marxismo', *Rinascita*, 6/1954.
Tošenovský, L. *Prispevky k základním otázkám teorie pravdy*. Prague, 1962.
Tsereteli, S. B. 'K ponyatiya dialekticheskoi logiki', *Voprosui filosofii*, 3/1966.
Vainshtein, I. 'K voprosu o metodologii politicheskoi ekonomii u Marksa i klassikov', *Pod znamenem marksizma*, 9/1929.
Várossová, E. 'Význam Hegelovy Fenomenologie ducha', *Otázky marxistické filosofie*, 2/1961.

della Volpe, G. 'Methodologische Fragen in Karl Marx' Schriften von 1843 bis 1859', *Deutsche Zeitschrift für Philosophie*, 5/1958.

Vorländer, K. *Kant und Marx*. Tübingen, 1926.

Vranicki, P. 'Über historischen Determinismus und menschliche Freiheit', *Praxis*, 4/1965.

Weil, E. *Hegel et l'etat*. Paris, 1950.

Wittich, D. *Praxis – Erkenntnis – Wissenschaft*. Berlin, 1965.

Yanovskaya, S. 'O matematicheskikh rukopisyakh K. Marksa', *Pod znamenem marksizma*, 1/1933.

Zelený, J. 'K problému logiky Marxova Kapitálu', *Filosofický časopis*, 2/1960.

——. Problém základů vědy u Hegela a Marxe', *Filosofický časopis*, 4/1964 and 2/1965.

——. 'Die Marxsche Hegelkritik in den Pariser Manuskripten', *Filosofický časopis*, 4/1966.

——. 'Hegels Logik und die Integrationstendenzen in der gegenwärtigen Grundlagenforschung', *Hegel-Jahrbuch*, 1961.

——. Kant und Marx als Kritiker der Vernunft', *Kant-Studien*, 3–4/1966.

——, and Materna, P. 'Zu Marxens Auffassung der Begründung eines Satzes', *The Foundation of Statements and Decisions*. Warsaw, 1965.

Zich, O., Málek, I. and Tondl, L. *K methodologii experimentálnich věd*. Prague, 1959.

Zlocisti, T. *Moses Hess*. Berlin, 1921.

Translator's
Bibliography

Descartes, R. *The Method, Meditations, and Selections from the Principles*. 16th edn. Trans. John Neitch. Edinburgh and London: Blackwood, 1925.

———. *Philosophical Writings*. Eds E. Anscombe and P. T. Geach. Edinburgh and London: Nelson, 1954.

Hegel, G. W. F. *The Phenomenology of Mind*. 2nd edn. Trans. Sir James Baillie. London and New York: George Allen and Unwin/Humanities Press, 1966.

———. *Science of Logic*. Trans. A. V. Miller. London and New York: George Allen and Unwin/Humanities Press, 1969.

Kant, I. *Critique of Practical Reason*. Trans. T. K. Abbott. 6th edn. London, 1909.

———. *Critique of Pure Reason*. Trans. N. K. Smith. London: Macmillan, 1933, repr. 1970.

Lenin, V. I. *Collected Works*, Moscow: Foreign Languages Publishing House, 1960 etc.

Marx, K. *Capital*. Vol. 1. Trans. Samuel Moore and Edward Aveling. London: George Allen and Unwin, 1957.

———. Idem. Trans. Ben Fowkes. Harmondsworth: Penguin and New Left Review, 1976.

———. *Capital*. Vol. 2. Trans. I. Lasker. London: Lawrence and Wishart, 1970.

———. *Capital*. Vol. 3, Moscow: Progress, 1971.

———. *A Contribution to the Critique of Political Economy*. Trans. S. W. Ryanzanskaya. London: Lawrence and Wishart, 1971.

———. *Early Writings*. Trans. Rodney Livingstone and Gregor Benton. Harmondsworth: Penguin and New Left Review, 1975.

———. *Grundrisse*. Trans. Martin Nicolaus. Harmondsworth: Penguin and New Left Review, 1974.

———. *Poverty of Philosophy*. Moscow: Progress, 1976.

———. *Texts on Method*. Trans. Terrell Carver. Oxford: Basil Blackwell, 1975.

———. *Theories of Surplus Value*. Vol. 1. Trans. Émile Burns. London: Lawrence and Wishart, 1969.

———. Idem. Vol. 2. Trans. Renate Simpson. Moscow: Progress, 1968.

———. Idem. Vol. 3. Trans. Jack Cohen. London: Lawrence and Wishart, 1972.

———, and Engels, F. *Collected Works*. Vol. 1. London: Lawrence and Wishart, 1975.

———. *The German Ideology*. Moscow: Progress, 1968.

———. *The Holy Family*. 2nd edn. Trans. Richard Dixon and Clemens Dutt. Moscow: Progress, 1975.

———. *Selected Correspondence*. 2nd edn. Trans. I. Lasker. Moscow: Progress, 1965.

——. *Selected Works* in one volume. London: Lawrence and Wishart, 1973.
Ricardo, D. *Principles of Political Economy and Taxation*. Ed. R. M. Hartwell. Harmondsworth: Penguin, 1971.
Spinoza, B. de. *The Chief Works*. 2 vols. Trans. R. H. M. Elwes. London: Bell, 1884.

Index